THE COMPLETE BARBECUE BOOK

NOTES

Nuts and nut derivatives
This book includes dishes made with nuts and nut derivatives. It is advisable for customers with known allergic reactions to nuts and nut derivatives and those who may be potentially vulnerable to these allergies, such as pregnant and nursing mothers, invalids, the elderly, babies and children, to avoid dishes made with nuts and nut oils. It is also prudent to check the labels of pre-prepared ingredients for the possible inclusion of nut derivatives.

Do not refreeze a dish that has been frozen previously.

Eggs should be large unless otherwise stated.

It is advised that eggs should not be consumed raw. This book contains dishes made with raw or lightly cooked eggs. It is prudent for more vulnerable people, such as pregnant or nursing mothers, invalids, the elderly, babies and young children, to avoid uncooked or lightly cooked dishes made with eggs. Once prepared, these dishes should be kept refrigerated and used promptly.

Milk should be whole unless otherwise stated.

Poultry should be cooked thoroughly. To test if poultry is cooked, pierce the flesh through the thickest part with a skewer or fork – the juices should run clear, never pink or red.

Fresh herbs should be used unless otherwise stated. If unavailable, use dried herbs as an alternative but halve the quantities stated.

THE COMPLETE BARBECUE BOOK

CHANCELLOR
PRESS

First published in 2003 by Chancellor Press,
an imprint of Bounty Books, a division of
Octopus Publishing Group Ltd,
2-4 Heron Quays, London E14 4JP

ISBN 0 7537 0808 6

Printed in Singapore

Contents

Introduction

There is something special about eating outdoors and something even more delightful about cooking outdoors. Everyone—young and old alike—loves a barbecue. You won't be short of offers to help, either, as the first whiff of burning charcoal brings out the chef in people who would never normally go near a kitchen stove. Make full use of willing helpers to transport plates and glasses, mix salads, and hand around dishes, but limit the numbers clustering around the fire for reasons of safety.

Barbecues can be as simple or as elaborate as you like. It's a great way to share a family supper on a midweek summer evening. You can leave some chicken or steaks marinating in the refrigerator when you go off to work, light the coals as soon as you get home, toss a few salad greens together, and then dine al fresco with very little extra effort. The kids might even be willing to do the dishes afterward. Equally, you can make a barbecue a grand occasion for family and friends with a wide selection of different dishes and several courses. If you have the space and the confidence, a three or four course meal can all be cooked on the barbecue, although you will need to do some careful planning. To make life simpler, you can prepare marinades, sauces, and salads one or two days in advance.

Whether your plan is a small gathering of friends or a large party, you will find everything you need to know in the pages of this book. There is advice on getting the most from your barbecue, useful equipment, and personal and food safety guidance, and this is followed by a superb collection of recipes. Individual chapters feature meat, poultry, fish, shellfish, vegetarian dishes, side dishes, and desserts for cooking on the barbecue. In addition, there are recipes for those all-important extras: Marinades, salads, dips and relishes, and even suggestions for drinks—both alcoholic and non-alcoholic.

Recipes range from the very simple, but nonetheless delicious, to splendid roasts and baked whole fish. They have been inspired by cuisines of countries across the world—Thailand, Malaysia, Indian, China, Australia, Italy, France, Greece, Spain, the Middle East, the Caribbean, Mexico—as well as including many homegrown, family favorites. There is sure to be something for everyone, whether hot and spicy, delicate and subtle, exotic and unusual, plain and simple, or extravagant and luxurious.

Some are specially designed for catering for large numbers of guests, while others are just right for couples and small families. There are perfect dishes for cooking on portable barbecues at the beach or lake and fabulous recipes for spit-roasting on large, sophisticated equipment in your own backyard.

There is no doubt that barbecues are great fun and they should be just as enjoyable for the host as they are for guests. This book is packed with information and recipes to guarantee success. The only limits to what you can do are your budget and the size of the barbecue grid. Even then, people are often quite happy to eat in relays throughout the course of a hot, lazy afternoon on the weekend, and a homemade hamburger is just as good as fresh lobster. However, if you are going to be supplying a steady stream of hungry people—and fresh air gives everyone a hearty appetite—exploit some of the offers of help to give yourself a break.

TYPES OF BARBECUE

The range of barbecues is extensive, from cheap, disposable ones to permanent, brick-built structures, with many variations in between. It's usually worth buying the largest one you can afford, as barbecues are often very sociable occasions and you may find yourself cooking for more people than you originally expected. The level of sophistication you choose—rotisserie, variable temperature controls, adjustable grills, or a "keep-warm" oven—depends on just what you want to get out of the occasion and, of course, your budget.

Hibachi

Inexpensive, lightweight, and small, this is a popular beginner's barbecue. It's simple to use, easily transported around the yard or on days out and picnics, and offers some heat control. A single grill hibachi is adequate for cooking for 4 people, and double and triple grill models are also available. A simple way to extend your range is just to buy a second hibachi.

Table-top portable

Usually consisting of a 10–16 inch diameter grill, with folding, telescopic, or screw-in legs, these are very popular, especially for those with limited space. They are adequate for cooking for 6 people and some have extra attachments, such as a mini-rotisserie and a small windshield.

Open brazier

Usually in the middle of the price range, the open brazier model offers plenty of scope for the keen barbecue cook. At its simplest, it is similar to the table-top portable, but is usually sturdier and often has a stainless steel fire bowl that will last longer. Some models have wheels, making them easy to move around the yard (not when lit). Many have extra attachments, including a half-hood, rotisserie, adjustable grills, and other controls, as well as clip-on trays and a condiments shelf.

Kettle

This is rather like an open brazier, but with a cover or hood that encloses the grill. This means that heat is reflected back down to the food as well as being supplied from underneath, so it's more like an oven. They are usually quite large —about 20 inches in diameter—and suitable for cooking for 12. Most models have wheels and a system of vents for controlling the temperature. A wide range of sophisticated extras is available.

Wagon

Also called a barbecue box, this tends to be like a rectangular version of the kettle. They are sturdily made and usually incorporate a wide range of accessories, making them quite expensive. A window in the cover, as well as adjustable controls, makes them very flexible.

Gas and electric

Cleaner and less effort than charcoal- or wood-burning barbecues, gas and electric models are just as effective in creating that special smoky flavor and are extremely easy to use. There have been suggestions that charcoal-cooked food may contain some carcinogenic agents, so these are good options for anyone concerned about that. Styles vary, but, inevitably the larger and more sophisticated models are more highly priced. Running costs, however, can sometimes be lower than for conventional barbecues.

Permanent

These are the first choice for people who love to do lots of outside entertaining and have plenty of space. It is best to get professional advice or buy a special kit. It is important to be sure that the foundations are secure and that fire-resistant bricks are used where necessary. A professional should also be able to advise you about safety features, such as overhanging branches and prevailing winds. A cover of some sort is advisable to keep off garden pests and neighborhood cats when the barbecue is not in use.

TYPES OF FUEL

Charcoal is by far and away the most common form of barbecue fuel used today, but wood is also quite popular.

Charcoal

Most charcoal available today is found in two forms—either as charcoal briquettes, which are solid, pillow-like squares of compressed charcoal, or as lumpwood charcoal, which are irregular chunks of light, wood-like charcoal. Briquettes have greater staying power and burn for longer but are more expensive. They may also be more difficult to light, although some are available impregnated with an ignition agent, which makes it easier.

Charcoal is the ideal fuel for the barbecue, since it gives off little odor and is safe and pleasant to use. However, it does give off carbon monoxide, so it should never be used indoors. For an average barbecue, you will probably need about 30 briquettes of compressed charcoal to make an adequate fire-bed, or about 9 briquettes for every 6 inch square of fire-bed.

Wood

If you have access to plenty of wood, this makes a good fuel for the barbecue. Soft woods, such as pine, are good for kindling the fire. Add harder woods later as they burn more slowly and produce a hotter fire for cooking. Never use wood that has been painted, varnished, or treated in any way.

Gas

Gas is quick and easy, although you have to remember to refill the gas bottle from time to time. Many people swear by their gas barbecues for the convenience they offer, but others feel that gas lacks the integrity and style of cooking over a real fire.

THE FIRE

An effective and useful trick is to make a shallow bed of sand or gravel in the base of the barbecue and place the charcoal or wood on top. This helps to soak up excess fat drippings which can cause flare-ups and charring of the food, and also helps protect the metal construction of the fire-bed from excess heat. To make clearing up afterward easier, line the fire-bed with foil, shiny side up, before adding the sand and charcoal.

LIGHTING

Whatever method you use to assist in lighting the fire always read the manufacturer's instructions first.

Lighting a gas barbecue

The gas jets on a gas barbecue are covered by lava rocks, which heat up and distribute the heat to the food more evenly and create that smoky flavor. Switch on the gas and light the barbecue about 15 minutes before you want to cook to allow the lava rocks to heat up evenly. When the coals are hot, brush a layer of oil on to the grill bars to prevent the food from sticking.

Firelighters

These are still probably the most popular, safe, and inexpensive way to ignite the fire without fear of sparks, chemical residue, or after-taste. Use about 3–4 blocks (measuring 1-2 inches) for an average fire-bed and simply light with a match. Coals ignited this way will be ready for cooking in 30–45 minutes.

Liquid fire starters

Available in plastic bottles, these are an easy way to ignite the coals for a barbecue. After laying the bed of charcoal, spray it liberally with the liquid. Wait for about 2 minutes while it soaks in, then ignite the charcoal, which will be ready for use in 30–45 minutes. Never spray the liquid fire starter onto burning charcoal and store it safely away from naked flames and heat. Use only the liquid manufactured specially for this purpose.

Jellied alcohol

This highly combustible, jelly-like fire starter is designed for use with barbecues. Use about 1 tablespoon, dotted over the briquettes at the base of the fire-bed, and light with a match. Coals ignited in this way will be ready for cooking in 30–45 minutes.

Electric fire starter

This consists of an electric ring with a long handle. It should be placed on a few coals on the fire-bed, with the remaining coals positioned on top of it. When plugged in and switched on, an electric fire starter will ignite the briquettes within about 10 minutes. It should then be unplugged and removed. The coals will be ready for cooking in a further 20–30 minutes.

Gas torch

Not specifically designed for the purpose, this can, however, be used to ignite a barbecue. Aim the flame at the briquettes and hold it in position until they begin to glow.

BUILDING THE FIRE BED

For best results position wood and charcoal like a teepee. When hot, the charcoal or wood can then be spread to make a solid flat bed. This provides good, even, consistent heat that works well for cooking most foods. Remember that the closer the briquettes or sticks are to each other, the more intense the heat.

If you want to cook by indirect heat where there is a likelihood of flare-ups, especially with fatty meats, build a divided bed of coals by banking a pile of them either side of a drip pan. For cooking on a rotisserie, build a fire-bed of solid coals to the back of the barbecue and place a metal drip pan under the rotating food in the center of the grill area.

MANAGING THE FIRE

As a general rule, you will need to light the barbecue 30–45 minutes before you want to start cooking. You will know the fire is ready when the charcoal or wood is covered in a fine, gray ash or, if at night, it glows red. Sometimes, when cooking for a large gathering, you may need to add more coals or wood. Add these to the edge, then move toward the center after they have started to burn—this will avoid reducing the temperature of the fire too quickly. Gas and electric barbecues usually heat more quickly than charcoal fires—about 10–15 minutes—although they do not cook the food any quicker. Check the manufacturer's instructions.

Cooking heat can be varied in a several ways:

- Adjust the distance between the grid and the fire-bed
- Increase or decrease the amount of fuel, or space the fuel pieces farther apart
- Brush away ash from the coals or use bellows to increase the heat

Many people find it convenient to have a hotter fire in the center of the barbecue and a slightly less intense one at the sides. Throughout this book, the term "sear" has been used to refer to cooking an ingredient, usually meat, over the very hottest part of the barbecue to seal it. "Grill" has been used to mean cooking directly over medium heat.

EXTINGUISHING THE FIRE

When you have finished cooking and if there is little fuel left, then leave the barbecue to die down as you would an ordinary fire. Protect with a fireguard if young children are around. If the fire-bed still has some good useable charcoal, then remove with tongs to a pail of cold water or a metal pail with a lid. Both will snuff out the coals and the wet ones can be dried for later use.

If you have a hooded barbecue model, simply cover with the hood and close all the vents.

PERSONAL SAFETY

Everyone hopes that their barbecue party will pass without any unfortunate accidents. However, it is sensible to take a few precautions and to have an assortment of burn sprays and dressings available, should they be required.

- Make sure that the barbecue is standing on a firm, level surface and is stable. If it has wheels, operate the locking mechanism

- Use only the recommended fuel and starters—read the manufacturer's instructions. Never add flammable liquid to the fire
- Once you have lit the fire, do not leave it unattended
- If there will be a large number of children present, designate someone "child wrangler" to keep an eye on their safety
- Keep pets away from the fire
- Have a pail of sand handy in case the fire gets out of control
- Be careful about positioning lanterns, lights, and candles
- Pin down tablecloths with thumb tacks
- Cooking on a barbecue can be very thirsty work, but watch your intake of alcohol

USEFUL EQUIPMENT

You don't need much in the way of extra tools—most of what you require you will already have in your kitchen.

Cooking equipment

- Long-handled tongs, fork, and spatula for food
- Long-handled tongs for rearranging, removing, or adding coals
- Potholders—thick, and with extra-long arms
- Long-handled basting brush
- Heavy-duty apron
- Spray bottle of water to douse over-exuberant flames
- Roll of aluminum foil, preferably heavy-duty
- Roll of plastic wrap
- Aluminum drip pans
- Table nearby for preparation work and holding flavorings and bastes
- Hinged wire basket for holding foods, such as fish, that break up
- Absorbent paper towels and damp rag for mopping up spills and wiping hands
- Trash can for the inevitable debris that must be discarded
- Fireproof containers for keeping sauces and other foods hot on the side of the barbecue

Serving equipment

- Knives and forks
- Plates, bowls, etc
- Glasses
- Container of ice or other means of keeping drinks cold
- Can openers and corkscrews
- Baskets for bread and rolls
- Napkins
- Condiments—salt, pepper, mustard, catsup and relishes

Cleaning up equipment

- Sturdy wire brush—to remove debris from the barbecue grid. Don't wash the grid
- Oven or barbecue cleaner—for the end of the barbecue season

FOOD SAFETY

Cooking on a barbecue is a safe and enjoyable experience when it is done sensibly, but there are a few extra precautions that you should taken note of. After all, no one wants their party to end up in the emergency room.

- Always marinate foods, especially meat, fish, and shellfish, in a cool place and if you intend to marinate for more than 1 hour, place the food in the refrigerator and bring it back to room temperature before you start cooking
- Keep foods refrigerated until you are ready to cook
- Keep foods that are waiting to be cooked covered with plastic wrap to prevent flies and other insects touching them
- Make sure that food is cooked through before you serve it. This is particularly important with chicken, pork, and sausages. As you probably have less control over the heat than when cooking conventionally, always check that food is cooked through before serving. Pierce the thickest part of the meat with the point of a sharp knife. If the juices run clear, it is cooked through. If there are traces

of pink in the juices—even if the outside of the meat looks well browned—continue cooking it for a little longer and check again carefully before serving

- Keep raw and cooked foods separate to prevent the possibility of cross contamination
- Don't leave sauces and dips, especially those, like mayonnaise that contain raw egg, standing in hot sunshine for prolonged periods
- Wash your hands frequently

IN CONCLUSION

Now you have read this far, you should be fully prepared to have a safe, successful barbecue.

Enjoy!

chapter 1

Marinades and Flavorings

Basic Red Wine Marinade

2/3 cup red wine

2/3 cup sunflower oil

2 garlic cloves, crushed

1 teaspoon sea salt

1 marjoram sprig

1 rosemary sprig

1 thyme sprig

4 tablespoons chopped parsley

1 teaspoon ground black pepper

2 bay leaves

1 small onion, sliced

Combine all the ingredients in a bowl. Pour over beef or lamb in a shallow dish, stirring and turning to coat. Cover and marinate in the refrigerator for at least 3 hours. Use on the day it is made.

Makes about 1 1/4 cups

Red Wine Marinade

2/3 cup red wine

2 tablespoons lemon juice

1 onion, sliced

1 carrot, sliced

1 celery stalk, sliced

1 parsley sprig

1 thyme sprig

1 bay leaf

6 black peppercorns, lightly crushed

3 tablespoons sunflower oil (optional)

Combine all the ingredients in a bowl, whisking well with a fork or balloon whisk. Add the oil only if the marinade is to be used with lean meat such as chicken or turkey. Let stand for 1 hour before pouring over chicken, turkey, beef, or lamb in a shallow dish, stirring and turning to coat. Cover and marinate in the refrigerator.

Makes about 1 1/4 cups

White Wine Marinade

2/3 cup dry white wine

2 tablespoons lemon juice

1 onion, sliced

1 carrot, sliced

1 celery stalk, chopped

1 tablespoon chopped parsley

6 black peppercorns, lightly crushed

3 tablespoons safflower oil

Combine all the ingredients in a bowl, whisking well with a fork or balloon whisk. Let stand for 1 hour before pouring over chicken or veal in a shallow dish, stirring and turning to coat. Cover and marinate in the refrigerator.

Makes about 1 1/4 cups

Vermouth Marinade

¼ cup olive oil

¼ cup dry vermouth

1 tablespoon lemon juice

1 garlic clove, minced

1 teaspoon Worcestershire sauce

dash of angostura bitters

pepper

Combine the oil, vermouth, lemon juice, garlic, Worcestershire sauce, and angostura bitters in a bowl, whisking to mix. Season with pepper. Pour over pork, veal, or chicken in a shallow dish, cover, and marinate for at least 1 hour.

Makes about ½ cup

Chive Mustard Marinade

4 tablespoons sunflower oil

3 tablespoons lemon juice

2 tablespoons chive mustard

1 teaspoon salt

½ teaspoon pepper

Combine all the ingredients in a bowl, whisking well with a fork or balloon whisk. Pour over steaks, lamb, chicken, or fish in a shallow dish, stirring and turning to coat. Cover and marinate in the refrigerator.

Makes about ½ cup

Herb Marinade

4 tablespoons sunflower oil

2 tablespoons lemon juice

½ teaspoon dried marjoram

½ teaspoon dried thyme

1 garlic clove, minced

1 onion, finely chopped

2 tablespoons chopped parsley

salt and pepper

Combine all the ingredients in a bowl, whisking well with a fork or balloon whisk, then season to taste with salt and pepper. Pour over lamb, chicken, or turkey in a shallow dish, stirring and turning to coat. Cover and marinate in the refrigerator.

Makes about ⅔ cup

Fresh Herb Marinade

4 tablespoons sunflower oil

2 tablespoons lime juice

2 tablespoons chopped mixed herbs, such as marjoram, thyme, mint and savory

2 tablespoons chopped fresh parsley

1 garlic clove, minced

1 onion, finely chopped

salt and pepper

Combine all the ingredients in a bowl, whisking well with a fork or balloon whisk, then season to taste with salt and pepper. Pour over lamb, chicken, or turkey in a shallow dish, stirring and turning to coat. Cover and marinate in the refrigerator.

Makes about 2/3 cup

Chili Marinade

1 teaspoon chili powder

1 teaspoon celery salt

2 tablespoons soft brown sugar

2 tablespoons white wine vinegar

2 tablespoons Worcestershire sauce

3 tablespoons tomato ketchup

2/3 cup beef broth or water

Combine all the ingredients in a bowl, whisking well with a fork or balloon whisk. Pour over poultry, steaks, spareribs, chops, or roasts in a shallow dish, stirring and turning to coat. Cover and marinate in the refrigerator.

Makes about 1 cup

Sweet and Sour Marinade

4 tablespoons tomato ketchup

2 tablespoons Worcestershire sauce

2 tablespoons white wine vinegar

2 tablespoons honey

2 tablespoons light brown sugar

Combine all the ingredients in a pitcher. Brush over meat, chicken, fish, or vegetables in a shallow dish, then cover, and marinate for at least 4 hours.

Makes 2/3 cup

Tenderizing Marinade

2/3 cup malt or wine vinegar

2/3 cup water

1 large onion, sliced

6 cloves

2 bay leaves

6 black peppercorns, lightly crushed

Combine all the ingredients in a bowl, whisking well with a fork or balloon whisk. Let stand for at least 12 hours before pouring over tougher cuts of meat and steaks, chops, or kabobs in a shallow dish, stirring and turning to coat. Cover and marinate in the refrigerator.

Makes about 1 1/4 cups

Hard Cider and Honey Marinade

2 tablespoons soy sauce

3 tablespoons apple vinegar

1 tablespoon honey

1 tablespoon safflower oil

2/3 cup hard cider

Combine all the ingredients in a bowl, whisking well with a fork or balloon whisk. Pour over steaks, duck, chicken, or spareribs in a shallow dish, stirring and turning to coat. Cover and marinate in the refrigerator.

Makes about 1/2 cup

Piquant Honey Marinade

2 tablespoons sunflower oil

1 onion, finely chopped

1 garlic clove, minced

4 tablespoons orange juice

2 tablespoons honey

3 tablespoon white wine vinegar

1 tablespoon Worcestershire sauce

1 teaspoon horseradish sauce

1 teaspoon mustard powder

large pinch of dried rosemary

large pinch of dried thyme

salt and pepper

Heat the oil in a pan, add the onion and garlic, and cook over low heat until soft. Stir in the remaining ingredients and season with salt and pepper. Simmer for 5 minutes, then remove from the heat, and cool. Chill for 4–6 hours before using to marinate chicken or shrimp.

Makes about 2/3 cup

Soy Sauce Marinade

2 tablespoons sunflower oil

2 tablespoons light soy sauce

1 tablespoon lemon juice

½ teaspoon ground cumin

1 teaspoon chopped chives

Combine all the ingredients in a bowl. Pour over fish, such as tuna or salmon steaks, cover, and marinate for at least 30 minutes.

Makes ⅓ cup

Chinese Marinade

4 tablespoons soy sauce

2 tablespoons honey

4 tablespoons Chinese rice wine or dry sherry

1 tablespoon ground cinnamon

½ teaspoon ground cloves

4 tablespoons cold tea

1 garlic clove, minced

Combine all the ingredients in a bowl, whisking well with a fork or balloon whisk. Pour over pork or beef in a shallow dish, stirring and turning to coat. Cover and marinate in the refrigerator.

Makes about 1 cup

Hoi-sin Marinade

½ cup hoi-sin sauce

3 tablespoons tomato paste

2 tablespoons lemon juice

2 tablespoons honey

2 tablespoons soy sauce

Combine all the ingredients in a pitcher. Pour over chicken or fish, stirring and turning to coat. Cover and marinate for at least 30 minutes.

Makes about 1 cup

Teriyaki Marinade

¾ inch piece of fresh ginger root, minced

2 tablespoons shoyu

1 tablespoon lemon juice

2 tablespoons sake or dry sherry

½ cup fish broth

Combine all the ingredients in a shallow dish. Add chicken, salmon, or shrimp and marinate, turning occasionally, for at least 30 minutes.

Makes scant 1 cup

Olive Oil Marinade

⅔ cup olive oil

1 garlic clove, sliced

1 small onion, sliced

1 bay leaf

2 teaspoons chopped parsley

grated zest of 1 lemon

2 teaspoons lemon juice

salt and pepper

Pour the oil into a shallow dish and add all the remaining ingredients, seasoning to taste with salt and pepper. Add pork, chicken, or vegetables, stirring and turning to coat. Cover and marinate in the refrigerator.

Makes about 2/3 cup

Spiced Oil

1 1/4 cups sunflower oil

1 garlic clove, halved

2 thyme sprigs

1 rosemary sprig

1 bay leaf

1 teaspoon mixed pickling spices

2 small dried red chilies

Pour the oil into a screw-top bottle. Add all the remaining ingredients, seal, and let steep. Use to brush all kinds of meat and fish for grilling on the barbecue.

Makes 1 1/4 cups

Aromatic Oil

2 cups olive oil

2 large rosemary sprigs

6 thyme sprigs

1 large garlic clove

1 green chili

5–6 small red chilies

6 black peppercorns

6 juniper berries

Pour the oil into a clear glass bottle with a tightly fitting lid or cork. Wash the herbs and pat dry with paper towels. Drop the herbs, garlic, chiles, peppercorns, and juniper berries into the oil and seal tightly. Let stand for 2 weeks, shaking the bottle every 2–3 days, before using in marinades for meat, poultry or fish.

Makes 2 cups

Sage and Onion Yogurt Marinade

⅔ cup plain yogurt

2 tablespoons sage and onion mustard

1 tablespoon brown sugar

salt and pepper

Combine all the ingredients in a bowl, whisking well with a fork or balloon whisk. Pour over pork or chicken in a shallow dish, stirring and turning to coat. Cover and marinate in the refrigerator.

Makes about ⅔ cup

Sour Cream Marinade

$^{2}/_{3}$ cup sour cream

1 tablespoon lemon juice

1 garlic clove, minced

1 celery stalk, thinly sliced

large pinch of paprika

$^{1}/_{2}$ teaspoon Worcestershire sauce

salt and pepper

Pour the sour cream into a bowl, add the lemon juice, garlic, and salt and pepper to taste and stir well. Stir in the remaining ingredients. Pour over steaks, lamb chops, or chicken. Cover and marinate in the refrigerator.

Makes about $^{2}/_{3}$ cup

Yogurt Marinade

2 cups plain yogurt

3 tablespoons olive oil

2 tablespoons lime juice

1 small onion, minced

1 teaspoon ground cloves

1 teaspoon cumin seeds, crushed

$^{1}/_{4}$ teaspoon ground cardamom

2 garlic cloves, minced

1 teaspoon ground cinnamon

1 teaspoon salt

1 teaspoon ground white pepper

Combine all the ingredients in a bowl, whisking well with a fork or balloon whisk. Pour over all kinds of meat and poultry in a shallow dish, stirring and turning to coat. Cover and marinate in the refrigerator.

Makes about 2 cups

Coconut Cream Marinade

2 garlic cloves, minced

½ inch piece of fresh ginger root, very finely shredded

2 tablespoons lime juice

2 teaspoons grated lemon zest

1–2 red chilies, deseeded and finely chopped

½ cup coconut cream

Combine all the ingredients in a shallow dish. Add chicken, fish, or shrimp, cover, and marinate for 1–2 hours.

Makes ½ cup

chapter 2

Meat

BEEF AND VEAL

Simple Spit-roasted Sirloin

3–4 pound beef sirloin, rolled and tied

2 tablespoons sunflower oil

2 teaspoons French mustard

2 teaspoons Worcestershire sauce

Attach the sirloin to a rotisserie. Combine the oil, mustard and Worcestershire sauce in a bowl and brush the mixture all over the beef. Cook, basting frequently, for 1–1¼ hours for rare meat. For well-done beef, cover the sirloin with foil and cook for a further 15–20 minutes.

8 servings

Mustard Sirloin

3–4 pound beef sirloin

3 tablespoons olive oil

1 tablespoon lemon juice

3 large onions, sliced

1 tablespoon all-purpose flour

1 teaspoon mustard powder

melted butter, for basting

salt and pepper

Brush the beef all over with the olive oil and sprinkle with the lemon juice. Place half the onion slices in the base of a shallow dish, put the beef on top, and cover with the remaining onion slices. Let stand for at least 3 hours. Either discard the onions or fry them to serve with the beef. Combine the flour and mustard in a bowl. Attach the beef to a rotisserie, baste with the butter, and cook for 20 minutes. Dust with the flour mixture and continue cooking until a crust forms, then baste again. Cook, basting occasionally, for 1 1/4 hours more, or until the beef is tender and to your liking. Season with salt and pepper.

6–8 servings

Succulent Sirloin

3–4 pound beef sirloin, rolled and tied

Red Wine Marinade (see page 18)

2 tablespoons sunflower oil

1 teaspoon Worcestershire sauce

pepper

Place the beef in a shallow dish, pour in the marinade, and marinate, turning occasionally, for 3–4 hours. Drain the beef and discard the marinade. Combine the oil and Worcestershire sauce. Season the beef with pepper and brush the oil mixture all over it. Grill, turning regularly and brushing with the oil mixture occasionally, for 50 minutes–1 1/4 hours, until tender and to your liking.

6–8 servings

Balsamic Steaks

4 tenderloin steaks, about 7–8 ounces each

2 red onions, thinly sliced into rings

3 tablespoons balsamic vinegar

1/4 cup red wine

generous 1/2 cup olive oil

1–2 garlic cloves, minced

2 cups basil leaves

2 pounds potatoes, cut into large chunks

salt and pepper

Place the steaks in a large shallow dish and sprinkle the onion rings over them. Combine the vinegar, wine and 2 tablespoons of the oil in a pitcher, add the garlic, and pour over the steaks. Turn to coat, cover, and marinate, turning once, for 1–1½ hours. Process the remaining oil and the basil leaves in a blender or food processor until smooth. Scrape into a bowl and set aside. Cook the potatoes in lightly salted, boiling water for 15–20 minutes, until tender. Drain, mash, beat in the basil oil, and season with salt and pepper. Cover tightly and keep warm on the side of the barbecue. Meanwhile, transfer the steaks to a plate and pour the marinade into a pan. Bring to a boil, then lower the heat, and simmer until reduced by half. Place the pan on the side of the barbecue to keep warm. Grill the steaks for 2–3 minutes on each side for rare, or 4–5 minutes on each side for medium. Transfer to plates, spoon over the sauce, and serve with the basil flavored potatoes.

4 servings

Quick-fry Steaks with Barbecue Glaze

1 tablespoon malt vinegar

1 teaspoon prepared mustard

1 tablespoon dark brown sugar

pinch of paprika

2 teaspoons Worcestershire sauce

1 teaspoon soy sauce

3 tablespoons tomato ketchup

6 quick-fry tenderized steaks

sunflower oil, for brushing

salt and pepper

Combine the vinegar, mustard, sugar, paprika, Worcestershire sauce, soy sauce, and ketchup in a bowl, adding a little water, if necessary, to make a thin sauce. Season the steaks with salt and pepper and brush with oil. Sear the steaks for 1 minute on each side. Brush with the sauce and grill for 4–5 minutes on each side, depending on how well done you like your steak. Brush frequently with the sauce while the steaks are cooking.

6 servings

Classic Steak au Poivre

4 tablespoons black peppercorns

4 round steaks, about 5 ounces each

sunflower oil, for brushing

light cream (optional)

salt

Lightly crush the peppercorns in a mortar with a pestle or by placing them between 2 sheets of waxed paper and hammering them with the side of a rolling pin. Spread them out on a plate and press the steaks firmly onto them to coat both sides. Season with salt and brush lightly with oil. Sear the steaks until browned on both sides, then grill for 2–5 minutes on each side, until cooked to your liking. Drizzle with a little light cream as you serve them, if you like.

4 servings

Carpetbag Steak

2 pounds round steak in 1 piece

8 ounces canned oysters in brine, drained

2 tablespoons lemon juice

3 tablespoons vegetable oil

salt and pepper

lemon wedges and chopped parsley, to garnish

Slit the steak horizontally, leaving 1 long edge uncut so that it can be opened out like a book. Place the oysters on 1 cut surface and sprinkle with the lemon juice. Cover with the other half of the steak and sew up with a trussing needle and fine string. Season the steak with salt and pepper and brush with the oil. Sear for 2 minutes on each side, then grill for 15–20 minutes more, until cooked to your liking. Season with salt, remove and discard the string, and cut the steak crosswise into 4 slices. Serve garnished with lemon wedges and parsley.

4 servings

Deviled Steaks

4 round steaks

4 teaspoons French mustard

4 tablespoons light brown sugar

salt and pepper

parsley sprigs, to garnish

Trim off any excess fat from the steaks and season them with pepper. Combine the mustard and sugar in a bowl and spread half the mixture on 1 side of each steak. Grill for 5 minutes, then turn the steaks over, and spread with the remaining mustard mixture. Grill for 5 minutes more, until to your liking. Season with salt and serve garnished with parsley sprigs.

4 servings

Peppered Steak Flamed with Brandy

4 tenderloin steaks, about 6 ounces each

1 tablespoon finely crushed black peppercorns

6 tablespoons/$^3/_4$ stick butter, melted

2 garlic cloves, minced

4 French bread slices, slightly larger than the steaks

4 tablespoons brandy

salt

Press both sides of each steak into the crushed peppercorns and season lightly with salt. Combine the melted butter and garlic in a small bowl and brush the mixture all over the steaks. Grill the steaks for $2^1/_2$–$3^1/_2$ minutes on each side, depending on how well done you like them. Just before they are ready, dip the bread slices into the remaining melted butter mixture and toast on both sides on the barbecue. Place the toasted bread on a platter and top each slice with a steak. Pour the brandy into a small pan or heatproof ladle and heat gently on the barbecue. Carefully set the brandy alight and pour it, flaming, over the steaks. Serve the steaks as soon as the flames die down.

4 servings

Beef Teriyaki

4 tablespoons shoyu

2 tablespoons dry sherry

2 teaspoons chopped fresh ginger root

1 garlic clove, minced

4 sirloin steaks, about 5 ounces each

scallion tassels, to garnish

Japanese Dipping Sauce (see page 268), to serve

Combine the shoyu, sherry, ginger, and garlic in a shallow dish. Add the steaks and marinate at room temperature, turning occasionally, for 2 hours. Remove the steaks, reserving the marinade. Grill, basting frequently with the reserved marinade, for 3–4 minutes on each side for medium steaks, longer for well done. Slice the steaks into thin strips, garnish with the scallion tassels, and serve with small bowls of the sauce for dipping.

4 servings

Apricot-topped Steaks

3 tablespoons Garlic and Herb Butter (see page 285)

4 sirloin steaks, about 4 ounces each

8 canned apricots in syrup, drained, plus 2 tablespoons syrup from the can

Cut the butter into 8 pieces. Brush the steaks with the apricot syrup and arrange them in a foil grill tray. Cook on the barbecue for 4 minutes, then turn them over. Place 2 apricot halves, cut sides up, on each steak. (If necessary, cut a sliver from the rounded sides of the apricots so that they will stand up.) Place a piece of garlic and herb butter in each cavity and cook for 4 minutes more, until they are cooked to your liking.

4 servings

Steak with Tomatoes and Red Wine

2 pounds sirloin steak in a single piece

½ cup olive oil

7 tablespoons chopped oregano

3 large garlic cloves, minced

1 small onion, finely chopped

1½ pounds tomatoes, skinned, deseeded, and chopped

6 tablespoons full-bodied red wine

salt and pepper

Place the steak in a shallow dish. Combine 6 tablespoons of the olive oil, 1 tablespoon of the oregano, and 1 garlic clove in a pitcher and season with salt and pepper. Pour the mixture over the steak, turning to coat. Cover and marinate, turning once, for 4–6 hours. Heat the remaining oil in a pan, add the onion, and cook for 3–4 minutes, until softened. Add the tomatoes, the remaining oregano, the remaining garlic, and the wine and simmer gently for 10 minutes. Transfer the pan to the side of the barbecue to keep warm. Drain the steak, reserving the marinade. Grill for 10–20 minutes, depending on how well done you like your steak, then turn over, brush with the marinade, and grill for 10–20 minutes more. To serve, cut the steak into fairly thick slices and top each portion with some of the hot sauce.

4–6 servings

Sweet and Sour Steaks

4 round or sirloin steaks, about 6 ounces each

2 tablespoons soy sauce

4 tablespoons pineapple juice

1 tablespoon ground ginger

2 tablespoons cream sherry

½ teaspoon mustard powder

1 garlic clove, minced

2 tablespoons/¼ stick butter, melted

Place the meat in a large, shallow dish. Combine the soy sauce, pineapple juice, ginger, sherry, mustard powder, and garlic in a pitcher and pour the mixture over the steaks. Cover and marinate for at least 4 hours. Drain the steaks, reserving the marinade in a small pan. Bring the marinade to a boil, then transfer the pan to the side of the barbecue to keep warm. Grill the steaks, brushing occasionally with melted butter, for 5–7 minutes, until cooked to your liking. Serve the steaks with a little of the marinade spooned over.

4 servings

Garlic Steaks

6 round or sirloin steaks, about 8 ounces each

¼ cup butter, melted

3 garlic cloves, minced

½ cup lemon juice

2 tablespoons Worcestershire sauce

salt and pepper

Beat the steaks with a meat bat or the side of a rolling pin until about ⅓ inch thick. Combine the butter and garlic in a small bowl and brush the mixture all over the steaks. Grill, brushing frequently with the garlic butter, for about 5 minutes on each side. Stir the lemon juice and Worcestershire sauce into the remaining garlic butter and season with salt and pepper. Spread a little of the mixture over each steak before serving.

6 servings

Western Steak

2 tablespoons corn oil

4 bacon strips, diced

1 onion, finely chopped

4 tablespoons lemon juice

1 tablespoon tomato ketchup

1 tablespoon Worcestershire sauce

1 tablespoon horseradish sauce

4 round steaks

salt and pepper

Heat the oil in a pan, add the bacon and onion, and cook over low heat for about 5 minutes, until the onion is softened and golden brown. Stir in the lemon juice, ketchup, Worcestershire sauce, and horseradish sauce and season with salt and pepper. Place the steaks in a shallow dish and pour the mixture over them. Cover and marinate, turning occasionally, for at least 1 hour. Drain the steaks, reserving the marinade. Grill, basting occasionally with the marinade, for 5–7 minutes on each side, depending on how well done you like your steaks.

4 servings

Barbecue Skewers

1½ pounds beef shoulder steak, cut into 1 inch cubes

Tenderizing Marinade (see page 23)

16 white mushrooms

pepper

Place the beef cubes in a shallow dish and pour the marinade over them. Marinate, stirring occasionally, for at least 36 hours. Drain the beef, reserving the marinade, and thread onto 4 oiled skewers, alternating with the mushrooms. Season with salt and pepper and grill, turning and brushing frequently with the reserved marinade, for 10–15 minutes, until tender.

4 servings

Russian Shashlik

2 pounds sirloin steak, cut into 1 inch cubes

4 ounces white mushrooms

1 onion, minced

4 tablespoons red wine vinegar

1 teaspoon salt

½ teaspoon ground coriander

sunflower oil, for brushing

pepper

lemon wedges, to garnish

Place the meat and mushrooms in a large shallow dish. Combine the onion, vinegar, salt, and coriander in a pitcher, season with pepper, and pour the mixture over the meat. Cover and marinate overnight. Drain the meat and mushrooms, thread them alternately onto skewers, and brush with oil. Grill, turning and brushing with oil frequently, for 10–15 minutes. Serve garnished with lemon wedges.

6–8 servings

The Great Steak Sandwich

6 tablespoons olive oil

2 teaspoons mustard seeds

2 large red onions, thinly sliced

2 garlic cloves, minced

½ cup Italian parsley, chopped

1 tablespoon balsamic vinegar

2 sirloin steaks, about 8 ounces each

8 olive bread or crusty bread slices

3 ounces fontina cheese, thinly sliced

2 beefsteak tomatoes, sliced

4 ounces arugula

sea salt and crushed black peppercorns

Heat 4 tablespoons of the oil in a skillet. Add the mustard seeds, cover, and cook over medium heat for about 30 seconds, until they start to pop. Add the onions and garlic, cover again, and cook over low heat for 30 minutes, until very soft but not colored. Transfer the mixture to a blender or food processor and process until smooth. Spoon the mixture into a bowl and stir in the parsley and vinegar. Season with salt and pepper. Cover and set aside. Brush the steaks with some of the remaining oil and season with crushed peppercorns. Grill for 2–6 minutes on each side, depending on how well done you like your steak. Toast the bread slices on both sides until lightly golden, then spread with the onion mixture. Slice the steaks thinly and divide among 4 of the bread slices. Top with the fontina and tomato slices and arugula. Season with sea salt and crushed peppercorns and top with the remaining bread slices.

4 servings

Indian-style Kabobs

1 pound ground beef

1 garlic clove, minced

1 inch piece of fresh ginger root, chopped

1 teaspoon paprika

1 tablespoon hot curry powder

½ teaspoon ground coriander

pinch of chili powder

1 egg, beaten

2 tablespoons lemon juice

salt and pepper

Yogurt Sauce (see page 281), to serve

Combine the beef, garlic, ginger, 1/2 teaspoon of the paprika, the curry powder, coriander, and chili powder in a bowl and season with salt and pepper. Gradually work in the beaten egg, then let stand for 5 minutes. Mold the mixture into long, thin shapes on 4–6 oiled skewers. Grill, turning frequently, for 15 minutes, until browned and cooked through. Sprinkle with the lemon juice and remaining paprika before serving with the yogurt sauce.

4–6 servings

Mexican Kabobs

4 tablespoons corn oil

1 small onion, finely chopped

4 tablespoons red wine vinegar

1/2 teaspoon dried oregano

1/2 teaspoon ground cumin

1/2 teaspoon ground cloves

1/2 teaspoon ground cinnamon

1 garlic clove, minced

1 3/4 pounds round steak, cut into 1 inch cubes

3 1/2 cups white mushrooms

salt and pepper

Guacamole (see page 269), to serve

Heat 2 tablespoons of the oil in a pan and cook the onion until golden brown. Stir in the vinegar, oregano, cumin, cloves, cinnamon, garlic, and salt to taste. Cover and simmer for 15 minutes, then remove the pan from the heat, and cool. Place the meat in a shallow dish, brush with the remaining oil, and sprinkle with pepper. Add the cooled marinade, cover and leave to marinate for 2–4 hours. Drain the steak, reserving the marinade. Thread the meat onto 4–6 skewers, alternating with the mushrooms. Brush with the reserved marinade. Grill, turning and brushing with the marinade frequently, for 12–20 minutes, depending on well done you like your steak. Serve the kabobs with guacamole.

4–6 servings

Beef Strips with Horseradish

12 ounces round steak, about 2 inches thick

8 scallions, cut into 1 inch lengths

4 tablespoons soy sauce

4 tablespoons dry sherry

1 tablespoon creamed horseradish

Trim off any excess fat from the steak, then wrap and place in the freezer for 3 hours, until firm but not frozen. Using a very sharp knife, cut the steak horizontally into wafer-thin slices. Thread the steak slices and scallions onto skewers, weaving the meat around the scallions. Combine the soy sauce, sherry, and horseradish in a bowl, brush the mixture liberally over the meat, and marinate for 30 minutes. Grill the kabobs, brushing frequently with the marinade, for 2–3 minutes on each side, until the steak is brown and just cooked.

6 servings

Tomato Beef Kabobs

¾ cup tomato juice

pinch of garlic salt

pinch of dried mixed herbs

1 tablespoon soy sauce

1 pound round steak, cut into 1 inch cubes

8 pearl onions, par-boiled

4 cherry tomatoes, halved

8 white mushrooms

1 green bell pepper, deseeded and cut into 8 pieces

1 red bell pepper, deseeded and cut into 8 pieces

pepper

Combine the tomato juice, garlic salt, herbs, and soy sauce in a pitcher and season with pepper. Place the steak in a shallow dish, pour in the tomato mixture, and marinate, turning several times, for at least 1 hour. Drain the steak, reserving the marinade. Thread the steak, onions, tomatoes, mushrooms, and bell peppers alternately onto 4 oiled skewers. Grill, turning and brushing with marinade occasionally, for 15–20 minutes.

4 servings

Beef Kabobs with Beet and Horseradish Salsa

1½ pounds sirloin steak, cut into 16 long, thin strips

8 long rosemary sprigs

4 tablespoons balsamic vinegar

¾ cup red wine

¼ cup olive oil

1 tablespoon cracked black pepper

8 ounces cooked beet, peeled and chopped

½ red onion, finely chopped

1–2 tablespoons finely grated fresh horseradish or horseradish relish

salt

Thread 2 pieces of steak onto each rosemary sprig, concertina style, and place in a shallow dish. Combine the vinegar, wine, olive oil, and pepper in a pitcher and pour the mixture over the steak, turning to coat. Cover and marinate for 1–2 hours. Meanwhile, combine the beet, red onion, and horseradish in a bowl and season to taste with salt. Remove the kabobs, reserving the marinade. Sprinkle the kabobs with salt and grill, basting frequently with the marinade, for 3–4 minutes on each side. Serve with the salsa.

4 servings

Beef, Ginger, and Soy Kabobs

2 pounds sirloin steak, trimmed of fat and cut into ¾ inch cubes

2 inch piece of fresh ginger root, very thinly sliced

scant ½ cup soy sauce

scant ½ cup sake or dry sherry

5 tablespoons peanut or sunflower oil

10 scallions, green tops only, finely chopped

Thread the steak cubes and ginger slices onto long, thin skewers, putting a slice of ginger after every 2–3 meat cubes. Place the skewers in a shallow dish. Combine the soy sauce, sake or sherry, and oil and pour the mixture over the skewers, turning to coat. Cover and marinate for at least 2 hours. Remove the skewers and grill for 4–5 minutes on each side. Serve sprinkled with the scallions.

4 servings

Malay Beef

1¼ cups milk

⅔ cup dry unsweetened shredded coconut

1 inch piece of fresh ginger root, finely chopped

2 small chilies, deseeded and finely chopped

1 tablespoon dark brown sugar

½ teaspoon cayenne pepper

4 small quick-fry tenderized steaks

salt and pepper

Pour the milk into a small pan, add the coconut, and heat gently. Stir in the ginger, chilies, sugar, and cayenne, then remove the pan from the heat. Reserve 4 tablespoons of the mixture and pour the remainder into a shallow dish. Cut the steak into long 1 inch wide strips. Season with salt and pepper, then add to the dish. Cover and marinate for at least 2 hours. Just before serving, heat the reserved coconut mixture in a small pan, then place on the side of the barbecue to keep warm. Drain the meat, reserving the marinade. Thread the meat onto 4 skewers and grill, basting occasionally with the reserved marinade, for 3–4 minutes on each side. Serve with the warm coconut sauce spooned over.

4 servings

Japanese Beef

½ inch piece of fresh ginger root, minced

1 garlic clove, minced

2 tablespoons honey

2 tablespoons shoyu

1 tablespoon dry sherry

1 pound lean braising steak, cut into thin strips

1 green bell pepper, halved, deseeded, and sliced

Combine the ginger, garlic, honey, shoyu, and sherry in a shallow dish. Add the meat, turning to coat, then cover, and marinate for 2 hours. Drain the meat, reserving the marinade. Thread the meat and bell pepper slices onto skewers. Grill, turning and brushing with the marinade frequently, for 10–12 minutes, until tender.

4 servings

Stuffed Bell Peppers

2 green bell peppers, halved lengthwise and deseeded

2 tablespoons olive oil

1 small onion, finely chopped

1 celery stalk, finely chopped

9 ounces ground beef

⅔ cup Tomato Sauce (see page 280)

1 teaspoon chopped oregano

salt and pepper

Blanch the bell pepper halves in boiling water for 2 minutes, then drain well. Heat half the oil in a skillet and cook the onion and celery for about 5 minutes, until softened. Add the beef and cook, breaking it up with a wooden spoon, until browned. Stir in the tomato sauce and oregano and season with salt and pepper. Spoon the meat mixture into the bell pepper halves and brush the skins with the remaining oil. Cook toward the edge of the barbecue grid for 1 hour.

4 servings

Beef Shish Kabob

1–2 garlic cloves, minced

2 onions, minced

juice and finely grated zest of 1 lemon

5 tablespoons olive oil

2 teaspoons drained bottled green peppercorns, crushed

2 tablespoons chopped oregano or parsley

1 pound sirloin steak, cut into 1 inch cubes

1 yellow bell pepper, deseeded and cut into 1 inch squares

salt

Combine the garlic, onions, lemon juice and zest, olive oil, peppercorns, and oregano or parsley in a bowl. Add the steak cubes, season well and toss to coat. Cover and marinate for 2–3 hours. Drain the beef cubes, reserving the marinade, and thread onto 4 skewers, alternating with the bell pepper squares. Grill the kabobs, brushing with the reserved marinade, for 3–4 minutes on each side.

4 servings

Cheese-stuffed Veal Chops

4 thick, lean veal chops

4 ounces fontina or Bel Paese cheese, cut into 4 slices

2 tablespoons chopped basil

1 large garlic clove, finely chopped

2–4 tablespoons olive oil

salt and pepper

Cut horizontally through each chop on the side without a bone to make a deep pocket. Press a slice of cheese into each pocket. Combine the basil and garlic in a small bowl and season with salt and pepper. Sprinkle the herb mixture into the pockets. Brush each chop all over with the olive oil, then grill them for about 5–10 minutes on each side.

4 servings

Veal Chops with Kirsch

4 veal chops

1 tablespoon olive oil

3 tablespoons kirsch

juice of 1 orange

salt and pepper

chopped parsley, to garnish

Brush the chops all over with the oil and season with salt and pepper. Grill for 9–12 minutes on each side, until cooked and tender. Transfer to a platter. Warm the kirsch in a small pan or heatproof ladle, pour it over the chops, and ignite. When the flames die down, add the orange juice and sprinkle with parsley.

4 servings

Veal Chops with Roquefort and Mushroom Stuffing

3 ounces bacon strips, finely diced

1½ cups sliced white mushrooms

1 onion, chopped

½ cup crumbled Roquefort cheese

2 cups parsley, chopped

4 veal chops

1 tablespoon olive oil

salt and pepper

Heat the bacon in a pan over low heat until the fat runs. Add the mushrooms and onion and cook for 2–3 minutes. (If the mixture seems too dry, add a little olive oil.) Remove the pan from the heat and cool slightly, then stir in the cheese and parsley, and season with salt and pepper. Make a horizontal slit in each chop and spoon in the stuffing. Brush both sides with olive oil, then secure each slit with a toothpick. Grill, turning once, for 30 minutes. Remove and discard the toothpicks before serving.

4 servings

Veal and Fontina Cheese Rolls

6 tablespoons/¾ stick sweet butter, softened

2 tablespoons chopped parsley

1 tablespoon chopped sage

1 garlic clove, minced

finely grated zest of 1 lemon

6 long, thin veal scallops, total weight about 1 pound

6 thin prosciutto slices

6 very thin fontina or mozzarella cheese slices, total weight about 6 ounces

4 tablespoons olive oil

salt and pepper

sage leaves and lemon slices, to garnish

Marsala Aioli (see page 282), to serve

Combine the butter, parsley, sage, garlic, and lemon rind in a bowl and season with salt and pepper. Beat each veal scallop into a rectangle measuring about 8 x 5 inches, then halve them widthwise. Halve the prosciutto and cheese slices so that they are about the same size as the pieces of veal. Spread each piece of veal with the flavored butter, top with a prosciutto slice, then a cheese slice. Roll up tightly and tie with fine string. Chill for at least 8 hours. Thread 3 veal rolls lengthwise onto each of 4 skewers, then brush them all over with oil. Grill, turning once, for 8–10 minutes. Remove the rolls from the skewers, then cut off and discard the string before garnishing with sage leaves and lemon slices. Serve the rolls with the Marsala aioli.

6 servings

Veal Liver and Prosciutto Kabobs with Onion Relish

¼ cup/½ stick butter

4 large red onions, sliced

4 tablespoons thyme leaves

1 tablespoon red wine vinegar

1 tablespoon superfine sugar

12 ounces veal liver, sliced

6–8 prosciutto slices

16 bay leaves

2 tablespoons olive oil

salt and pepper

To make the onion relish, melt the butter in a large skillet. Add the onions and half the thyme, stir well, cover, and cook gently, stirring once, for 40 minutes. Remove the lid and stir in the vinegar and sugar. Bring to a boil and boil rapidly until reduced. Spoon into a bowl and let cool. Cut the liver and prosciutto into 3 x 1 inch strips. Place a strip of liver on top of a strip of prosciutto, sprinkle with a little of the remaining thyme, and season with salt and pepper. Roll up from the short end and thread onto a skewer. Repeat with the remaining liver and prosciutto, adding bay leaves at regular intervals, until 4 skewers have been filled. Brush the kabobs with the oil and grill, turning frequently, for 5–6 minutes. Serve the kabobs with warm or cold onion relish.

4 servings

Foil-wrapped Veal

4 veal loin chops

3 tomatoes, skinned and chopped

1 large onion, finely chopped

1 tablespoon finely chopped chives

½ teaspoon dried tarragon

½ teaspoon dried marjoram

4 tablespoons sunflower oil

4 tablespoons cream sherry

Cut 4 large squares of double-thickness foil and put a chop into the center of each. Combine the tomatoes, onion, chives, tarragon, and marjoram in a bowl. Divide this mixture among the chops. Combine the oil and sherry in another bowl, then spoon 2 tablespoons of the mixture over each chop. Fold the foil up and over the chops and crimp the edges to seal. Cook on the barbecue, turning once, for 30 minutes, until the chops are tender.

4 servings

Veal Scallops with Artichoke Paste

4 ounces drained bottled artichokes in oil, plus 1 tablespoon oil from the jar

4 sun-dried tomato halves in oil, drained

4 veal scallops, about 4 ounces each, pounded until thin

2 prosciutto slices, halved

4 bocconcini, or 1 mozzarella cut into fourths

olive oil, for brushing

salt and pepper

Place the artichokes, the oil from the jar, and sun-dried tomatoes in a blender or food processor and process to a smooth paste. Scrape into a bowl and season with salt and pepper. Spread each veal scallop evenly with the paste, then top with half a prosciutto slice and a bocconcini or piece of mozzarella. Fold the veal over to make a neat packet and seal each end with a toothpick. Brush the packets with oil and grill, turning frequently, for 4–5 minutes.

4 servings

SIZZLING LAMB

Apricot and Rosemary Spit-roasted Leg of Lamb

4 tablespoons sunflower oil

1 small onion, finely chopped

3 rosemary sprigs, chopped

1 cup fresh bread crumbs

14 ounce can apricot halves in fruit juice

4 pound leg of lamb, boned

salt and pepper

Heat half the oil in a small skillet and cook the onion for about 5 minutes, until soft. Stir in the rosemary and bread crumbs. Drain the apricots, reserving the can juice. Chop half the fruit, reserving the remaining apricots for garnish. Add the chopped apricots to the bread crumb mixture and stir in enough of the can juice to make a soft stuffing. Season with salt and pepper. Spoon the stuffing into the center of the lamb, then tie into a neat shape with fine string. Secure the ends with toothpicks, making sure it is tight or it will lose its shape. Combine the remaining oil and remaining can juice in a bowl and brush it all over the lamb. Attach the lamb to a rotisserie and cook over the barbecue, brushing occasionally with the fruit juice mixture, for 1 1/2 hours. Serve garnished with the reserved apricot halves.

8 servings

French Leg of Lamb

2 tablespoons sunflower oil

2 tablespoons white wine

3–4 pound leg of lamb

2 garlic cloves, cut into thin slivers

10 small rosemary sprigs

salt and pepper

Combine the oil and wine in a pitcher, season with salt and pepper, and brush all over the lamb. Make small slits in the lamb and insert the garlic slivers and rosemary sprigs. Place the lamb in a plastic bag, add the remaining oil and wine mixture, secure the top, and marinate, turning occasionally, for 2–4 hours. Drain the lamb, reserving the marinade, and attach to a rotisserie. Cook, basting occasionally with the marinade, for 1 1/2–2 hours, until tender and to your liking.

4–6 servings

Minted Leg of Lamb

4–5 pound leg of lamb, boned and rolled

¼ cup brown sugar

3 tablespoons sunflower oil

1 teaspoon grated lemon zest

3 tablespoons white wine vinegar

4 tablespoons chopped mint

1 teaspoon chopped tarragon

1 teaspoon salt

1 teaspoon mustard powder

mint leaves (optional)

Place the lamb in a shallow dish. Combine the sugar, oil, lemon zest, vinegar, mint, tarragon, salt, and mustard in a pan and heat gently until the sugar has dissolved. Bring to a boil, then simmer for 5 minutes. Remove the pan from the heat and cool. Pour the cooled mixture over the lamb and marinate for 24 hours. Drain the lamb, reserving the marinade. Attach to a rotisserie and cook, brushing frequently with the reserved marinade for 1¼–2 hours, until cooked according to your liking. Occasionally throw handfuls of mint leaves onto the coals for extra flavor and aroma, if you like.

6–8 servings

Marinated Leg of Lamb with Cream Sauce

4 pound leg of lamb

1¼ cups dry white wine

1 onion, thinly sliced

handful of celery leaves, coarsely chopped

2 teaspoons juniper berries, crushed

6 tablespoons olive oil

scant 1 cup heavy cream

salt and pepper

Make several deep widthwise slits in the leg of lamb at regular intervals, then place it in a shallow dish. Combine the wine, onion, celery leaves, and juniper berries in a bowl and season with salt and pepper. Pour the mixture over the lamb and marinate, turning occasionally, for at least 6 hours. Drain the lamb, reserving the marinade. Attach the lamb to a rotisserie, brush with oil and cook for 1 1/2 hours. Meanwhile, pour the marinade into a pan, adding any cooking juices from the lamb if you have a drip pan. Stir in the cream and heat gently without boiling. Transfer the pan to the side of the barbecue to keep warm. Carve the lamb and serve with the cream sauce.

6–8 servings

Lamb Shoulder with Potato Slices

4 pound shoulder of lamb

6 rosemary sprigs

6 thyme sprigs

3 garlic cloves, thinly sliced

1/2 cup olive oil

2 pounds potatoes, scrubbed

salt and pepper

Trim off any excess fat from the lamb, then cut 2–3 deep slashes through the meat to the bone. Place the rosemary and thyme sprigs in the cuts. Make small slits all over the meat and place a garlic slice in each. Brush the lamb with olive oil and sprinkle with salt and pepper. Grill the lamb, turning it every 10 minutes and brushing frequently with oil, for about 40 minutes, until cooked according to your liking. Remove the lamb from the heat, tent with foil, and let rest for 15 minutes before carving. Meanwhile, thickly slice the potatoes, brush with oil, and grill, turning once, for 15 minutes. Carve the lamb into slices and serve with the grilled potatoes.

6–8 servings

Greek Lamb with Olives

2 pound lamb half-leg or shank

2 garlic cloves, minced

$\frac{1}{3}$ cup/$\frac{3}{4}$ stick butter

1 cup pitted Greek black olives, finely chopped

6 tablespoons dry white wine

4 tablespoons lemon juice

1 tablespoon chopped parsley

2 tablespoons chopped mint

1 teaspoon dried oregano

1 bay leaf

salt and pepper

Season the lamb with salt and pepper. Gently heat the garlic and butter in a skillet until the butter melts. Add the lamb and cook, turning frequently, until browned on all sides. Place the lamb on a large sheet of foil and fold up the edges slightly. Combine the olives, wine, lemon juice, parsley, mint, oregano, and bay leaf in a pitcher and season with salt and pepper. Pour the mixture over the meat, then fold the foil around the lamb. Wrap the packet in a second piece of foil. Cook on the barbecue grid, turning every 30 minutes, for $1\frac{1}{2}$ hours, until tender.

8 servings

Breast of Lamb in a Piquant Sauce

2 x 4 pound breasts of lamb

4 cups boiling water

3 tablespoons white wine vinegar

2 tablespoons soy sauce

2 tablespoons honey

2 tablespoons plum jelly

1 teaspoon Worcestershire sauce

1 teaspoon mustard powder

1 teaspoon tomato ketchup

dash of lemon juice

Trim off the excess fat from the lamb and cut the meat into thick strips. Place in a pan, pour in the boiling water and 2 tablespoons of the vinegar, and bring to a boil. Lower the heat and simmer for 15 minutes. Meanwhile, combine all the remaining ingredients in another pan and heat gently. Drain the lamb and brush with the sauce. Grill, turning occasionally and brushing with more of the sauce, for 15–20 minutes.

6 servings

Spicy Lamb Ribs

4 pound breast of lamb

⅔ cup hard cider

2 tablespoons Worcestershire sauce

1 tablespoon brown sugar

2 tablespoons sunflower oil

2 tablespoons white wine vinegar

1 onion, finely chopped

½ teaspoon dried rosemary

salt and pepper

Trim off any excess fat from the lamb, cut into pieces between the bones, and place in a shallow dish. Combine the hard cider, Worcestershire sauce, sugar, oil, vinegar, onion, and rosemary in a pan, season with salt and pepper, and bring to a boil. Lower the heat and simmer for 3–4 minutes. Remove the pan from the heat and cool. Pour the cooled mixture over the lamb and marinate, turning occasionally, for 3 hours. Drain the lamb, reserving the marinade. Grill the lamb, turning and brushing with the marinade occasionally, for 45–60 minutes, until crisp. Serve garnished with lemon wedges.

4–6 servings

Lamb Chops with Green Peppercorn Glaze

4 lean lamb chops

3 teaspoons dried green peppercorns

½ teaspoon salt

1 tablespoon vegetable oil

4 tablespoons red currant jelly

Trim off any excess fat from the chops. Put the peppercorns and salt in a mortar and crush with a pestle. Press the mixture onto both sides of the chops. Brush the lamb with the oil and grill for about 10 minutes on each side, until cooked to your liking. Meanwhile, heat the red currant jelly in a small pan until melted. Serve the chops with the jelly spooned over.

4 servings

Lamb Chops with Peach and Ginger

14 ounce can peach slices in fruit juice

¼ cup dry white wine

1 teaspoon ground ginger

½ teaspoon dried oregano

2 tablespoons sunflower oil

1 onion, chopped

1 bay leaf

6 lamb leg chops

1 garlic clove, halved

salt and pepper

Drain the peach slices, reserving the juice. Place 4 tablespoons of the juice in a shallow dish, add the wine, ginger, oregano, oil, onion, and bay leaf, and mix well. Add the chops, turning to coat, then marinate for 2 hours. Drain the chops, reserving the marinade, and pat dry with paper towels. Rub the chops all over with the cut sides of the garlic. Grill, turning and basting with the reserved marinade frequently, for 10–15 minutes, until tender. Season with salt and pepper, place the peach slices on top of the chops and grill for 5 minutes more.

6 servings

Deviled Lamb Chops

4 lamb leg chops

4 teaspoons prepared hot or medium mustard

4 tablespoons brown sugar

mint sprigs, to garnish

Spread 1 side of each of the chops with half the mustard and sprinkle with half the sugar. Grill for 5 minutes. Turn the chops over, spread with the remaining mustard, and sprinkle with the remaining sugar. Grill for 5 minutes more. Serve garnished with mint sprigs.

4 servings

Spicy Lamb Packets

6 lamb loin chops

1/4 cup/1/2 stick butter, melted

2 onions, sliced into rings

2 garlic cloves, minced

1 teaspoon ground ginger

1 ground allspice

1 teaspoon dried rosemary

2 tablespoons honey

salt and pepper

rosemary sprigs, to garnish

Cut 6 squares of double-thickness foil. Brush the chops with melted butter on both sides, season with salt and pepper, and place 1 chop on each foil square. Heat the remaining butter in a pan, add the onions and garlic and cook, stirring occasionally, for 3 minutes. Stir in the ginger, allspice, and rosemary and cook for 1 minute. Stir in the honey. Divide the mixture among the foil squares, spooning it over the chops. Fold up the sides of the foil and crimp the edges to seal. Place the packets on the barbecue grid and cook for about 30 minutes. Serve garnished with rosemary sprigs.

6 servings

Grilled Lamb Steaks

3 pound boned leg of lamb

1/4 cup/1/2 stick butter, softened

1 tablespoon chopped parsley

salt and black pepper

Cut the lamb into steaks about 1 inch thick. Trim off any excess fat and rub both sides with salt and pepper. Mash the butter and parsley together and spread over the steaks. Grill, turning occasionally, for 15–20 minutes, until cooked to your liking.

4–6 servings

Lamb Noisettes with Mint Pesto

1 cup mint

1/2 cup Italian parsley

1/4 cup shelled pistachios

2 garlic cloves

2/3 cup olive oil

1/3 cup grated Parmesan cheese

8 lamb noisettes

salt and pepper

Place the mint, parsley, pistachios, and garlic in a blender or food processor and process until finely chopped. With the motor running, gradually add 1/2 cup of the olive oil in a thin, steady stream. Scrape the pesto into a bowl, stir in the Parmesan, and season with salt and pepper. Brush the noisettes with the remaining olive oil, season with pepper, and grill for 4–5 minutes on each side. Transfer to plates and top with the pesto before serving.

4 servings

Summer Lamb Packets

4 lamb leg steaks

2 onions, sliced

4 ounces sharp Cheddar cheese, sliced

1 tablespoon chopped parsley

salt and pepper

Cut 4 squares of double-thickness foil, place a leg steak in the center of each, and season with salt and pepper. Divide the onion among the steaks and top each with sliced cheese. Bring up the sides of the foil and crimp to seal. Cook the packets on the barbecue, turning twice, for 30 minutes. Remove the meat from the packets to serve and sprinkle with chopped parsley.

4 servings

Lamb Noisettes with Eggplant and Olive Paste

1 large eggplant, about 8 ounces

1 cup pitted black olives

1 cup parsley

1 tablespoon coarse grain mustard

2 garlic cloves, minced

8 lamb noisettes

2 tablespoons olive oil

salt and pepper

Place the eggplant under a preheat broiler and broil, turning occasionally, for about 20 minutes, until the skin is charred and the flesh is soft. Cool slightly, then slit the skin, and squeeze the eggplant over the sink to remove the bitter juices. Cut in half and scoop out the flesh into a blender or food processor. Add the olives, parsley, mustard, and garlic, and season with salt and pepper. Process until smooth, then spoon into a bowl. Brush the noisettes with the olive oil, season with pepper, and grill for 4–5 minutes on each side. Transfer to plates and top the noisettes with the eggplant paste before serving.

4 servings

Minted Lamb Noisettes

8 lamb noisettes

1 tablespoon white wine vinegar

1 large bunch of mint, finely chopped

⅔ cup plain yogurt

salt and pepper

mint sprigs, to garnish

Place the noisettes in a shallow dish. Combine the vinegar, mint, and yogurt in a pitcher and season with salt and pepper. Pour the mixture over the noisettes, turning to coat, and marinate for 2–4 hours. Grill the noisettes for about 5 minutes on each side. Serve garnished with mint sprigs.

4 servings

Classic Shish Kabob

2 pounds lean lamb, cut into 1 inch cubes

⅔ cup plain yogurt

4 tablespoons lemon juice

1 tablespoon olive oil

4 rosemary or marjoram sprigs

4 lemon wedges, to garnish

shredded salad greens and pitted black olives, to serve

Place the lamb in a shallow dish, add the yogurt, lemon juice, and olive oil, and season with salt and pepper. Stir well to mix, cover, and marinate for 8 hours or overnight. Drain the lamb, reserving the marinade, and thread onto skewers. Place the herb sprigs on the barbecue grid and place the kabobs on top. Grill, turning and basting with the marinade occasionally, for 15–20 minutes. Serve garnished with lemon wedges, on a bed of shredded salad, sprinkled with black olives.

4 servings

Middle Eastern Kabobs

2 onions, coarsely chopped

2/3 cup olive oil

grated zest and juice of 1 lemon

1 teaspoon ground cinnamon

2 pounds boneless shoulder of lamb, cubed

4 zucchini

salt and pepper

Place the onions in a blender or food processor and process until very finely chopped. Press through a wire strainer over a large bowl to extract the juice. Add the oil, lemon zest and juice, and cinnamon to the bowl, season with salt and pepper, and mix well. Add the lamb, turning to coat, cover, and marinate for 3–4 hours or overnight. Cut off 6 long thin strips of peel from each zucchini, then slice them. Drain the meat. Thread the lamb cubes and zucchini slices onto 8 skewers. Grill, turning frequently, for about 10 minutes, until cooked to your liking.

8 servings

Greek Kabobs

4 tablespoons olive oil

2 tablespoons white wine vinegar

2 tablespoons lemon juice

1 garlic clove, minced

1 small onion, finely chopped

2½ pounds lamb tenderloin, cut into 1 inch cubes

2 onions, divided into layers and cut into 1 inch squares

8 bay leaves

salt and pepper

lemon wedges, to garnish

Combine the oil, vinegar, lemon juice, garlic, and chopped onion in a shallow dish and season with salt and pepper. Add the lamb, stir to coat, cover, and marinate, turning occasionally, for at least 2 hours. Blanch the onion pieces in boiling water for 1 minute, then drain. Drain the lamb, reserving the marinade. Thread the lamb, onion squares, and bay leaves onto 6–8 skewers. Grill, turning and basting with the marinade frequently, for 10–15 minutes. Serve garnished with the lemon wedges.

6–8 servings

Lamb and Feta Kabobs

2 pounds lean lamb, cut into 1½ inch cubes

6 tablespoons olive oil

4 tablespoons lemon juice

2 large garlic cloves, minced

1 tablespoon chopped oregano

1 tablespoon chopped thyme

1 tablespoon chopped marjoram

1 cup crumbled feta cheese

4 bay leaves, crumbled

salt and pepper

Trim off any excess fat from the meat cubes and place them in a shallow dish. Combine the olive oil, lemon juice, garlic, oregano, thyme, and marjoram in a pitcher and season with salt and pepper. Pour the mixture over the lamb, cover, and marinate for at least 4 hours. Drain the lamb, reserving the marinade. Thread the meat onto 4 long skewers and brush with some of the marinade. Grill for about 5 minutes on each side. Transfer the skewers to serving plates and sprinkle with the feta and bay leaves.

4 servings

Lamb Sate

1¼ pounds lean lamb, cut into 1 inch cubes

⅔ cup soy sauce

2 tablespoons lemon juice

1 tablespoon minced fresh ginger root

1 garlic clove, minced

salt and pepper

Place the lamb in a shallow dish and season with salt and pepper. Combine the soy sauce, lemon juice, ginger, and garlic in a pitcher. Pour the mixture over the lamb and marinate, turning occasionally, for 2–3 hours. Drain the meat and thread the cubes onto skewers. Grill, turning occasionally, for 10–15 minutes, until tender.

4–6 servings

Korean Kabobs

1 large garlic clove, minced

4 tablespoons soy sauce

4 tablespoons vegetable oil

2 tablespoons peanut butter

2 tablespoons finely chopped scallion

1 teaspoon sesame seeds

pinch of chili powder

1½ pounds lean lamb, cut into ½ inch cubes

salt and pepper

Combine the garlic, soy sauce, oil, and peanut butter in a bowl, whisking well. Gradually whisk in the scallion, sesame seeds, and chili powder and season with salt and pepper. Add the meat, turning to coat, then marinate for 2–4 hours. Thread the lamb onto 4 skewers. Grill, turning frequently, for 10–15 minutes, until it is cooked to your liking.

4 servings

Mini Kabobs

2 tablespoons sunflower oil

1 tablespoon white wine vinegar

1 garlic clove, minced

1½ pounds boned shoulder of lamb, cut into ½ inch cubes

1 red bell pepper, deseeded and cut into 8 squares

8 white mushrooms

4 small tomatoes

4 bay leaves

salt and pepper

Combine the oil, vinegar, and garlic in a plastic bag and season with salt and pepper. Add the lamb cubes, seal the top and chill overnight. Drain the lamb, reserving the marinade. Thread the meat onto 4 skewers, alternating with the bell pepper squares and mushrooms. Add a tomato and bay leaf to each skewer. Grill, turning and brushing with the reserved marinade occasionally, for 10 minutes.

4 servings

Kofta Kabobs

1 pound ground lamb

1 onion, minced

½ cup pine nuts, roasted and chopped

1 tablespoon chopped oregano

½ teaspoon ground cumin

½ teaspoon ground coriander

salt and pepper

Middle Eastern Yogurt Dip (see page 268), to serve

Place the lamb in a food processor and grind to a smooth paste. Alternatively, pass through the finest blade of a meat grinder. Scrape into a bowl and stir in the onion, pine nuts, oregano, cumin, and coriander. Season with salt and pepper. Mold the mixture around 4 long skewers, shaping it into "sausage" shapes. Grill for 10–12 minutes, turning frequently, until cooked through. Serve with the yogurt dip.

4 servings

Skewered Lamb Meatballs

¾ cup golden raisins

1½ pounds ground lamb

4 cups soft white bread crumbs

2 eggs, beaten

1 tablespoon curry powder

2 onions, cut into squares

salt and pepper

Place the golden raisins in a bowl, cover with water and soak for 1 hour, then drain. Combine the lamb, bread crumbs, eggs, curry powder, and golden raisins and season with salt and pepper. Shape the mixture into 24 balls and thread onto 6 skewers, alternating with the onion slices. Grill, turning frequently, for 15–20 minutes.

6 servings

Sheftalia

2 garlic cloves

2¾ pounds lean lamb

1 large onion, chopped

6 tablespoons chopped parsley

1 medium egg, beaten

1 teaspoon ground allspice

seasoned all-purpose flour, for coating

sunflower oil, for brushing

salt and pepper

Using the flat of a knife blade, crush the garlic cloves with 1 teaspoon salt. Place the lamb, onion, parsley, and garlic in a food processor and process until finely ground and smooth. Alternatively, grind together several times in a meat grinder. Place the mixture in a bowl, stir in the egg and allspice, and season with pepper. Shape the mixture into thin "sausages" about 2$^1/_2$ inches long and roll between well-floured hands until they are firm and lightly coated with flour. Chill for 24 hours. Thread the "sausages" lengthwise onto oiled skewers and lightly brush with oil. Grill, turning and brushing with oil occasionally, for 10–15 minutes, until cooked through.

8 servings

Lamb Kabobs with Mint Dip

1$^1/_2$ pounds lamb tenderloin, cut into 1 inch cubes

1$^1/_4$ cups plain yogurt

1 tablespoon olive oil

2 teaspoons concentrated mint sauce

$^1/_4$ cup cream cheese, softened

salt and pepper

Place the lamb in a shallow dish. Combine half the yogurt, the olive oil, and 1 teaspoon of the mint sauce in a pitcher. Pour the mixture over the lamb, turning to coat. Cover and marinate for 1 hour. Drain the meat and thread onto 4 oiled skewers. Grill, turning frequently, for 15 minutes, until cooked and tender. Meanwhile, combine the remaining yogurt, and mint sauce with the cream cheese. Season to taste. Serve the kabobs with the mint dip.

4 servings

Lamb Kabobs Marinated in Yogurt

2 pounds boneless leg of lamb, cut into $^3/_4$ inch cubes

1$^1/_4$ cups plain yogurt

2 garlic cloves, minced

grated zest of 1 lemon

salt and pepper

1 bunch of cilantro, coarsely chopped, and lime wedges, to garnish

Thread the lamb cubes onto long skewers and place in a shallow dish. Combine the yogurt, garlic, and lemon zest in a pitcher and season with salt and pepper. Pour the yogurt mixture over the lamb, turning to coat. Cover and marinate for at least 12 hours. Grill the kabobs, turning frequently, for about 15 minutes, or until cooked to your liking. Serve sprinkled with the coriander and garnished with lime wedges.

4 servings

Kibbeh

1 cup finely ground couscous

1 small onion, minced

8 ounces ground lamb

1½ teaspoons salt

½ teaspoon pepper

½ teaspoon ground cinnamon

½ teaspoon paprika

Place the couscous in a bowl, pour in cold water to cover, and soak for 30 minutes. Drain well, pressing out as much water as possible. Combine the onion, lamb, salt, pepper, cinnamon, and paprika in a bowl and knead together. Gradually knead in the couscous. Continue to knead for about 10 minutes, until the mixture forms a soft "dough." With damp hands, divide the mixture into 8 portions and roll each between your palms into a long oval shape. Mold each oval onto a metal skewer, pressing it on firmly. Grill, turning frequently, for about 10 minutes.

8 servings

Souvlakia

2 pounds boneless leg of lamb, cut into 1 inch cubes

2 onions, cut into fourths

4 tablespoons lemon juice

4 tablespoons olive oil

1 garlic clove, minced

1 teaspoon chopped oregano

1 tablespoon chopped parsley

3 tomatoes, cut into fourths

4 bay leaves

salt and pepper

Place the lamb in a shallow dish and add the onions. Combine the lemon juice, oil, garlic, oregano, and parsley in a pitcher and season with salt and pepper. Pour the mixture over the lamb, cover, and marinate for at least 12 hours. Drain the lamb and thread onto 4 skewers, alternating with the onions and tomatoes and finishing with a bay leaf on each skewer. Grill, turning frequently, for 10–20 minutes.

4 servings

Lamb and Mushroom Kabobs

1 onion, chopped

1 garlic clove, minced

2 teaspoons dried mixed herbs

4 tablespoons vegetable oil

6 tablespoons red wine

1 tablespoon lemon juice

1½ pounds boneless leg of lamb, cut into 1 inch cubes

8 fatty bacon strips

16 mushrooms

salt and pepper

Combine the onion, garlic, herbs, oil, wine, and lemon juice in a shallow dish and season with salt and pepper. Add the lamb cubes and stir to coat. Cover and marinate, turning once or twice, for 4–6 hours. Drain the lamb, reserving the marinade. Roll up the bacon strips. Thread the lamb, bacon rolls, and mushrooms alternately onto 4 long skewers and brush with the marinade. Grill, turning and brushing with the marinade occasionally, for 10–15 minutes, until tender and cooked to your liking.

4 servings

Liver and Bacon Skewers

4 ounces bacon strips

12 ounces lamb's liver, cut into bitesize pieces

1½ cups small white mushrooms

¼ cup/½ stick butter, melted

pepper

Cut the bacon strips in half and roll up. Thread the liver, bacon, and mushrooms alternately onto 4 skewers. Brush with melted butter and season with pepper. Grill, turning frequently, for 8–10 minutes.

4 servings

Liver and Bacon Kabobs with Tomatoes

1 pound lamb's liver, cut into 1 inch cubes

4 tablespoons sunflower oil

2 tablespoons lemon juice

12 fatty bacon strips

8 large white mushrooms

8 bay leaves

4 large tomatoes, halved

Place the liver in a shallow dish. Combine the oil and lemon juice in a pitcher, pour the mixture over the liver, and marinate for 1–2 hours. Roll up the bacon strips. Drain the liver, reserving the marinade. Thread the liver, bacon, mushrooms, and bay leaves onto 4 skewers. Grill, turning and brushing with the reserved marinade frequently, for 10 minutes. Grill the tomatoes alongside the kabobs and serve with them.

4 servings

Liver Shashlik

1 pound lamb's liver, cut into 1 inch cubes

8 pearl onions, blanched

8 small tomatoes, skinned

3½ cups white mushrooms

16 bay leaves

1 tablespoon sunflower oil

1 tablespoon white wine vinegar

4 tablespoons lemon juice

1 tablespoon chopped parsley

salt and pepper

Thread the liver, onions, tomatoes, mushrooms, and bay leaves onto 8 skewers. Brush with oil, sprinkle with vinegar, and season with salt and pepper. Grill, turning frequently, for 10 minutes. Serve sprinkled with lemon juice and parsley

4 servings

Liver with Lemon, Sage, and Black Pepper

1 pound lamb's liver, thinly sliced

3 tablespoons lemon juice

2 sage sprigs, very finely chopped

2 tablespoons sunflower oil

2 tablespoons/¼ stick butter, melted

salt and pepper

Brush the liver generously with lemon juice and sprinkle with a little salt and plenty of black pepper. Combine the sage, oil, and butter in a bowl and brush the mixture over the liver. Grill, brushing frequently with the sage mixture, for 6 minutes on each side under tender and cooked through.

6 servings

PORK DISHES

Orange-glazed Pork Tenderloin

3–5 pound pork tenderloin in a single piece

3 tablespoons/⅓ stick butter

½ cup brown sugar

¾ cup frozen concentrated orange juice

2 teaspoons cornstarch

4 ounces seedless green grapes, halved

Calculate the cooking time, allowing 25–30 minutes per pound of meat. Score the fat on the pork tenderloin at 1 inch intervals. Place the meat, fat side up, on the barbecue grid and cook, turning occasionally, for the calculated time (1¼–2½ hours). Toward the end of the cooking time, melt the butter in pan and stir in the sugar and concentrated orange juice. Brush some of the mixture over the pork, then return the pan to the heat. Stir the cornstarch with 4½ tablespoons water to make a smooth paste, then stir the paste into the orange mixture. Cook stirring constantly, until thickened, then simmer for 8 minutes more. Stir in the grapes and serve with the pork.

6–8 servings

Stuffed Pork Tenderloin

¾ cup ground almonds

4 large oranges

2 tablespoons honey

½ cup olive oil

2 tablespoons chopped oregano

1 pound pork tenderloin, trimmed

4 garlic cloves, thinly sliced

1 tablespoon butter, diced

salt and pepper

Spread out the ground almonds on a cookie sheet and toast in a preheated oven, 350°F, for 10 minutes, until golden Remove from the oven and cool then tip into a bowl. Finely grate the zest of 2 of the oranges into the bowl, stir in the honey to make a paste, and season with salt and pepper. Remove the white pith from these 2 oranges and separate them into segments. Squeeze the juice from the remaining oranges into a pitcher and stir in the olive oil and oregano. Slice the pork tenderloin lengthwise almost all the way through, then open out like a book. Divide the almond mixture between the halves of the tenderloin. Drain the orange segments, adding any juice to the pitcher of marinade, and divide them and the garlic slivers between the halves of the tenderloin, placing them on top of the almond mixture. Bring the edges of the meat together and tie the tenderloin with string at 1 inch intervals. Place in a shallow dish, pour the marinade over it, turning to coat, cover, and marinate for 8 hours or overnight. Drain the tenderloin, reserving the marinade, and season with salt and pepper. Grill, basting frequently with the marinade, for 40–45 minutes. Transfer the meat to a platter, tent with foil, and let stand for 10–15 minutes. Tip the remaining marinade into a pan and bring to a boil. Boil rapidly until reduced by half, then gradually whisk in the butter. To serve, remove and discard the string from the meat and cut into slices. Serve with the sauce.

4 servings

Honey Ribs

3 pounds country-style pork ribs in 2 pieces

½ cup soy sauce

2 garlic cloves, minced

2 tablespoons honey

2 tablespoons dry sherry

Wipe the ribs with damp paper towels and place on a rack in a shallow roasting pan. Bake in a preheated oven, 350°F, for 45 minutes. Pour off the fat from the roasting pan. Combine the soy sauce, garlic, honey, and sherry in a pitcher and pour the mixture over the ribs. Marinate for at least 1 hour, turning occasionally. Grill the ribs, turning and basting with the marinade occasionally, for 10–15 minutes, until they are crisp and brown.

6 servings

Simple Ribs

1½ pounds country-style pork ribs, separated between the bones

Basic Barbecue Sauce (see page 270)

Place the ribs in a pan, add water to cover, and bring to a boil. Simmer for 10 minutes, drain, and cool. Trim off any excess fat, then place the ribs in a shallow dish and pour the barbecue sauce over them, turning to coat. Marinate for 1 hour. Drain the ribs, reserving the marinade. Sear the ribs for 6–8 minutes on each side, then grill, turning and brushing with the reserved marinade frequently, for 15–20 minutes more, until crisp.

4 servings

Sichuan Ribs

4 tablespoons hoi-sin sauce

2 tablespoons honey

4 tablespoons soy sauce

4 teaspoons white wine vinegar

½ cup chicken broth

¼ teaspoon Chinese five-spice powder

3 pounds country-style pork ribs, separated between the bones

salt and pepper

Chili Dipping Sauce (see page 268), to serve

Combine the hoi-sin sauce, honey, soy sauce, vinegar, chicken broth, and five-spice powder in a pitcher. Rub the ribs all over with salt and season with pepper, then place in a shallow dish. Pour the marinade over them, cover, and marinate, turning once, for 4 hours. Drain the marinade into a pitcher, place the ribs in a hinged rack, and grill for 10 minutes. Turn the rack over and grill the ribs for 10 minutes more. Baste the ribs with the marinade, turn the rack over, and grill for 15 minutes. Baste the ribs with the marinade, turn the rack over, and grill for a final 10 minutes. Serve with small bowls of chili dipping sauce.

4–6 servings

Cantonese Ribs

4 pounds country-style pork ribs, separated between the bones

2 x quantity Chinese Marinade (see page 25)

Place the ribs and marinade in a large plastic bag, seal the top and marinate for 4–8 hours. Remove the ribs, reserving the marinade. Place the ribs on the barbecue grid or on a spit and grill for 1–1½ hours. Brush with the marinade toward the end of the cooking time.

4–6 servings

Sweet and Sour Ribs

⅔ cup white wine vinegar

2 teaspoons prepared mustard

3 tablespoons brown sugar

3 tablespoons Worcestershire sauce

5 tablespoons tomato paste

3 tablespoons lemon juice

1 small onion, finely chopped

2 pounds country-style pork ribs

salt and pepper

Combine the vinegar, mustard, sugar, Worcestershire sauce, tomato paste, lemon juice, and onion in a pan, season with salt and pepper, and bring to a boil, then lower the heat, and simmer, stirring occasionally, for 30 minutes. Make deep slits all over the ribs with a sharp knife, then brush all over with the sauce. Grill, turning and brushing with the sauce frequently, for 1–1¼ hours.

4 servings

Ribs with Spicy Orange Sauce

2 pounds country-style pork ribs, separated between the bones

sunflower oil, for brushing

2 tablespoons honey

3 tablespoons soy sauce

3 tablespoons tomato ketchup

dash of Tabasco sauce

1 small garlic clove, minced

pinch of mustard powder

pinch of paprika

¼ cup orange juice

¼ cup white wine vinegar

salt and pepper

Brush the ribs with a little oil and grill, turning several times, for 15 minutes, until browned. Meanwhile, make the sauce. Combine the honey, soy sauce, tomato ketchup, Tabasco, garlic, mustard, and paprika in a bowl and season with salt and pepper. Stir in the orange juice and vinegar. Brush the sauce over the ribs. Continue to grill, turning and brushing with the sauce occasionally, for 30 minutes more.

4 servings

Spit-roasted Ribs

1 rack of pork ribs

Spicy Barbecue Sauce (see page 271)

Trim off any excess fat from the ribs, then attach to a rotisserie, threading the spit through the meat between every second pair of ribs. Cook the ribs for 20 minutes, then brush them all over with the spicy barbecue sauce. Continue to cook, brushing with the sauce every 10 minutes, for 30–40 minutes more, until crisp on the outside. Cut into individual ribs to serve.

4 servings

Pork and Juniper Kabobs and Ruby Grapefruit Salsa

3 ruby grapefruit

2 tablespoons chopped chives

2 tablespoons very finely chopped red onion

2 tablespoons lime juice

3 tablespoons honey

2 garlic cloves, minced

6 juniper berries, finely crushed

7 tablespoons walnut or olive oil

1 pound pork tenderloin, cut into 1½ inch cubes

16 bay leaves

pepper

Squeeze the juice from 1 grapefruit. Peel the remaining grapefruit, then cut into segments, working over a bowl to catch the juice. Chop the grapefruit segments and place in another bowl with the chives and onion. Season with pepper and set aside. Combine the grapefruit juice, lime juice, honey, garlic, juniper berries, and oil in a shallow dish. Add the pork cubes, turning to coat, and marinate for 1–2 hours. Drain the pork, reserving the marinade. Thread the pork onto 4 skewers, placing a bay leaf between each piece. Grill, basting with the reserved marinade frequently, for 15–20 minutes, until cooked through and tender. Serve with the grapefruit salsa.

4 servings

Chinese Pork Kabobs

1 pound pork tenderloin, cut into 1 inch cubes

1 green bell pepper, halved, deseeded, and cut into 1 inch squares

7 ounce can pineapple chunks, drained

Chinese Marinade (see page 25)

4 small tomatoes

Sweet and Sour Sauce (see page 277), to serve

Put the pork, bell pepper, and pineapple in a shallow dish and pour in the marinade, turning to coat. Marinate, turning and basting occasionally, for 2 hours. Drain the pork, bell pepper, and pineapple, reserving the marinade, and thread alternately onto long skewers, leaving room at the end. Grill, turning and brushing with the reserved marinade occasionally, for 15 minutes. Place the tomatoes on the ends of the skewers and grill for 5 minutes more. Serve with sweet-and-sour sauce.

4 servings

Pork Sate

3 tablespoons smooth or crunchy peanut butter

2 tablespoons soy sauce

1 tablespoon vinegar

1 tablespoon chicken broth or water

1 teaspoon curry powder

1 pound pork tenderloin, cut into ½ inch cubes

salt and pepper

lemon wedges and cucumber chunks, to garnish

Combine the peanut butter, soy sauce, vinegar, stock or water, and curry powder in a pan and season with a little salt and some pepper. Stir over low heat until the mixture is thick and creamy. Remove the pan from the heat and cool. Stir the pork cubes into the cooled mixture, tip into a shallow dish, cover, and marinate for 4 hours. Thread the pork cubes onto 12 wooden skewers and grill for 2 minutes. Turn the skewers and cook for 2 minutes more. Serve garnished with lemon wedges and chunks of cucumber.

6 servings

Fruity Pork Kabobs

¾ cup light brown sugar

4 tablespoons apricot jelly

2 tablespoons Worcestershire sauce

⅓ cup white wine vinegar

1 teaspoon mustard powder

1 pound pork tenderloin, cut into 1 inch cubes

8 ounce can apricots in fruit juice, drained

8 ready-to-eat prunes

Combine the sugar, apricot jelly, Worcestershire sauce, vinegar, and mustard in a small pan and heat gently until the sugar dissolves. Thread the pork, apricots and prunes alternately onto 4 oiled skewers, brush with the sugar mixture, and grill, turning and brushing with the sugar mixture frequently, for 15 minutes.

4 servings

Japanese Pork Kabobs

1 inch piece of fresh ginger root, minced

1 scallion, finely chopped

5 tablespoons shoyu

4 tablespoons sugar

4 tablespoons rice wine or dry sherry

2 pounds pork tenderloin, thinly sliced

Combine the ginger, scallion, shoyu, sugar, and rice wine or sherry in a shallow dish. Add the meat, turning to coat, then cover, and marinate for at least 1 hour. Drain the meat, reserving the marinade. Thread it onto 4 skewers. Grill, turning and brushing with the marinade frequently, for about 10 minutes.

4 servings

Pork and Lemon Brochettes

1½ pounds pork tenderloin, cut into 1½ inch strips

2 onions, thickly sliced and blanched

7 teaspoons lemon juice

sunflower oil, for brushing

scant 1 cup chicken or vegetable broth

1 tablespoon soy sauce

1/4 teaspoon Worcestershire sauce

1 teaspoon cornstarch

2 tomatoes, skinned, deseeded, and chopped

salt and pepper

lemon wedges, to garnish

Thread the meat onto 4 long skewers, interspersing it with the onion slices. Reserve 1 teaspoon of the lemon juice, brush the remainder over the meat, then brush with oil. Grill, turning and brushing with oil frequently, for 20 minutes. Meanwhile, combine the broth, soy sauce, Worcestershire sauce, and reserved lemon juice in a pan and bring to a boil. Stir the cornstarch with 2 tablespoons cold water to make a smooth paste, then stir the paste into the pan. Add the tomatoes and simmer for 5 minutes. Serve the brochettes with the sauce, garnished with lemon wedges.

4 servings

Pork, Ham, and Sage Rolls

scant 1/2 cup golden raisins

4 tablespoons Marsala

4 long, thin pork scallops, about 3 ounces each

4 thin prosciutto slices

1 tablespoon chopped sage

16 white bread cubes, about 1 inch square

4 tablespoons olive oil

8 thin fatty bacon strips, halved crosswise

salt and pepper

Combine the golden raisins and Marsala in a small bowl and soak for 1 hour. Cut each pork scallop in 4 long strips and cut the prosciutto into strips about the same size. Place a strip of prosciutto on top of each pork strip, sprinkle with sage and few golden raisins, and season with salt and pepper. Roll up each strip neatly. Lightly brush each bread cube with olive oil, then roll up in a half-strip of bacon. Thread 4 pork and ham rolls and 4 bread and bacon rolls alternately onto each of 4 skewers. Brush the rolls with olive oil. Grill for 3–4 minutes on each side.

4 servings

Sweet and Sour Pork Kabobs

7 ounce can pineapple cubes in syrup

1 pound pork tenderloin, cubed

1 green bell pepper, halved, deseeded, and cut into 1 inch squares

1 red bell pepper, halved, deseeded, and cut into 1 inch squares

1 tablespoon tomato paste

2 tablespoons brown sugar

2 tablespoons white wine vinegar

2 teaspoons Worcestershire sauce

pinch of chili powder

2 teaspoons cornstarch

salt and pepper

Drain the syrup from the can of pineapple into a pan. Thread the pork, bell pepper squares, and pineapple cubes alternately onto 8 metal skewers. Stir the tomato paste, sugar, vinegar, Worcestershire sauce, and chili powder into the pineapple syrup and bring to a boil. Stir the cornstarch with 1 tablespoon cold water in a small bowl to a paste. Stir the paste into the pineapple syrup mixture and cook, stirring constantly, for 1 minute, until thickened and smooth. Brush the sauce over the kabobs. Grill the kabobs, turning and brushing with the sauce frequently, for 10–12 minutes.

4 servings

Blue Cheese Chops

6 pork chops

4 tablespoons olive oil

4 ounces Roquefort or other blue cheese, cut into 6 slices

¼ cup walnut pieces

salt and pepper

chopped basil, to garnish

Brush the chops with olive oil and season with salt and pepper. Grill for about 7 minutes on each side, until browned and the juices run clear when the meat is pierced with the point of a sharp knife. Place a slice of cheese on top of each chop, sprinkle with the walnuts, and cook for 2–3 minutes more, until the cheese melts. Serve garnished with basil.

6 servings

Pork Chops Provençal

8 ounce can tomatoes

1 small onion, finely chopped

2 tablespoons white wine

1 tablespoon tomato paste

1 teaspoon paprika

1 teaspoon dried herbes de Provence

1 teaspoon olive oil

6 pork loin chops

Drain the tomatoes, reserving their can juice. Chop the tomatoes and combine them with the onion, wine, tomato paste, paprika, herbes de Provence, and olive oil in a bowl, then stir in 2 tablespoons of the can juice. Brush both sides of the chops with the tomato mixture and grill, turning and brushing with the tomato mixture occasionally, for 25 minutes, until tender and cooked through. Heat the remaining sauce in a small pan and serve separately with the chops.

6 servings

Honeyed Pork

4 lean center cut pork chops

4 tablespoons honey

1 tablespoon sunflower oil

1–2 garlic cloves, minced

3 tablespoons cream sherry

¼ cup sliced almonds

salt and pepper

Place the chops in a shallow dish. Combine the honey, oil, garlic, and sherry in a pitcher and season with salt and pepper. Pour the mixture over the chops, cover, and marinate, turning occasionally, for 5–6 hours. Drain the chops, reserving the marinade. Grill, basting frequently with the marinade, for 10–12 minutes on each side. Serve sprinkled with the almonds.

4 servings

Pork Chops with Caper and Gherkin Marinade

4 pork rib chops

1 bay leaf

2 tablespoons drained capers

2 gherkins, chopped

4 tablespoons dry white wine or hard cider

2 teaspoons superfine sugar

2 tablespoons olive oil

½ teaspoon French mustard

grilled onion rings, to serve

Place the chops in a large, shallow dish with the bay leaf. Sprinkle the capers and gherkins on top. Combine the wine or hard cider, sugar, oil, and mustard in a pitcher and pour the mixture over the chops. Cover and marinate for about 2 hours. Drain the chops, reserving the marinade. Sear the chops for 6–7 minutes on each side, then grill, turning and brushing with reserved marinade occasionally, for 10–15 minutes more on each side. Serve topped with the onion rings.

4 servings

Saucy Pork Chops

6 pork rib chops

1 teaspoon mustard powder

1 teaspoon salt

¼–½ teaspoon chili powder

1 tablespoon dark brown sugar

10½ ounce can condensed tomato soup

2 tablespoons white wine vinegar

2 tablespoons Worcestershire sauce

2 tablespoons soy sauce

Place the chops in a large, shallow dish. Combine all the remaining ingredients in a pitcher, pour the mixture over the chops, turning to coat, then cover, and marinate for 1–2 hours. Drain the chops, reserving the marinade. Grill, basting frequently with the reserved marinade, for 10 minutes on each side, until tender and cooked through.

6 servings

Chili Pork

1 small green bell pepper, halved and deseeded

2 small green chilies, deseeded

1 garlic clove, peeled

4 tomatoes, skinned and deseeded

1 small onion

4 tablespoons medium sweet white wine

6 boneless pork chops

salt and pepper

cilantro sprigs, to garnish

Place the bell pepper, chilies, garlic, tomatoes, onion, and wine in a blender or food processor, season with salt and pepper, and process to a paste. Place the chops in a shallow dish and spread the spice paste over them. Cover and marinate for 2 hours. Remove the chops and drain off the marinade into a small pan. Heat the marinade gently, until just at boiling point, then transfer to the barbecue to keep warm. Sear the chops for 3–4 minutes on each side, then grill for 10–12 minutes more, until golden and cooked through. Serve with the marinade, garnished with cilantro.

6 servings

Ginger Pork Chops

4 pork loin chops

2 tablespoons preserved ginger, chopped

1 tablespoon soy sauce

1 tablespoon tomato paste

2 scallions, chopped

1/3 cup white wine

salt and pepper

Place the chops in a shallow dish. Combine the ginger, soy sauce, tomato paste, scallions, and white wine in a small pan and season with salt and pepper. Heat gently for 5 minutes, then pour the mixture over the chops. Cover and marinate for 2–3 hours or overnight. Drain the chops, reserving the marinade. Grill, brushing frequently with the reserved marinade, for about 12 minutes on each side, until cooked through.

4 servings

Pork and Rice Packets

4 pork loin chops

1 tablespoon soy sauce

1 1/2 cups cooked long grain rice

12 ounce can corn, drained

4 scallions, chopped

4 tablespoons hard cider

salt and pepper

Cut 4 large squares of double-thickness foil. Place a chop on the center of each square, then sprinkle them with soy sauce, salt, and pepper. Combine the rice, corn, and scallions in a bowl, then divide the mixture equally among the chops. Add 1 tablespoon hard cider to each chop, then fold up the sides of the foil, and crimp the edges to seal. Place the packets on the barbecue grid and cook for about 35 minutes, until tender.

4 servings

Pork and Sage Packets

4 lean center cut pork chops

2 onions, finely chopped

1 cup grated sharp Cheddar cheese

1 tablespoon chopped sage

2 tablespoons lemon juice

1 tart apple, peeled, cored, and sliced

salt and pepper

Cut 4 large squares of double-thickness foil. Place a chop on the center of each square and season with salt and pepper. Combine the onions, cheese, and sage in a bowl, then divide the mixture equally among the chops. Pour the lemon juice into a shallow dish, add the apple slices, and toss well. Top the chops with the apple slices, fold up the sides of the foil, and crimp the edges to seal. Place the packets on the barbecue grid and cook for 30–35 minutes, until tender.

4 servings

Spiced Pork

1 tablespoon juniper berries

1 teaspoon black peppercorns

4 allspice berries

1 teaspoon dried thyme

2 bay leaves

6 tablespoons coarse salt

6 thick slices pork side

sunflower oil, for brushing

Grind the juniper berries, peppercorns, allspice berries, thyme, and bay leaves in a spice grinder or blender until coarsely ground. Combine the spice mix with the salt. Coat the pork all over with the spice mix, place in a shallow, nonmetallic dish, and marinate for 2 days. Shake off the excess spice mix from the pork, brush with oil, and sear for 5–8 minutes on each side. Turn the pork slices over and grill for 15–20 minutes more.

6 servings

BACON, SAUSAGES AND HAMBURGERS

Onion-smothered Bacon Chops

6 unsmoked bacon chops

1¼ cups beer

1 bay leaf

3 onions, sliced

2 tablespoons molasses

1 tablespoon lemon juice

2 tablespoons sunflower oil

pepper

Put the chops in a shallow dish, pour in the beer, and season well with pepper. Add the bay leaf and one-third of the onion slices. Cover and marinate for 8 hours. Drain the bacon chops and strain the marinade into a small pan. Bring the marinade to a boil and continue to boil until reduced by half. Stir in the molasses and lemon juice and remove the pan from the heat. Heat the oil in a skillet, add the remaining onions, and cook until softened. Transfer the skillet to the side of the barbecue to keep warm. Grill the bacon chops, brushing frequently with the beer mixture, for about 10 minutes. Turn the chops, brush with the beer mixture again, then top with the onions, and spoon over more of the beer mixture. Grill for 10 minutes more, until tender and well glazed.

6 servings

Spicy Ham Steaks

4 cured ham steaks, about 1 inch thick

⅔ cup sherry

⅔ cup pineapple juice

2 tablespoons olive oil

pinch of ground cloves

1 tablespoon mustard powder

4 tablespoons brown sugar

1 teaspoon paprika

4 canned pineapple slices or peach halves

Snip around the edges of the ham steaks with kitchen scissors to prevent them from curling up, and place in a shallow dish. Combine the sherry, pineapple juice, oil, cloves, mustard, sugar, and paprika in a pitcher and pour the mixture over the ham steaks, turning to coat. Marinate, turning occasionally, for 2–3 hours. Drain the ham steaks, reserving the marinade. Grill the ham steaks, turning and basting with the marinade occasionally, for 20 minutes. Serve topped with a pineapple slice or a peach half.

4 servings

Ham Steaks with Lemon Glaze

½ cup light brown sugar

3 tablespoons prepared mild mustard

2 tablespoons lemon juice

½ teaspoon grated lemon zest

6 cured ham steaks

lemon slices and mizuna, to garnish

Combine the sugar, mustard, lemon juice, and zest in a small bowl. Snip the fat around the steaks at regular intervals with kitchen scissors. Brush the lemon glaze over the steaks and grill, basting frequently, for 8 minutes on each side, until golden brown and sticky. Serve, garnished with lemon slices and mizuna.

6 servings

Apple and Raisin Stuffed Bacon Chops

1 tablespoon butter

1 large cooking apple, peeled, cored and sliced

⅓ cup raisins

4 thick bacon chops

sunflower oil, for brushing

Melt the butter in a small skillet, add the apple slices, and cook over low heat until tender. Break up with a fork and stir in the raisins. Cut into the side of each bacon chop, without cutting all the way through, to make a pocket. Pack the apple and raisin mixture into the pockets. Brush the chops with oil and grill for 6–8 minutes on each side, or until the meat feels firm.

4 servings

Blue Cheese Ham Steaks

1/3 cup/3/4 stick butter, softened

3/4 cup crumbled blue cheese

4 cured ham steaks

sunflower oil, for brushing

6 scallions, chopped

grated zest and juice of 2 oranges

4 thick orange slices

salt and pepper

Combine the butter and cheese in a bowl and season with salt and pepper. Shape into a log, wrap in waxed paper or foil, and chill for 30 minutes–1 hour in the freezer. Snip the fat around the meat at regular intervals with kitchen scissors. Brush with oil and grill for about 6 minutes. Turn the steaks over, brush with oil, and sprinkle with the scallions, orange zest, and juice. Grill for 4–6 minutes more, until tender and cooked through. Serve each steak topped with a slice of orange and a slice of the blue cheese butter.

4 servings

Hot Ham and Fruit Packets

4 cured ham steaks, about 6 ounces each

4 canned pineapple rings, drained

4 canned peach halves, drained

2 tablespoons molasses sugar

2 tablespoons Worcestershire sauce

1 teaspoon mustard powder

Cut 4 squares of double-thickness foil large enough to enclose a ham steak. Place the steaks on the foil squares and top each with a pineapple ring and a peach half. Combine the sugar, Worcestershire sauce, and mustard powder in a bowl and spoon the mixture evenly over the fruit. Bring up the sides of the foil and crimp the edges to seal. Cook on the barbecue for 15 minutes. Serve straight from the foil packets.

4 servings

Prosciutto and Pear Sucks

6 prosciutto slices

2 ripe pears

Romano or Parmesan shavings

cracked black pepper

extra virgin olive oil

Halve each prosciutto slice lengthwise. Cut each pear into 6 wedges and remove the cores. Wrap a piece of prosciutto around each pear wedge and thread 3 wedges onto each skewer. Grill for 2–3 minutes on each side. Before serving, sprinkle with cheese shavings and cracked black pepper and drizzle with a little olive oil.

4 servings

Bacon Kabobs with Orange Sauce

1 tablespoon sunflower oil

2 tablespoons Worcestershire sauce

grated zest and juice of 1 large orange

1 pound vacuum-packed smoked picnic shoulder bacon, cut into 1 inch cubes

4 thin, skinless pork sausage links, halved

8 pearl onions

12 white mushrooms

2 teaspoons cornstarch

⅔ cup water

3 tablespoons chunky marmalade

salt and pepper

Combine the oil, Worcestershire sauce, orange zest, and orange juice in a shallow dish and season with salt and pepper. Add the bacon and marinate, turning occasionally, for at least 2 hours. Drain the bacon cubes, reserving the marinade, and thread onto 4 oiled skewers, alternating with the sausage pieces, onions, and mushrooms, then set aside. Stir the cornstarch and a little of the water together to make a paste. Pour the reserved marinade into a pan, add the cornstarch paste, remaining water, and marmalade, and bring to a boil. Lower the heat and simmer gently for 2 minutes, then transfer to the side of the barbecue to keep warm. Grill the kabobs, turning frequently, for 12–15 minutes. Serve with the sauce.

4 servings

Bacon Bites

½ cup lemon juice

¼ teaspoon ground ginger

2 avocados, halved, pitted, and peeled

18 fatty bacon strips

salt and pepper

Combine the lemon juice and ginger in a bowl and season with salt and pepper. Cut each avocado half into 9 equal pieces—it does not matter if they are not the same shape. Toss in the lemon juice mixture. Lay the bacon strips on a counter and stretch each slightly with the back of a large knife, then cut in half crosswise. Place a piece of avocado on each piece of bacon and roll up. Thread the bacon bites onto 6 oiled skewers and grill, turning occasionally, for 2–3 minutes.

6 servings

Bacon Coils

1½ pounds fatty bacon strips

2 tablespoons whole-grain mustard

12 ounces bulk pork sausage

2 tablespoons finely chopped parsley

2 tablespoons chopped chives

2 canned anchovy fillets, pounded to a paste

pepper

Lay the bacon strips on a counter and stretch each slightly with the back of large knife. Season with pepper, then spread each strip with about ¼ teaspoon mustard. Combine the bulk sausage, parsley, chives, and anchovy paste in a bowl. Spread about 1 tablespoon of the mixture onto each bacon strip, then roll up tightly. Thread onto bamboo skewers, making sure that the end of each bacon coil is held firmly. Grill, turning frequently, for about 20 minutes.

Makes 25 coils

Sausage and Ham Skewers

¾ inch thick cured ham steak, about 10–12 ounces

15 ounce can peach halves in fruit juice

8 ounces small pork sausage links, halved crosswise

8 bay leaves

8 pearl onions

Italian Coleslaw (see page 299), to serve

Cut the ham steak into ¾ inch cubes. Drain the peaches, reserving the can juice, and cut them in half. Thread the ham cubes, peach halves, sausage link halves, bay leaves, and onions alternately onto 4 skewers. Grill, turning and brushing with the reserved can juice frequently, for about 15 minutes, until the sausages and bacon are cooked. Serve on a bed of Italian coleslaw.

4 servings

Bacon-wrapped Sausages

1 pound pork sausage links

4 ounces Monterey jack or Cheddar cheese, sliced

4 teaspoons French mustard

8 bacon strips

Grill the sausages, turning occasionally, for about 15 minutes, until evenly browned. Remove them from the heat and split them lengthwise without cutting all the way through. Fill with the cheese slices, then press the sausages back together. Spread the mustard over the bacon strips and wrap around the sausages, securing the ends with toothpicks. Grill, turning occasionally, for 5 minutes more, until the cheese melts and the bacon is crisp.

4 servings

Brunch Kabobs

8 lambs' kidneys, skinned, halved, and cored

8 mushrooms

4 small tomatoes, halved

8 small pork sausage links

olive oil, for brushing

salt and pepper

Garlic Bread (see page 329), to serve

Thread the kidneys, mushrooms, tomato halves, and sausages alternately onto skewers. Brush with oil, season with salt and pepper, and grill, turning occasionally, for 15–20 minutes. Serve with garlic bread.

4 servings

Chorizo Kabobs with Celery Root and Garlic Relish

8 large garlic cloves, unpeeled

1½ pounds celery root, cut into 1 inch cubes

2 tablespoons/¼ stick butter

3 red onions, unpeeled

4 large chorizo sausages, cut into 1 inch lengths

1 bunch of sage, leaves stripped from stalks

salt and pepper

Place the garlic cloves on a cookie sheet and bake in a preheated oven, 350°F, for 10–15 minutes, until soft. When cool enough to handle, squeeze out the flesh into a bowl. Meanwhile, put the celery root in a pan, pour in cold water to cover, add a pinch of salt, and bring to a boil. Lower the heat and simmer for 15–20 minutes, until tender. Drain well and add to the garlic. Add the butter and mash, then season to taste with salt and pepper. Transfer the mixture to a clean pan and place on the side of the barbecue to keep warm. Cut each onion into 8 wedges without cutting all the way through. Wrap in a double thickness of foil and place in the embers for 20 minutes, until tender. Thread the sausage pieces onto skewers, alternating with the sage leaves. Grill for 8–10 minutes, turning occasionally, until slightly crisp and heated through. Serve the hot kabobs with the baked onions and the celery root and garlic relish.

4 servings

Skewered Sausage Meatballs

4 tablespoons sage and onion stuffing mix

½ cup boiling water

1 pound bulk pork sausage

1 egg yolk

2 red-skinned apples, halved, cored, and cut into wedges

4 tablespoons lemon juice

olive oil, for brushing

salt and pepper

Combine the stuffing mix and boiling water in a bowl and let stand until the water has been absorbed. Stir in the bulk sausage and egg yolk and season with salt and pepper. Form the mixture into balls about the size of a chestnut, then cover and chill for 1 hour. Toss the apple wedges in the lemon juice. Thread the meatballs and apple wedges alternately onto 4 skewers. Brush the skewers with olive oil and grill for 5 minutes, then turn, brush with more oil, and grill for 5–6 minutes more.

4 servings

Kabanos and Pineapple Kabobs

3 kabanos, cut into 1 inch pieces

7 ounce can pineapple chunks, drained

2 cooked chicken breast portions, cut into 1 inch chunks

1 tablespoon sunflower oil

Thread the kabanos pieces, pineapple chunks, and chicken chunks alternately onto 8 small metal skewers and brush with oil. Grill, turning and brushing with oil occasionally, for 10 minutes.

4 servings

Italian Sausages with Stuffed Mushrooms and Polenta

3 cups water

1⅔ cups cornmeal mush

2 tablespoons olive oil

8 large cremini or portabello mushrooms

8 sun-dried tomato halves in oil, chopped, plus 4 tablespoons oil from the jar

2 cups crumbled Gorgonzola cheese

½ cup pine nuts, toasted

8 Italian sausages

salt and pepper

Bring the measured water to a boil in a large pan and add 1 teaspoon salt. Lower the heat slightly and add the cornmeal in a thin stream, beating constantly with a wooden spoon. Cook, stirring constantly, for 20–30 minutes, until the mixture comes away from the sides of the pan. Tip the mixture onto a board or cookie sheet and let cool. Cut into thick slices, brush with the olive oil, and set aside. Remove the stems from the mushrooms and chop them finely. Brush the mushroom caps all over with the oil from the tomatoes. Combine the mushroom stems, sun-dried tomatoes, Gorgonzola, and pine nuts in a bowl and season with salt and pepper. Stuff the mushroom caps with this mixture, then place 2 stuffed mushrooms on a piece of foil large enough to enclose them, bring up the edges, and crimp together to seal. Repeat with the remaining stuffed mushrooms. Place the polenta slices, mushrooms packets, and the sausages on the barbecue grid and cook, turning the sausages frequently, for 15–20 minutes until tender and cooked through. Divide among serving plates and serve immediately.

4 servings

Hot Dogs

4 large frankfurter sausages or wieners

4 hot dog rolls

4 tablespoons tomato ketchup

Prick the sausages all over with a fork, then grill, turning frequently, for about 5–8 minutes. Meanwhile, slit the rolls and heat on the edge of the barbecue. Place the sausages in the rolls, top with the ketchup, and serve.

4 servings

Bacon Dogs

4 lean bacon strips

14½ ounce can hot dog sausages

6 tablespoons tomato ketchup

2 tablespoons French mustard

2 small onions, minced

Halve each bacon strip lengthwise. Wrap a piece of bacon around each sausage and secure firmly with toothpicks. Combine the tomato ketchup, mustard and onions in a bowl. Grill the bacon-wrapped sausages, turning and brushing frequently with the ketchup mixture, for 7–11 minutes, until golden brown on all sides. Serve with the remaining sauce.

6–8 servings

Franks 'n' Cheese

8 frankfurter sausages

8 narrow strips of processed cheese slices

8 bacon strips

8 hot dog rolls

Split the sausages lengthwise without cutting right through and insert a strip of cheese in each. Wrap each sausage in a bacon strip and grill, turning frequently, for about 7 minutes, until the bacon is cooked. Meanwhile, slit the rolls and heat on the edge of the barbecue. Serve the sausages in the rolls.

8 servings

Homemade Sausages with Mustard Aioli

sausage casings, soaked in cold water for 20 minutes

1 pound lean pork blade shoulder, trimmed and coarsely chopped

6 ounces back fat without rind, trimmed and coarsely chopped

1½ tablespoons coarse sea salt

4 tablespoons thyme leaves

½ teaspoon ground bay

4–6 garlic cloves, minced

2 egg yolks

2 tablespoons lemon juice, plus extra to taste

1¼ cups extra virgin olive oil

2 tablespoons coarse grain mustard

salt and pepper

Rinse the sausage casings by pulling 1 end over the faucet and running cold water through it. Pass the meat and back fat through the medium blade of a meat grinder or finely chop by hand. Combine the ground meat with the sea salt, thyme, and bay and season with pepper. Spoon the mixture into a large pastry bag fitted with a plain tip and squeeze gently to remove excess air. Wrinkle the open end of a sausage casing onto and up the nozzle and, holding the casing onto the nozzle, squeeze in the filling to make a long sausage. Twist or knot the sausage to make 8 large or 12 small links. Set aside. To make the aioli, place the garlic, egg yolks, and lemon juice in a blender or food processor and process briefly to mix. With the motor running, gradually add the olive oil in a thin stream until the mixture forms a thick cream. Scrape the aioli into a bowl, season with salt and pepper, and stir in the mustard. Taste and add more lemon juice, if necessary. Grill the sausages, turning frequently, for 10–15 minutes, until cooked through. Serve with the aioli.

4 servings

Sausages Basted with Beer

3 pounds pork sausage links

1¼ cups dark beer

2 garlic cloves, minced

1½ teaspoons ground allspice

1 inch piece of orange zest

8 soft rolls

whole-grain mustard, to serve

Prick the sausage links all over with a fork and place in a shallow dish. Combine the beer, garlic, allspice, and orange zest in a pitcher and pour the mixture over the sausage links. Cover and marinate, turning frequently, for 4 hours. Drain the sausage links, reserving the marinade. Grill, turning and basting with the marinade frequently, for 30 minutes. Serve the sausages in the rolls with the mustard.

8 servings

Beefy Barbecue Sausages

2 tablespoons/¼ stick butter

1 small onion, chopped

2 bacon strips, chopped

1 tablespoon tomato paste

4 beef bouillon cubes, crumbled

1½ cups hard cider

2 tablespoons raw sugar

1 teaspoon Worcestershire sauce

8 thick beef sausage links

sunflower oil, for brushing

Melt the butter in a pan, add the onion and bacon, and cook over low heat, stirring occasionally, for 5 minutes, until the onion is softened. Add the tomato paste, bouillon cubes, hard cider, sugar, and Worcestershire sauce, bring to a boil, then lower the heat, and simmer, stirring occasionally, for 15 minutes. Pour the mixture into a blender or food processor and process until smooth, then divide among individual bowls. Brush the sausage links with oil and grill, turning frequently, for about 15 minutes, until brown and cooked through. Serve with the bowls of dipping sauce.

4–8 servings

Herbed Sausage Patties

1 pound bulk pork sausage

2 teaspoons dried mixed herbs

1 garlic clove, minced

2 tablespoons chopped parsley

16 ounce can baked beans

salt and pepper

Combine the bulk sausage, mixed herbs, garlic, and parsley in a bowl and season with salt and pepper. Divide the mixture into 6 portions and shape into neat rounds. Grill for about 7 minutes on each side. Meanwhile, heat the beans in a pan and serve poured over the patties.

6 servings

Swedish Meat Patties

3 white bread slices, crusts removed

⅔ cup club soda

8 ounces ground veal

8 ounces ground pork

⅓ cup finely chopped cured ham

1 teaspoon juniper berries, crushed

2 egg yolks

sunflower oil, for brushing

onion rings and sliced dill pickles, to garnish

4 large slices rye bread and sour cream, to serve

Tear the bread into pieces and place in a shallow bowl. Add the club soda and soak for 20 minutes. Combine the veal, pork, ham, juniper berries, and egg yolks in a bowl and season with salt and pepper. Add the moistened bread and beat the mixture until smooth. Divide into 4 portions and shape into neat rounds. Brush both sides of the patties with oil and grill for 4 minutes. Turn them over, brush with a little more oil, and grill for 4 minutes more. To serve, place a slice of rye bread on each of 4 plates, top each with a patty, garnish with onion rings and dill pickles, and add a swirl of sour cream.

4 servings

Basic Hamburgers

1 onion, finely chopped

1½ pounds lean ground beef

2 teaspoons salt

½ teaspoon pepper

Combine all the ingredients in a bowl. Divide into 6 and pat each portion into a neat round about ½ inch thick. Chill for 1 hour. Grill the hamburgers for 2 minutes on each side for rare, 4 minutes on each side for medium, and 6 minutes on each side for well done.

6 servings

Tangy Hamburgers

1 cup soft white bread crumbs

3 tablespoons milk

1 pound ground beef

1 onion, finely chopped

½ teaspoon dried basil

½ teaspoon finely grated lemon zest

¼ cup grated Cheddar cheese

sunflower oil, for brushing

salt and pepper

Place the bread crumbs in small bowl, add the milk, and soak for 5 minutes. Stir in the beef, onion, basil, lemon zest, and cheese and season with salt and pepper. Transfer to a food processor and process until smooth. Divide the mixture into 8 portions and shape each into a neat round. Chill for 12 hours. Brush the hamburgers with oil and grill for 5 minutes. Turn them over, brush with oil, and grill for 5–8 minutes more, until cooked to your liking.

4 servings

Basic Cheeseburgers

1 pound ground beef

½ cup grated Cheddar or Monterey Jack cheese

1 onion, minced

4 tablespoons crushed cornflakes

dash of Worcestershire sauce

salt and pepper

Combine all the ingredients in a bowl and season well. Divide into 8 portions and shape each into a round. Chill for 1 hour. Grill for 5 minutes on each side.

4–8 servings

Mustard Cheeseburgers

1½ pounds ground beef

1 onion, finely chopped

½ cup grated sharp cheese

1 teaspoon prepared hot mustard

6 slices cheese

salt and pepper

Combine the beef, onion, grated cheese, and mustard in a bowl and season with salt and pepper. Divide the mixture into 6 and pat each portion into a neat round about ½ inch thick. Chill for 1 hour. Grill for about 5 minutes on each side, then top each cheeseburger with a slice of cheese and grill for 1–2 minutes more, until the cheese is just melted.

6 servings

Hamburgers with Onions

1½ pounds ground beef

½ cup soft bread crumbs

¼ teaspoon dried thyme

1 egg, lightly beaten

2 tablespoons/¼ stick butter

1 large onion, sliced into rings

salt and pepper

Combine the beef, bread crumbs, thyme, and egg in a bowl and season with salt and pepper. Divide the mixture into 4 portions and shape into neat rounds. Chill for 30 minutes. Just before cooking the hamburgers, melt the butter in a skillet. Add the onion rings and cook, stirring occasionally, over low heat for about 10 minutes, until softened and lightly golden. Transfer to a heatproof plate and keep warm on the side of the barbecue. Grill the hamburgers for 5–6 minutes on each side. Top with the onion rings before serving.

4 servings

Swiss Cheeseburgers

1 pound lean ground beef

½ cup soft white bread crumbs

1 tablespoon tomato paste

1 cup grated Swiss cheese

4 scallions, finely chopped

2 tablespoons Worcestershire sauce

1 egg, beaten

salt and pepper

tomato and cucumber slices, to garnish

Combine the beef, bread crumbs, tomato paste, cheese, scallions, Worcestershire sauce, and egg in a bowl and season with salt and pepper. Divide the mixture into 4 portions and shape into neat rounds about ½ inch thick. Chill for 30 minutes. Grill the burgers, turning once, for 12–15 minutes, until cooked to your taste. Serve garnished with tomato and cucumber slices.

4 servings

Italian-style Cheeseburgers

1 pound lean ground beef

1 onion, minced

1 garlic clove, minced

1 tablespoon tomato paste

½ teaspoon dried oregano

vegetable oil, for brushing

3 ounces mozzarella cheese, cut into 4 slices

4 tomato slices

salt and pepper

Combine the beef, onion, garlic, tomato paste, and oregano in a bowl and season with salt and pepper. Divide the mixture into 4 portions and shape each into a neat round. Chill for at least 1 hour. Brush the hamburgers with the oil and grill for 5 minutes, then turn them over, and grill for 3 minutes more. Place a slice of cheese on top of each hamburger and grill for 8 minutes more, until the cheese is melted and the hamburgers are cooked to your liking. Top each hamburger with a tomato slice before serving.

4 servings

Relishburgers

2 cups soft white bread crumbs

2 pounds ground beef

3 tablespoons bottled barbecue relish, plus extra to serve

1 onion, finely chopped

1 egg, beaten

rolled oats, for coating

parsley sprigs, to garnish

Combine the bread crumbs, beef, relish, onion, and egg in a bowl. Divide the mixture into 12 portions and shape each into a neat round about 1 inch thick. Coat with the rolled oats, patting them on firmly. Cover and chill for 1 hour. Grill, turning once, for about 15 minutes, depending on how well done you like your hamburgers. Serve with extra relish.

12 servings

Hamburgers au Poivre

1 onion, finely chopped

1½ pounds lean ground beef

2 teaspoons Worcestershire sauce

1 teaspoon French mustard

coarsely ground black pepper, to coat

salt

Combine the onion, beef, Worcestershire sauce, and mustard in a bowl and season with salt. Divide into 6 and pat each portion into a neat round about ½ inch thick. Chill for 1 hour. Spread out the coarsely ground pepper on a plate and coat the hamburgers on both sides. Grill for 2–6 minutes on each side, depending on how well done you like your hamburgers.

6 servings

Mint and Curryburgers

2 onions, finely chopped

1½ pounds ground beef

1 teaspoon mild curry powder

1 tablespoon chopped mint

1 tablespoon lemon juice

salt and pepper

Combine all the ingredients in a bowl and season with salt and pepper. Divide the mixture into 6–8 portions and shape each into a neat round. Chill for 1 hour. Grill for about 5 minutes on each side.

6–8 servings

St Louis Rice Burgers

1 pound ground beef

½ teaspoon dried mixed herbs

1 small onion, finely chopped

1 garlic clove, minced

1½ cups cooked long grain rice

1 egg, beaten

4 tablespoons white wine

1 tablespoon chopped parsley

salt and pepper

Combine all the ingredients in a bowl and season with salt and pepper. Cover and let stand for 30 minutes. Divide the mixture into 4 portions and shape each into a neat round. Grill for about 7 minutes on each side, until cooked to your liking.

4 servings

Herb and Caper Hamburgers

1 onion, finely chopped

1½ pounds lean ground beef

2 tablespoons drained bottled capers

1 teaspoon chopped sage

½ teaspoon chili powder

1 egg

salt and pepper

Combine the onion, beef, capers, sage, chili powder, and egg in a bowl and season with salt and pepper. Divide into 6 and pat each portion into a neat round about 1/2 inch thick. Chill for 1 hour. Grill for 2–6 minutes on each side, depending on how well done you like your hamburgers.

6 servings

Hot Chiliburgers

1 pound lean ground beef

8 ounces bulk pork sausage

1 onion, minced

1 garlic clove, minced

8 ounce can kidney beans, drained and chopped

2 teaspoons chili powder

vegetable oil, for brushing

salt and pepper

Combine the beef, bulk sausage, onion, garlic, beans, and chili powder in a bowl and season with salt and pepper. Divide the mixture into 6–8 portions and shape into neat rounds. Brush with oil and grill for about 7 minutes on each side.

6–8 servings

Irish Hamburgers

1 pound ground beef

2 potatoes, grated

1 onion, finely chopped

2 tablespoons chopped parsley

dash of Worcestershire sauce

salt and pepper

tomato slices, to garnish

Combine the beef, potatoes, onion, parsley, and Worcestershire sauce in a bowl and season with salt and pepper. Divide the mixture into 8 portions and shape each into a neat round. Chill for 1 hour. Grill for about 5 minutes on each side. Top with sliced tomato before serving.

4 servings

Spinach Burgers

10 ounces frozen spinach, thawed

1¼ pounds ground beef

1 cup soft bread crumbs

1 onion, finely chopped

1 teaspoon Worcestershire sauce

1 egg, lightly beaten

1 tablespoon chopped parsley

6 mozzarella cheese slices

salt and pepper

Place the spinach in a strainer and press firmly to squeeze out as much moisture as possible, then tip into a bowl. Add the beef, bread crumbs, onion, Worcestershire sauce, egg, and parsley and season with salt and pepper. Mix well, then divide into 6 portions and shape each into a neat round. Chill for 1 hour. Grill the burgers for 5–6 minutes on each side. (You may need to place them on sheets of foil, as these burgers are quite moist.) Top each burger with a cheese slice and grill for 1–2 minutes more, until just melted.

6 servings

Tomato Burgers

1¼ pounds ground beef

1 cup soft bread crumbs

⅔ cup Tomato Sauce (see page 280)

1 large onion, finely chopped

1 tablespoon chopped parsley

1 teaspoon Tabasco sauce

salt and pepper

Combine the beef, bread crumbs, tomato sauce, onion, parsley, and Tabasco in a bowl and season with salt and pepper. Divide into 10 portions and shape each into a neat round. Chill for 1 hour. Grill the burgers for 5 minutes on each side.

5–10 servings

Lamb Burgers

1¼ pounds finely ground lamb

2 tablespoons olive oil

1 large garlic clove, minced

2 tablespoons chopped parsley

large pinch of dried mint

salt and pepper

Combine the lamb with 1 tablespoon of the oil, the garlic, parsley, and mint, and season with salt and pepper. Divide the mixture into 8 portions and shape each into a neat round. Chill for 1 hour. Brush the lamb burgers with the remaining oil and grill, turning occasionally, for 15 minutes, until golden brown.

4–8 servings

Lamb Burgers with Rosemary

1 garlic clove, minced

2 onions, very finely chopped

1½ pounds ground lamb

2 teaspoons chopped thyme

1½ teaspoons chopped rosemary

salt and pepper

Combine the garlic, onions, lamb, and herbs in a bowl and season with salt and pepper. Divide the mixture into 8 portions and shape into neat rounds about 1 inch thick. Chill for 1 hour. Grill for 5 minutes on each side, or until cooked to your liking.

4–8 servings

Pork Burgers

1 pound bulk pork sausage or ground pork

2 bacon strips, ground

2 teaspoons Worcestershire sauce

1 small onion, minced

2 tablespoons soft white bread crumbs

2 teaspoons sunflower oil

salt and pepper

Combine all the ingredients in a bowl and season with salt and pepper. Divide the mixture into 8 portions and shape each into a neat round. Chill for 1 hour. Brush the burgers with the oil and grill, turning occasionally, for about 15 minutes, until cooked through. Top with a tomato slice to serve.

4–8 servings

chapter 3
Poultry

CHICKEN DISHES

Orange and Lemon Chicken

3½ pound chicken

2 tablespoons lemon juice

1 bunch of mixed herbs, such as parsley, thyme, marjoram, and chervil

Orange and Lemon Barbecue Sauce (see page 274)

salt and pepper

Sprinkle the inside of the chicken with the lemon juice, season inside and out with salt and pepper, and place the bunch of herbs in the cavity. Attach the chicken to a rotisserie and brush with the barbecue sauce. Cook, brushing occasionally with the sauce, for 1–1½ hours, until tender. Test by inserting the point of a sharp knife into the thickest part; if the juices run clear, the chicken is cooked through. Transfer to a carving dish, tent with foil, and let stand for 10 minutes. Reheat any remaining sauce. Carve the chicken into portions and serve with the sauce.

4 servings

Chicken with Macaroon and Raisin Stuffing

4 pound chicken

1 cup crushed macaroons

1 cup soft bread crumbs

⅔ cup raisins

1 tablespoon chopped basil

1 egg, beaten

4 tablespoons olive oil

3 tablespoons honey, melted

1 tablespoon lemon juice

1 teaspoon ground cinnamon

salt and pepper

Rub the chicken inside and out with salt and pepper. Combine the crushed macaroons, bread crumbs, raisins, basil, and egg in a bowl and season with salt and pepper. Stuff the chicken with this mixture, then secure the opening with small metal skewers. Rub some olive oil all over the chicken, then attach to a rotisserie and cook for about 45 minutes. Combine the melted honey and lemon juice and brush the mixture all over the chicken. Sprinkle with cinnamon. Continue to cook for 45 minutes or until tender and cooked through. Test by inserting the point of a sharp knife into the thickest part; if the juices run clear, the chicken is cooked through. Transfer to a carving dish, tent with foil, and let stand for 10 minutes before carving and serving.

6 servings

Tarragon Chicken

3 pound chicken

2 tablespoons lemon juice

2 tablespoons chopped tarragon

½ cup/1 stick butter

Rub the inside of the chicken with lemon juice and season inside and out with salt and pepper. Combine the tarragon with half the butter and place the mixture in the cavity. Melt the remaining butter. Attach the chicken to a rotisserie and brush with the melted butter. Cook, brushing occasionally with the butter, for 1–1½ hours, until the chicken is cooked through and tender. Test by inserting the point of a sharp knife into the thickest part; if the juices run clear, the chicken is cooked through. Transfer to a carving dish, tent with foil, and let stand for 10 minutes.

4 servings

Kentucky Spit-roasted Chicken

1 lemon, halved

3 pound chicken

pinch of grated nutmeg

½ teaspoon celery salt

1 teaspoon paprika

1 tablespoon brown sugar

¼ cup/½ stick butter, melted

salt and pepper

Place 1 half lemon inside the cavity of the chicken and season inside and out with salt and pepper. Truss the chicken with string and attach to a rotisserie. Squeeze the juice from the remaining half lemon into a bowl and stir in the nutmeg, celery salt, paprika, sugar, and butter. Cook the chicken, brushing frequently with the spice mixture, for 1–1½ hours, until cooked through and tender. Test by inserting the point of a sharp knife into the thickest part; if the juices run clear, the chicken is cooked through. Transfer to a carving dish, tent with foil, and let stand for 10 minutes before carving.

4 servings

Maple Chicken with Orange and Watercress

4 chicken legs

scant 1 cup orange juice

1 onion, thinly sliced

1 garlic clove, minced

pinch of ground nutmeg

4 tablespoons maple syrup

salt and pepper

Prick the chicken legs with a fine skewer and place in a shallow dish. Add the orange juice, onion, garlic, and nutmeg and season with salt and pepper. Cover and marinate for 8 hours or overnight. Drain the chicken and grill, flesh side down, for 15 minutes. Turn the legs over, brush with the maple syrup, and grill for another 15–20 minutes, until tender. Test that the chicken is cooked by inserting the point of a sharp knife into the thickest part; if the juices run clear, it is cooked through.

4 servings

Chicken on a Spit

3 pound chicken

2 tablespoons lemon juice

1 bunch of mixed herbs

Smoky Barbecue Sauce (see page 272)

salt and pepper

Rub the inside of the chicken with lemon juice and season inside and out with salt and pepper. Place the herbs in the cavity. Attach the chicken to a rotisserie and brush with the sauce. Cook, brushing occasionally with the sauce, for 1–1½ hours, until the chicken is cooked through and tender. Test by inserting the point of a sharp knife into the thickest part; if the juices run clear, the chicken is cooked through. Transfer to a carving dish, tent with foil, and let stand for 10 minutes. Reheat any remaining sauce. Carve the chicken into portions and serve with the sauce.

4 servings

Rosemary Chicken

4 tablespoons white wine vinegar

1 tablespoon molasses sugar

1 tablespoon Worcestershire sauce

1 tablespoon tomato paste

1 teaspoon paprika

1 small onion, finely chopped

4 chicken portions

6 rosemary sprigs

salt and pepper

Orange and Lemon Barbecue Sauce (see page 274), to serve

Combine the vinegar, sugar, Worcestershire sauce, tomato paste, paprika, and onion in a pan, season with salt and pepper, and bring to a boil. Lower the heat and simmer for 10 minutes. Brush the glaze all over the chicken portions. Grill, turning occasionally and basting frequently with the glaze, for 20–25 minutes. About 10 minutes before the end of the cooking time, add a few rosemary sprigs to the coals and to the chicken. Test that the chicken is cooked by inserting the point of a sharp knife into the thickest part; if the juices run clear, it is cooked through. Serve the chicken with the sauce.

4 servings

Herbed Chicken

4 chicken portions

scant 1 cup sunflower oil

4 tablespoons lemon juice

1 teaspoon chili powder

2 garlic cloves, minced

generous pinch each of rosemary, oregano, tarragon, and parsley

salt and pepper

Score the chicken skin in several places with a sharp knife and place the portions in a shallow dish. Combine the oil, lemon juice, chili powder, garlic, and herbs in a bowl and season with salt and pepper. Pour the mixture over the chicken, turning to coat, cover, and marinate for at least 4 hours. Drain the chicken portions, reserving the marinade. Grill the chicken, turning and brushing with the marinade frequently, for 20 minutes, until it is cooked through and tender. Test that the chicken is cooked by inserting the point of a sharp knife into the thickest part; if the juices run clear, it is cooked through.

4 servings

Orange Rosemary Chicken

5 tablespoons orange juice

¼ cup dry white wine

1 tablespoon Dijon mustard

1 teaspoon honey

1 tablespoon soy sauce

1 garlic clove, minced

2 tablespoons finely chopped rosemary

4 chicken portions, about 5–6 ounces each

sea salt and pepper

Put the orange juice, wine, mustard, honey, soy sauce, garlic, and rosemary in a blender or food processor and process until thoroughly combined. Put the chicken portions in a shallow dish and pour the mixture over them. Cover and marinate for 30 minutes. Drain the chicken, reserving the marinade. Grill, skin side up, for 15 minutes. Turn the chicken over, and grill, basting frequently with the marinade, for 12–15 minutes more, until golden brown and cooked through. Season with salt and pepper before serving.

4 servings

Citrus Chicken

1 garlic clove, minced

3 tablespoons lemon juice

4 tablespoons grapefruit juice

pinch of ground cinnamon

4 skinless chicken portions

sunflower oil, for brushing

salt and pepper

Combine the garlic, lemon juice, grapefruit juice, and cinnamon in a pitcher and season with salt and pepper. Place the chicken portions in a shallow dish and pour the mixture over them, then marinate for 4 hours. Drain the chicken, reserving the marinade, and brush the portions all over with oil. Grill, basting frequently with the marinade, for about 10 minutes on each side. Test that the chicken is cooked by inserting the point of a sharp knife into the thickest part; if the juices run clear, it is cooked through.

4 servings

Mint-stuffed Chicken

4 slices of bread

1 lemon

2 teaspoons bottled mint sauce

4 chicken portions

¼ cup/½ stick butter, melted

2 tablespoons sunflower oil

Tear the bread into pieces and place in a bowl. Coarsely grate the lemon zest into the bowl. Squeeze the juice and add to the bowl with the mint sauce. Mash with a fork until combined. Carefully lift the skin of the main part of the chicken portions, without tearing, and pack the stuffing underneath it. Grill, bone side down, brushing occasionally with melted butter and oil, for 15 minutes. Turn over and grill, brushing occasionally with the butter and oil, for 10 minutes more.

4 servings

Orange-glazed Chicken

4 tablespoons honey

2 tablespoons lemon juice

grated zest of 1 orange

juice of 2 oranges

2 tablespoons Worcestershire sauce

1 tablespoon soy sauce

4 skinless chicken portions

salt and pepper

Combine the honey, lemon juice, orange zest and juice, Worcestershire sauce, and soy sauce in a pan and heat gently for 2 minutes. Remove from the heat and let the mixture cool. Place the chicken in a shallow dish, pour the cooled mixture over it, and marinate, turning occasionally, for 12–24 hours. Drain the chicken, reserving the marinade. Place the chicken portions in a roasting pan and cook in a preheated oven, 350°F, for 1 hour. Brush the hot chicken with the reserved marinade and season with salt and pepper. Grill the portions, turning and brushing frequently with the marinade, for 10–15 minutes.

4 servings

Patio Chicken

6 chicken portions

1 onion, finely chopped

2/3 cup lime juice cordial

1 teaspoon chopped tarragon

1 teaspoon salt

1/2 teaspoon Tabasco sauce

Place the chicken portions in a shallow dish. Combine the onion, lime juice cordial, tarragon, salt, and Tabasco sauce in a bowl and pour the mixture over the chicken, turning to coat. Cover and marinate overnight. Drain the chicken portions, reserving the marinade. Grill, turning once or twice and brushing frequently with the marinade, for about 15–20 minutes, until they are tender. Test that the chicken is cooked by inserting the point of a sharp knife into the thickest part; if the juices run clear, it is cooked through.

6 servings

Deviled Chicken

4 large chicken portions

2 teaspoons salt

2 teaspoons sugar

1 teaspoon pepper

1 teaspoon ground ginger

1 teaspoon mustard powder

1/2 teaspoon curry powder

1/4 cup/1/2 stick butter

2 tablespoons tomato ketchup

1 tablespoon mushroom ketchup

1 tablespoon Worcestershire sauce

1 tablespoon soy sauce

1 tablespoon plum preserve

dash of Tabasco sauce

Place the chicken portions in a large, shallow dish. Combine the salt, sugar, pepper, ginger, mustard, and curry powder in a bowl and rub the mixture into the chicken. Marinate for 1 hour. Melt the butter and brush it all over the chicken portions, then grill, turning occasionally, for 20 minutes, until crisp. Combine the rest of the ingredients in a bowl, adding any remaining melted butter, and brush the mixture over the chicken portions. Grill, basting occasionally, for 10 minutes more. Test that the chicken is cooked by inserting the point of a sharp knife into the thickest part; if the juices run clear, it is cooked through.

4 servings

Golden Tandoori Chicken

8 small chicken portions

3 tablespoons lemon juice

1 teaspoon salt

2 cups plain yogurt

½ onion, finely chopped

1 garlic clove, minced

1 teaspoon minced fresh ginger root

½ teaspoon ground cardamom

½ teaspoon ground cinnamon

pinch of ground cloves

pinch of ground nutmeg

pinch of pepper

Place the chicken portions in a large, shallow dish and sprinkle both sides with the lemon juice and salt. Set aside for 30 minutes. Combine the yogurt, onion, garlic, ginger, cardamom, cinnamon, cloves, nutmeg, and pepper in a bowl. Spoon the mixture over the chicken, turning to coat, and marinate for 6–24 hours. Drain the chicken portions and grill, bone side down, for 20 minutes, then turn them over, and grill for 10–15 minutes more, until tender. Test that the chicken is cooked by inserting the point of a sharp knife into the thickest part; if the juices run clear, it is cooked through.

8 servings

Stuffed Chicken Rolls

3 tablespoons butter

1 small onion, finely chopped

generous ½ cup brown or white rice

1 teaspoon ground turmeric

1 bay leaf

3 cloves

2 cardamom pods

1½ cups water

4 skinless, boneless chicken breast portions

salt

Melt the butter in a pan, add the onion and rice, and cook, stirring frequently , until the onion is translucent. Stir in the turmeric, bay leaf, cloves, and cardamom and season with salt. Pour in the measured water, bring to a boil, then lower the heat and simmer until the rice is tender and the water has been absorbed. Place the chicken between 2 sheets of waxed paper and beat until thin. Spoon a little stuffing onto each chicken portion, roll up, and secure with a skewer or toothpick. Grill, turning once, for about 20 minutes.

4 servings

Sesame Chicken

8 chicken portions

4 garlic cloves, finely chopped

4 tablespoons lemon juice

2 teaspoons ground ginger

1 cup sunflower oil

3 tablespoons sesame seeds

½ cup soy sauce

Place the chicken in a large dish. Combine all the remaining ingredients in a pitcher and pour the mixture over the chicken. Marinate for at least 30 minutes. Cut 8 squares of double-thickness foil. Place a chicken portion and 1 tablespoon of marinade on each square, bring up the sides, and crimp the edges to seal. Reserve the remaining marinade. Cook on the barbecue for 40–50 minutes. Unwrap the chicken, base with the reserved marinade, and grill for a few minutes more until the sesame seeds are golden.

8 servings

Chicken in a Green Almond Sauce

1 cup whole blanched almonds

2 garlic cloves, minced

1 small onion, coarsely chopped

2 green chilies, deseeded and chopped

1 cup cilantro

1 cup Italian parsley

6 tablespoons olive oil

4 skinless, boneless chicken breast portions, about 6 ounces each

salt and pepper

Place the almonds, garlic, onion, chilies, cilantro, parsley, and oil in a blender or food processor and process until smooth. Season with salt and pepper. Cut out 4 squares of double-thickness foil and place a chicken portion in the center of each. Divide the almond sauce among them. Bring up the sides of the foil and crimp the edges to seal. Place the packets on the barbecue grid and cook for 20–25 minutes, until the chicken is tender and cooked through.

4 servings

Goat Cheese Stuffed Chicken with a Tomato and Chive Vinaigrette

4 boneless chicken breast portions, about 6–8 ounces each

4 ounces soft goat cheese

1/4 cup finely chopped walnuts

2 tablespoons chopped Italian parsley

2/3 cup olive oil

½ cup chives

juice and finely grated zest of 1 lime

1 pound ripe tomatoes, skinned, deseeded, and chopped

2 tablespoons Dijon mustard

1 garlic clove, minced

salt and pepper

young spinach leaves, to serve

Pull away the small fillets from the flesh of the chicken portions. Place them between 2 sheets of plastic wrap and flatten gently with a meat bat or a rolling pin. Set aside. Place the chicken portions skin side down, insert a small knife into the thickest part of the flesh, and slice along to create a pocket, taking care not to make any holes. Combine the cheese, walnuts, and parsley in a small bowl and season with salt and pepper. Divide the mixture among the chicken pockets. Place the small chicken fillets on top of each pocket and draw the edges of the chicken portions around them. Cover and chill for 30 minutes. Reserve 3 tablespoons of the oil and pour the remainder into a blender or food processor. Add the chives and process until smooth. Transfer the mixture to a bowl and stir in the lime juice and zest. Season with salt and pepper and stir in the tomatoes. Combine the mustard, garlic and reserved oil in another bowl. Brush this mixture all over the chicken. Place the chicken, skin side down, on the barbecue grid and grill, turning once and basting occasionally with the remaining glaze. Serve the chicken on a bed of spinach leaves sprinkled with the tomato and chive vinaigrette.

4 servings

Blue Cheese Chicken

6 chicken breast portions

⅔ cup French Dressing (see page 280)

6 tablespoons/¾ stick butter

¾ cup crumbled blue cheese

1 tablespoon chopped chives

1 garlic clove, finely chopped

2 tablespoons brandy

salt and pepper

lime or lemon wedges, to garnish

Place the chicken portions in a shallow dish, pour the dressing over them, and season with salt and pepper. Cover and marinate, turning once, for 4 hours. Meanwhile, beat the butter with the cheese, chives, garlic, and brandy and season with salt and pepper. Place on a sheet of foil or plastic wrap and form into a roll about 1 inch in diameter. Wrap tightly and chill until firm. Drain the chicken portions and grill, skin side up, for 10 minutes. Cut half of the blue cheese butter into 12 pieces. Place 1 piece on each chicken portion and grill for 5 minutes more. Turn the chicken portions over, place a piece of butter on each, and grill for another 15 minutes, or until cooked through and tender. Test by inserting the point of a sharp knife into the thickest part; if the juices run clear, the chicken is cooked through. Cut the remaining blue cheese butter into 6 pieces. Arrange the chicken portions on a serving dish, top each with a piece of the butter, and garnish with lime or lemon wedges.

6 servings

Marinated Chicken with Mushrooms and Marsala Sauce

4 large boneless chicken breast portions

7 tablespoons lemon juice

6 tablespoons olive oil

1 tablespoon chopped rosemary

2 tablespoons/¼ stick butter

1 onion, finely chopped

1 garlic clove, minced

3 lean bacon strips, finely chopped

1½ cups sliced white mushrooms

2 ounces chicken livers, chopped

1 tablespoon all-purpose flour

scant 1 cup red wine

4 tablespoons Marsala

salt and pepper

Place the chicken portions in a shallow dish. Combine the lemon juice, 5 tablespoons of the olive oil, and the rosemary in a bowl and season with salt and pepper. Spoon the mixture over the chicken, cover and marinate, turning once, for 3–4 hours. Heat the butter and remaining oil in a pan, add the onion, garlic, and bacon, and cook over low heat for 5 minutes. Add the mushrooms and chicken livers and cook for 2 minutes more. Stir in the flour, then gradually stir in the wine and Marsala. Simmer gently for 15 minutes. Transfer the pan to the side of the barbecue to keep warm. Drain the chicken portions, reserving the marinade. Brush the skinless side of each portion with the marinade and grill, skinless side down, for about 7 minutes. Brush both sides of the chicken portions with the marinade, place on the grid skin side down, and grill for 3–5 minutes more, until cooked and tender. Serve with the hot Marsala sauce.

4 servings

Southeast Asian Chicken with Pineapple and Peanut Relish

4 part-boned chicken breast portions

2 lemongrass stalks

7 tablespoons lime juice

2 red chilies, deseeded and chopped

3 garlic cloves, minced

1 inch piece of fresh ginger root, finely chopped

2 tablespoons dark brown sugar

2 tablespoons chopped cilantro

2/3 cup coconut milk

1 small pineapple, peeled, cored, and finely chopped

1 red onion, chopped

3 tablespoons lime juice

1 tablespoon light soy sauce

1/4 cup roasted unsalted peanuts, chopped

Cut 3 diagonal slits in each piece of chicken and place in a shallow dish. Put the lemongrass, 4 tablespoons of the lime juice, the chilies, 3 of the garlic cloves, the ginger, sugar, cilantro, and coconut milk in a blender or food processor and process until smooth. Pour the mixture over the chicken, cover, and marinate for 1–1 1/2 hours. Combine all the remaining ingredients in a bowl to make the relish. Cover and set aside. Drain the chicken, reserving the marinade. Grill the chicken, turning and brushing with the marinade occasionally, for 25–30 minutes, until cooked through and tender. Serve with the relish.

4 servings

Glazed Chicken Drumsticks

8 chicken drumsticks

1/4 cup/1/2 stick butter

1 onion, minced

7 ounce can tomatoes

2 tablespoons Worcestershire sauce

2 tablespoons raw sugar

1 teaspoon salt

pepper

Trim off any excess skin from the chicken drumsticks. Combine all the remaining ingredients in a small pan, cover, and simmer for 30 minutes. Push the mixture through a wire strainer or process in a blender or food processor until smooth. Brush the glaze all over the drumsticks. Grill, brushing frequently with the glaze, for 15–20 minutes on each side, or until cooked through and tender.

4 servings

Molasses-glazed Drumsticks

4 tablespoons tomato ketchup

4 tablespoons fruity brown sauce

1 tablespoon malt vinegar

1 tablespoon molasses

10 chicken drumsticks

Combine the ketchup, brown sauce, vinegar, and molasses in a bowl. Brush the glaze all over the drumsticks. Grill, turning and brushing with the glaze frequently, for 15–20 minutes, or until cooked through and tender.

10 servings

Chicken Drumsticks with Honey and Tomato Sauce

¼ cup/½ stick butter

1 onion, minced

13 ounce can tomatoes

2 tablespoons Worcestershire sauce

1 tablespoon honey

4 chicken drumsticks, scored

salt and pepper

Put the butter, onion, tomatoes and their juice, Worcestershire sauce, and honey in a pan, season with salt and pepper, and cook gently, stirring occasionally, for 30 minutes. Place the drumsticks on the barbecue grid and spread the sauce over them. Grill, basting frequently with the sauce, for 10 minutes on each side.

4 servings

Tandoori Chicken

2 inch piece of fresh ginger root, chopped

3 garlic cloves, chopped

3 black peppercorns

2 teaspoons chili powder

2 teaspoons ground coriander

1 teaspoon ground cumin

finely grated zest and juice of 1 lemon

1–2 drops red food coloring

10 skinless chicken drumsticks

⅔ cup plain yogurt, plus extra to serve

salt

Pound the ginger, garlic, and peppercorns in a mortar with a pestle. Combine the chili powder, coriander, cumin, lemon zest and juice, and food coloring in a bowl, season with salt, and stir in the ginger paste. Score the chicken flesh with the point of a sharp knife, then rub the spice mixture into the flesh. Brush each drumstick with 1 tablespoon yogurt, then marinate for 24 hours. Grill the chicken drumsticks, turning frequently, for about 20 minutes, until the outsides are charred and the meat is cooked through. Test that the chicken is cooked by inserting the point of a sharp knife into the thickest part; if the juices run clear, it is cooked through. Serve the drumsticks with extra yogurt.

10 servings

Drumsticks with Red Wine Sauce

8 chicken drumsticks

Red Wine Marinade (see page 18)

2/3 cup chicken broth

1 tablespoon tomato paste

1 tablespoon butter

2 teaspoons all-purpose flour

salt and pepper

Place the chicken drumsticks in a shallow dish, pour in the marinade, and marinate for 2–4 hours. Drain the chicken, reserving the marinade in a small pan. Grill the drumsticks, turning occasionally, for about 20 minutes, until cooked through and golden brown. Test by inserting the point of a sharp knife into the thickest part; if the juices run clear, the chicken is cooked through. Meanwhile, stir the broth and tomato paste into the reserved marinade and bring to a boil. Boil for 10 minutes, until reduced, then strain into a pitcher. Melt the butter in the rinsed-out pan and stir in the flour. Cook, stirring constantly, for 1 minute. Gradually stir in the marinade mixture. Simmer until thickened and season with salt and pepper. Serve the chicken drumsticks with the sauce spooned over them.

8 servings

Jamaican Jerk Chicken

12 chicken drumsticks

2 tablespoons canola oil

1 small onion, finely chopped

10 allspice berries

2 red chilies, deseeded and coarsely chopped

3 tablespoons lime juice

1 teaspoon salt

Score the chicken drumsticks with a sharp pointed knife, cutting right down as far as the bone, and place in a dish. Put all the remaining ingredients into a food processor and grind to a paste. Alternatively, grind in a spice mill. Coat the chicken with the jerk seasoning mixture, brushing it into the slashes in the meat. Cover and marinate overnight. Grill, turning frequently, for 20 minutes, until the drumsticks are charred on the outside and the flesh is cooked through. Test that the chicken is cooked by inserting the point of a sharp knife into the thickest part; if the juices run clear, it is cooked through.

4–6 servings

Spiced Chicken

8 chicken drumsticks

1 tablespoon sunflower oil

1 onion, sliced

1–2 garlic cloves, minced

1 teaspoon chili powder

10½ ounce can condensed cream of chicken soup

1 tablespoon mild curry powder

Place the chicken drumsticks in a shallow dish. Heat the oil in a pan and cook the onion over a low heat until softened. Add the garlic, chili powder, soup, and curry powder and bring to a boil. Lower the heat and simmer for 5 minutes. Remove the pan from the heat and cool, then pour the mixture over the chicken. Cover and marinate for at least 1 hour. Drain the drumsticks, reserving the marinade. Grill, turning and basting with the marinade frequently, for about 15 minutes, until cooked through and tender.

4–8 servings

Parmesan Chicken Drumsticks

½ cup soft white bread crumbs

⅓ cup grated Parmesan cheese

1 tablespoon all-purpose flour

4 large skinless chicken drumsticks

1 egg, beaten

salt and pepper

Combine the bread crumbs and Parmesan in a shallow dish. Season the flour with salt and pepper. Coat the drumsticks with seasoned flour, dip into the egg, then roll in the bread crumb mixture, pressing on the coating with your fingers. Chill for 30 minutes. Grill, turning frequently, for 20–30 minutes, until cooked through.

4 servings

Crispy Chicken with Mayonnaise

5 tablespoons Worcestershire sauce

2 tablespoons sugar

1 tablespoon tomato paste

6 chicken drumsticks

1/4 cup/1/2 stick butter

1 cup soft bread crumbs

1/4 cup chopped walnuts

2/3 cup Mayonnaise (see page 281)

2 tablespoons lemon juice

3 tablespoons light cream

Combine 2 tablespoons of the Worcestershire sauce, the sugar, and tomato paste in a pitcher. Place the drumsticks in a shallow dish and pour the mixture over them. Cover and marinate for 30 minutes. Melt the butter in a pan, add the bread crumbs and nuts, stir well, and cook over low heat until the crumbs are golden. Remove the pan from the heat. Drain the drumsticks, reserving the marinade. Grill, turning and basting with the marinade occasionally, for 15–20 minutes. Cool the drumsticks slightly, then coat in the bread crumb mixture. Whisk together the remaining Worcestershire sauce, the mayonnaise, lemon juice, and cream in a small bowl. Serve the drumsticks with the mayonnaise.

6 servings

Chicken and Zucchini Packets

8 chicken drumsticks

sunflower oil, for brushing

8 zucchini, cut into 1/2 inch slices

4 garlic cloves, finely chopped

1 tablespoon tomato paste

1 teaspoon chopped basil

2 teaspoons sugar

salt and pepper

Cut 8 squares of double-thickness foil. Brush the drumsticks with oil and grill for 2 minutes on each side. Place a drumstick on each foil square, arrange the zucchini slices around them, sprinkle with the garlic, and season with salt and pepper. Add a dab of tomato paste and sprinkle with a little basil and sugar. Bring up the sides and crimp the edges to seal. Cook the packages on the barbecue for about 10 minutes on each side until the chicken is cooked through.

8 servings

Drumsticks and Wings

6 chicken drumsticks

6 chicken wings

2 teaspoons dried thyme

2 tablespoons olive oil

2 tablespoons lemon juice

salt and pepper

lemon wedges, halved, to garnish

Prick the drumsticks and wings with a skewer or large needle and place in a dish. Add the thyme, oil, and lemon juice, season with salt and pepper, and turn to coat. Cover and marinate for at least 2 hours. Grill the drumsticks and wings, turning occasionally, for 10–15 minutes until cooked through. Serve the drumsticks garnished with half lemon wedges.

6 servings

Sate Spiced Wings

8 chicken wings

1 tablespoon ground almonds

1 tablespoon ground ginger

1 teaspoon ground coriander

1 teaspoon ground turmeric

1¼ cups coconut milk

2 onions, coarsely chopped

1 cup roasted peanuts

pinch of chili powder

2 tablespoons sunflower oil

⅔ cup water

2 teaspoons brown sugar

1 tablespoon soy sauce

2 tablespoons lemon juice

salt and pepper

Season the wings with salt and pepper and place in a shallow dish. Combine the almonds, ginger, coriander, and turmeric in a bowl and gradually stir in the coconut milk. Pour the mixture over the chicken, turning to coat. Marinate for 2 hours. Place half the chopped onions in a blender or food processor and add the peanuts and chili powder. Process to a paste. Heat the oil in a pan, add the remaining onion, and cook, stirring occasionally, for about 5 minutes, until softened. Stir in the paste and cook for 3 minutes. gradually stir in the measured water, then half the sugar, and, finally, the soy sauce and lemon juice. Stir well, then transfer the pan to the side of the barbecue to keep warm. Drain the chicken wings, reserving the marinade. Sprinkle with the remaining sugar and grill, turning and brushing with the marinade frequently, for 15–20 minutes, until brown and crisp. Serve with the sauce.

8 servings

Cinnamon-spiced Wings

1 garlic clove

2 inch piece of fresh ginger root, chopped

juice and finely grated zest of 2 limes

2 tablespoons light soy sauce

2 tablespoons peanut oil

2 teaspoons ground cinnamon

1 teaspoon ground turmeric

2 tablespoons honey

8 large chicken wings

salt

Yellow Bell Pepper Dip (see page 269), to serve

Place the garlic, ginger, lime juice and zest, soy sauce, peanut oil, cinnamon, turmeric, and honey in a blender or food processor, add a pinch of salt, and process until very smooth. Place the chicken wings in a shallow dish and pour the mixture over them. Toss well, cover, and marinate for 1–2 hours. Drain the chicken, reserving the marinade. Grill the chicken wings, brushing occasionally with the marinade, for 4–5 minutes on each side. Serve with the dip.

4 servings

Caribbean Chicken Thighs

6 chicken thighs

1 tablespoon dark rum

1 tablespoon soy sauce

1 small can pineapple rings in juice, drained and juice reserved

4 tablespoons sunflower oil

salt and pepper

Make 2 slits on each side of the chicken thighs and place them in a shallow dish. Combine the rum, soy sauce, and pineapple juice in a bowl and brush the mixture over the chicken. Cover and marinate for 2 hours. Season the chicken with salt and pepper, then grill, turning and brushing with oil frequently, for 15–20 minutes, until cooked through and tender. Test by inserting the point of a sharp knife into the thickest part; if the juices run clear, the chicken is cooked through. Grill the pineapple rings for 2–3 minutes on each side and serve with the chicken.

6 servings

Chicken and Pancetta Kabobs with Parsley Pesto

4 skinless, boneless chicken thighs

1 tablespoon chopped rosemary

3/4 cup olive oil

1/4 cup lemon juice

4 garlic cloves, minced

2 cups Italian parsley

1/4 cup pine nuts

1/3 cup grated Parmesan cheese

16 very thin pancetta or fatty bacon slices

salt and pepper

Cut each of the chicken thighs into 4 pieces. Combine the rosemary, 1/4 cup of the oil, the lemon juice, and half the garlic in a bowl. Add the chicken pieces, cover, and marinate for 2–4 hours. Put the parsley, pine nuts, and remaining garlic in a blender or food processor and process until finely chopped. With the motor running, gradually add the remaining olive oil in a thin stream until fully incorporated. Scrape the parsley pesto into a bowl. Stir in the Parmesan, and season with salt and pepper. Drain the chicken, reserving the marinade. Wrap a piece of pancetta or bacon around each piece and thread 2 pieces onto each of 8 skewers. Grill, turning and brushing with the marinade frequently, for 10–15 minutes, until tender. Serve with the parsley pesto.

4 servings

Maryland Kabobs

12 baby corn cobs

2 bananas

1 tablespoon lemon juice

8 smoked bacon strips, halved crosswise

2 large skinless, boneless chicken breast portions, cut into 1 inch cubes

1/4 cup/1/2 stick butter, melted

1 tablespoon honey

salt and pepper

Blanch the corn in boiling water for about 2 minutes, then drain. Peel the bananas and cut into 1/2 inch thick slices. Dip them into the lemon juice to prevent discoloration, then wrap half a slice of bacon around each one. Thread the corn, bacon-wrapped banana slices, and chicken onto oiled skewers. Season with salt and pepper and brush with melted butter and honey. Grill, turning and brushing with melted butter and honey frequently, for 8–10 minutes.

4 servings

Chicken Kabobs with Carrot Rice

1 cup long grain rice

2½ cups water

1 tablespoon white wine vinegar

1 teaspoon honey

1 tablespoon sunflower oil

pinch of ground ginger

8 ounces carrots, cut into julienne strips

1 pound skinless, boneless chicken breast portions, cubed

4 onions, each cut into 8 wedges

3½ cups mushrooms

1 tablespoon paprika

dash of Tabasco sauce

salt and pepper

Put the rice into a pan, pour in the water, and add a pinch of salt. Bring to a boil, stir once, then lower the heat, cover, and simmer for about 15 minutes until the rice is tender and the water has been absorbed. Remove from the heat and cool. Combine the vinegar, honey, 1 teaspoon of the oil, and the ginger in a large bowl and season with pepper. Add the rice and carrots and let stand for 2 hours. Thread the chicken, onions, and mushrooms alternately onto oiled skewers. Combine the remaining oil, the paprika, and Tabasco in a bowl and season with salt. Brush the mixture over the kabobs. Grill, turning and basting occasionally, for about 15 minutes. Serve with the carrot rice.

4 servings

Chicken Tikka

3 skinless, boneless chicken breast portions, cut into 1 inch cubes

1 teaspoon salt

4 tablespoons lemon juice

1 inch piece of fresh ginger root, minced

2 garlic cloves, minced

⅔ cup plain yogurt

1 teaspoon ground cumin

pinch of curry powder

pinch of cayenne pepper

orange food coloring (optional)

½ cup/1 stick butter, melted

Thread the chicken loosely onto skewers and sprinkle with the salt and lemon juice. Let stand for 15–20 minutes. Combine the ginger, garlic, yogurt, cumin, curry powder, cayenne, and food coloring, if using, in a bowl and brush the mixture over the chicken. Marinate for several hours or overnight, then grill, turning and brushing frequently with melted butter, for 10–15 minutes.

6 servings

Chicken Tikka with Nan Bread

1 onion, coarsely chopped

1 inch piece of fresh ginger root, coarsely chopped

2 garlic cloves, minced

⅔ cup plain yogurt

2 red chilies, deseeded and chopped

2 teaspoons ground coriander

1 teaspoon ground cumin

½ teaspoon ground turmeric

4 tablespoons lemon juice

1 teaspoon salt

½ pound skinless, boneless chicken breast portions, cut into 1 inch cubes

4 nan breads

lemon or lime wedges, to garnish

Put the onion, ginger, garlic, yogurt, chilies, coriander, cumin, turmeric, lemon juice, and salt in a blender or food processor and process until smooth. Place the chicken in a shallow dish, pour the mixture over it, cover, and marinate overnight. Wrap the nan breads in foil. Drain the chicken, reserving the marinade. Thread the chicken onto oiled metal skewers and grill, basting with the marinade, for 6 minutes on each side. Place the packets of nan bread on the side of the barbecue to heat through. Serve the kabobs with the nan bread, garnished with lemon or lime wedges.

4 servings

Classic Chicken Sate

4 large skinless, boneless chicken breast portions, cut into 1 inch cubes

4 large garlic cloves

¾ cup soy sauce

3 tablespoons dark brown sugar

4 tablespoons molasses

grated zest of 1 lemon

3 tablespoons lemon juice

1 inch piece of fresh ginger root, minced

2 cups dry roast peanuts or rinsed and drained salted peanuts

3 dried red chilies, deseeded and crumbled

1 onion, coarsely chopped

1 teaspoon salt

4 tablespoons peanut oil

7 tablespoons chicken broth

2 tablespoons lime juice

Thread the chicken cubes onto wooden skewers and place in a shallow dish. Mince 2 garlic cloves and halve the others. Combine 2/3 cup of the soy sauce, 2 tablespoons of the sugar, the molasses, minced garlic, lemon zest, lemon juice, and ginger in a pitcher. Pour the mixture over the skewers, turning to coat. Cover and marinate, turning 2–3 times, for 1 hour. Grind the peanuts in a food processor, then add the halved garlic, chilies, onion, salt, and half the oil. Process to a thick paste, adding 1 tablespoon of the chicken broth if necessary. Heat the remaining oil in a small pan, pour in the paste, and cook gently, stirring constantly, for 3–4 minutes. Add the chicken broth, bring to a boil, then lower the heat, and simmer gently for 5–10 minutes, until the sauce is very thick and smooth. Remove the pan from the heat and stir in the remaining sugar and soy sauce and the lime juice. Place the pan on the side of the barbecue to keep warm. Drain the skewers, reserving the marinade. Grill, turning and basting with the marinade frequently, for 5–6 minutes. Serve the skewers with the sauce.

4 servings

East Indian Sate

1½ teaspoons ground coriander

½ teaspoon salt

1 onion, chopped

1 garlic clove, chopped

2 tablespoons soy sauce

1 tablespoon lemon juice

½ cup roast salted peanuts, ground

2 tablespoons brown sugar

3 tablespoons peanut oil

1½ pounds skinless, boneless chicken breast portions, cut into 1 inch cubes

squares of red, green, and yellow bell pepper

pepper

Put the coriander, salt, onion, garlic, soy sauce, lemon juice, peanuts, sugar, and oil in a blender or food processor and process until sooth. Season with pepper to taste. Place the chicken cubes in a shallow dish and pour the mixture over them. Stir to coat, cover, and marinate, turning the cubes occasionally, for about 4 hours. Drain the chicken, reserving the marinade, and thread it onto skewers alternating with the bell pepper squares. Grill, turning and brushing with the marinade frequently, for 20 minutes, until browned.

4 servings

Curried Chicken Kabobs

12 pearl onions or shallots

¼ cup/½ stick butter

2 teaspoons curry powder

dash of lemon juice

4 small, skinless, boneless chicken breast portions, cut into 1 inch cubes

4 chicken livers, trimmed and halved

8 white mushrooms

1 green bell pepper, deseeded and diced

salt and pepper

Simmer the onions in a little water for 3 minutes, then drain. Melt the butter, then combine it with the curry powder and lemon juice in a bowl, and season with salt and pepper. Add the chicken cubes, stir, and marinate for 10 minutes. Thread the chicken, livers, mushrooms, and bell peppers alternately onto 4 skewers, Brush with any remaining curry butter. Grill, turning frequently, for about 10 minutes.

4 servings

Yakitori – Japanese Chicken

12 ounces skinless boneless chicken breast portions, cut into 1 inch cubes

1½ cups white mushrooms

4 scallions, cut into 1 inch lengths

4 tablespoons shoyu

3 tablespoons cream sherry

pinch of ground ginger

2 teaspoons brown sugar

Thread the chicken, mushrooms, and scallions onto skewers. Combine the remaining ingredients in a bowl and brush the mixture all over the kabobs. Grill, turning and basting with the shoyu mixture frequently, for 10–12 minutes.

2–4 servings

Spicy Kabobs

$1\frac{1}{2}$ pounds skinless, boneless chicken breast portions, cut into 1 inch cubes

2 tablespoons lime juice

$\frac{1}{2}$ teaspoon salt

2 teaspoons tandoori powder

1 teaspoon garam masala

3 tablespoons plain yogurt

1 teaspoon honey

Place the chicken in a dish and sprinkle with the lime juice and salt. Stir and let stand for 10 minutes. Combine the tandoori powder, garam masala, yogurt, and honey in a bowl and spoon over the chicken. Cover and marinate for 2 hours. Thread the chicken onto 4 oiled skewers and grill, turning several times, for 8–10 minutes.

4 servings

Honey and Orange Chicken Sticks with Toasted Corn Salsa

4 skinless, boneless chicken breast portions

1 inch piece of fresh ginger root, minced

2 garlic cloves, minced

finely grated zest and juice of 1 orange

2 tablespoons olive oil

2 tablespoons honey

2 corn cobs

3 tablespoons sunflower oil

4 scallions, chopped

3 tablespoons chopped cilantro

2 teaspoons toasted sesame seeds

1 tablespoon lime juice

1 tablespoon light soy sauce

1 teaspoon sesame oil

salt and pepper

Cut each chicken portion into 8 long thin strips. Combine the ginger, garlic, orange zest and juice, olive oil, and honey in a bowl. Add the chicken strips, turning to coat, then cover, and marinate for 1–2 hours. Brush the corn cobs with 2 tablespoons of the sunflower oil, place under a preheated broiler, and cook, turning frequently, for 10–15 minutes, until charred and the kernels are tender. Remove from the heat and when cool enough to handle remove the kernels with a sharp knife. Combine the corn kernels, the remaining sunflower oil, the scallions, cilantro, sesame seeds, lime juice, soy sauce, and sesame oil in a bowl and season with salt and pepper to taste. Drain the chicken, reserving the marinade. Thread 2 strips of chicken onto each of 16 skewers. Grill, brushing occasionally with the marinade, for 2–3 minutes on each side. Serve the chicken with the corn relish.

4 servings

Sicilian Kabobs

4 skinless, boneless chicken breast portions

12 bacon strips

4 continental or grilling sausage links, thickly sliced

6 chicken livers, halved

18 large mushroom caps

12 fresh bay leaves

6 tablespoons/¾ stick butter, melted

pinch of dried mixed herbs

2 teaspoons paprika

Cut each portion of chicken into 6 chunks and cut each bacon strip into 4. Thread the chicken, sausages, chicken livers, bacon, mushroom caps, and bay leaves onto 6 skewers. Brush with melted butter and sprinkle with the mixed herbs. Grill until tender, turning once or twice and brushing frequently with the butter and sprinkling with the paprika.

6 servings

Crispy Chicken on Sticks

1½ cups cornflakes, finely crushed

1 teaspoon curry powder

½ teaspoon salt

2 skinless, boneless chicken breast portions, cut into 1 inch cubes

1 egg, beaten

1 red bell pepper, cored, deseeded, and cut into 1 inch strips

scant 1 cup white mushrooms, halved

Combine the cornflake crumbs, curry powder, and salt in a bowl. Dip the chicken cubes into the beaten egg and then toss them in the cornflake mixture, pressing it onto the chicken with your fingers. Thread the chicken cubes, bell pepper strips, and mushrooms halves onto 8 wooden skewers. Cover and chill for 2 hours. Grill the skewers, turning frequently, for about 20 minutes, until cooked through and crisp.

4 servings

Chicken Burgers with Deviled Pineapple Relish

1 tomato, skinned and finely chopped

½ red or green bell pepper, deseeded and finely chopped

6 tablespoons well-drained, canned crushed pineapple

1 tablespoon prepared mild mustard

12 ounces skinless, boneless chicken breast portions, finely chopped or ground

12 ounces pork bulk sausage

salt and pepper

Combine the tomato, bell pepper, pineapple, and mustard in a bowl. Cover and set aside. Combine the chicken and bulk sausage in another bowl and season with salt and pepper. Divide the mixture into 8 portions and shape into neat rounds with lightly floured hands. Grill for 4–6 minutes on each side. Serve with a little devilled pineapple relish on the side.

4–8 servings

Chicken and Corn Burgers

1 pound skinless, boneless chicken breast portions, coarsely chopped

2 tablespoons sunflower oil, plus extra for brushing

1 onion, finely chopped

¾ cup drained canned corn

1 extra large egg, beaten

6 tablespoons soft bread crumbs

salt and pepper

Grind the chicken in a food processor or with the fine blade of a meat grinder, then place in a bowl. Heat the oil in a skillet, add the onion, and cook over low heat until soft and translucent. Add to the chicken with the corn, egg, and bread crumbs and mix well, seasoning with salt and pepper. Divide the mixture into 6 portions and shape each into a neat round. Brush lightly with oil and grill the burgers for about 4 minutes on each side.

6 servings

Chicken Liver Roll-ups

1 tablespoon white wine vinegar

3 tablespoons sunflower oil

8 ounces ready-to-eat prunes

1 pound chicken livers, trimmed

8 ounces bacon strips

salt and pepper

Whisk together the vinegar and oil in a bowl and season with salt and pepper. Add the prunes and set aside. Halve the chicken livers if large and cut the bacon into pieces 3–4 inches long. Wrap a chicken liver and a prune in each piece of bacon and secure each roll with a toothpick. Grill the rolls, brushing once or twice with the vinegar and oil mixture during cooking, for about 3–4 minutes on each side.

6–8 servings

Chickens with Lemon Butter Baste

3 broiling chickens

6 tablespoons/¾ stick butter, softened

6 tarragon sprigs

1 lemon, thinly sliced

4 tablespoons sunflower or corn oil

salt and pepper

Using poultry shears or strong kitchen scissors, cut the chickens along the backbone. Place each flat on a board, cut side down, press firmly on the breastbone to flatten, and cut in half. Gently lift the skin away from the breast and spread the softened butter underneath. Place a lemon slice and a tarragon sprig under the skin of each half bird. Season with salt and pepper and brush with oil. Grill the chicken halves, brushing frequently with oil, for 10–15 minutes on each side, until the flesh is firm and the skin is crisp.

6 servings

CORNISH HENS

Butterflied Cornish Hens

2 Cornish hens

6 tablespoons sunflower oil

1 tablespoon Worcestershire sauce

2 garlic cloves, minced

2 tablespoons lemon juice

1 tablespoon French mustard

salt and pepper

Using poultry shears or strong kitchen scissors, cut the Cornish hens along each side of the backbone and remove it. Place each bird flat on a board, cut side down, and press firmly on the breastbone to flatten. Open out each Cornish hen and place, skin side up, on the board. Fold the wingtips under the wings so that they lie flat. Insert 2 skewers, crisscross fashion, through the birds to hold them rigid and place in a shallow dish. Combine the oil, Worcestershire sauce, garlic, lemon juice, and mustard in a bowl and season with salt and pepper. Spoon the mixture over the Cornish hens, then cover, and marinate for 4–6 hours or overnight. Drain the

Cornish hens, reserving the marinade. Grill, skin side down, for 10 minutes, then turn the birds over, baste with the marinade, and grill for 10 minutes more, until tender and cooked through. Test that the Cornish hens are cooked by inserting the point of a sharp knife into the thickest part; if the juices run clear, they are cooked.

2 servings

Butterflied Cornish Hens with Tarragon and Lemon Butter

½ cup/1 stick butter, softened

3 tablespoons coarsely chopped tarragon

2 shallots, chopped

finely grated zest and juice of 1 lemon

4 Cornish hens, about 1 pound each

salt and pepper

Place the butter, tarragon, shallots, and lemon zest and juice in a blender or food processor and process until smooth. Using poultry shears or strong kitchen scissors, cut the Cornish hens along each side of the backbone and remove it. Place each flat on a board, cut side down, and press firmly on the breastbone to flatten. Lift the skin covering the breast and gently push your fingers between the flesh and skin to make a pocket. Divide the flavored butter equally among the birds, pushing it underneath the skin. Thread a skewer through a drumstick, under the breastbone, and through the second drumstick. Thread a second skewer through the wings, catching the flap of skin underneath. Repeat with the other Cornish hens. Grill the birds for 15–20 minutes, until cooked through and tender. Test by inserting the point of a sharp knife into the thickest part; if the juices run clear, the Cornish hens are cooked through.

4 servings

Cornish Hens Stuffed with Goat Cheese

4 Cornish hens

6 ounces soft goat cheese

1 tablespoon thyme leaves

3 thin cured ham slices, finely chopped

1 lemon, cut into 8 wedges

scant 1 cup olive oil

finely grated zest of 1 lemon

1 tablespoon chopped basil

salt and pepper

Rub the inside and outside of the Cornish hens with salt and pepper. Carefully slip your fingers between the skin and flesh of each bird, starting at the neck end, and gently ease your fingers along the breastbone and down. Combine the goat cheese, thyme, and ham in a bowl and season with salt and pepper. Ease some of the cheese mixture evenly between the skin and flesh of each Cornish hen. Stuff each body cavity with 2 lemon wedges. Place the birds in a shallow dish. Combine the olive oil, lemon zest, and basil in a pitcher and season with salt and pepper. Pour the mixture over the Cornish hens, cover, and marinate for 4 hours. Drain the birds, reserving the marinade. Place the Cornish hens breast side down onto the barbecue grid and grill, brushing occasionally with the marinade, for 10 minutes. Turn the birds over and grill, brushing occasionally with the marinade, for 15–20 minutes more, until cooked. Test by inserting the point of a sharp knife into the thickest part; if the juices run clear, the Cornish hens are cooked through.

4 servings

Butterflied Cornish Hens with Sun-dried Tomato and Basil Butter

3 sun-dried tomato halves in oil, drained and chopped, plus a little oil from the jar

½ cup/1 stick butter, softened

3 tablespoons coarsely chopped basil

4 Cornish hens, about 1 pound each

salt and pepper

Place the sun-dried tomatoes, butter, and basil in a blender or food processor and process until smooth. Using poultry shears or strong kitchen scissors, cut the Cornish hens along each side of the backbone and remove it. Place each flat on a board, cut side down, and press firmly on the breastbone to flatten. Lift the skin covering the breast and gently push your fingers between the flesh and skin to make a pocket. Divide the flavored butter equally among the birds, pushing it underneath the skin. Thread a skewer through a drumstick, under the breastbone, and through the second drumstick. Thread a second skewer through the wings, catching the flap of skin underneath. Repeat with the other Cornish hens. Brush the birds with the oil from the tomatoes and season with salt and pepper. Grill for 15–20 minutes, until they are cooked through and tender. Test by inserting the point of a sharp knife into the thickest part; if the juices run clear, the Cornish hens are cooked through.

4 servings

Cornish Hens Stuffed with Pâté

4 Cornish hens

6 ounces smooth chicken liver pâté

2 teaspoons sage leaves

3 thin cured ham slices, finely chopped

1 lemon, cut into 8 wedges

scant 1 cup olive oil

finely grated zest of 1 lemon

2 teaspoons chopped tarragon

salt and pepper

Rub the inside and outside of the Cornish hens with salt and pepper. Carefully slip your fingers between the skin and flesh of each bird, starting at the neck end, and gently ease your fingers along the breastbone and down. Combine the pâté, sage, and ham in a bowl and season with salt and pepper. Ease some of the pâté mixture evenly between the skin and flesh of each Cornish hen. Stuff each body cavity with 2 lemon wedges. Place the birds in a shallow dish. Combine the olive oil, lemon zest, and tarragon in a pitcher and season with salt and pepper. Pour the mixture over the Cornish hens, cover, and marinate for 4 hours. Drain the birds, reserving the marinade. Place the Cornish hens breast side down onto the barbecue grid and grill, brushing occasionally with the marinade, for 10 minutes. Turn the birds over and grill, brushing occasionally with the marinade, for 15–20 minutes more, until cooked. Test by inserting the point of a sharp knife into the thickest part; if the juices run clear, the Cornish hens are cooked through.

4 servings

Cornish Hens with Gin, Juniper, and Herbs

4 Cornish hens

3 tablespoons sunflower oil

2 garlic cloves, minced

1 tablespoon chopped tarragon

1 tablespoon chopped thyme

1 tablespoon chopped parsley

1 tablespoon chopped rosemary

1 tablespoon gin

4 juniper berries

salt and pepper

Using poultry shears or strong kitchen scissors, cut the Cornish hens along each side of the backbone and remove it. Place each bird flat on a board, cut side down, press firmly on the breastbone to flatten, and cut in half. Insert 2 skewers, crisscross fashion, through the birds to hold them rigid, then place in a large shallow dish and season with salt and pepper. Add the oil, garlic, herbs, and gin. Turn the birds to coat well, add the juniper berries, cover, and marinate for at least 1 hour. Drain the Cornish hens and thread onto long skewers. Grill, turning frequently, for about 20 minutes, until cooked through. Test by inserting the point of a sharp knife into the thickest part; if the juices run clear, the Cornish hens are cooked through. Remove the skewers before serving

4 servings

TASTY TURKEY

Red Hot Turkey Focaccia Sandwich

2 red chilies

2 egg yolks

1 tablespoon white wine vinegar

scant 1 cup sunflower oil

2 garlic cloves, minced

1/4 cup pine nuts

4 tablespoons grated Parmesan cheese

8 sun-dried tomato halves in oil, drained, plus 3 tablespoons of the oil from the jar

4 turkey scallops, about 4 ounces each

4 tablespoons olive oil

3 tablespoons orange juice

1 large focaccia or olive bread loaf

4 artichokes in oil, drained and sliced

1 red onion, thinly sliced into rings

4 ounces arugula

salt and pepper

Place the chilies under a preheated broiler and broil, turning once, for 5–7 minutes, until charred and blistered. Transfer to a plastic bag, seal the top, and let cool. When cool, rub off the charred skins, slit the chilies, and deseed. Whisk the egg yolks with the vinegar in a bowl until slightly thickened. Gradually whisk in the oil, adding it in a steady stream, until the mixture is thick. Cover and set aside. Place the garlic, pine nuts, and Parmesan in a blender or food processor and process until smooth. Add the sun-dried tomatoes and chilies and process again. With the motor running, add the oil from the jar, then spoon the mixture into the mayonnaise. Place the turkey in a shallow dish. Combine the olive oil and orange juice in a pitcher and pour the mixture over the turkey, turning to coat. Marinate for 30–60 minutes. Drain the turkey, reserving the marinade. Grill, basting frequently with the marinade, for 3–4 minutes on each side. Remove the turkey from the barbecue, cut into thin strips, place in a bowl, and keep warm. Slice the bread in half, toast both halves, crumb side down, on the barbecue. Spread both halves with the mayonnaise mixture, then pile the artichokes, red onion, arugula, and turkey slices on the bottom half and sprinkle with salt and pepper. Re-form the sandwich and cut it into 4 chunks to serve.

4 servings

Spit-roast Turkey with Spiced Apple

9 pound turkey

2 large, tart apples, peeled, cored, and chopped

2/3 cup apple juice

2 tablespoons brown sugar

½ teaspoon ground allspice

Fill the turkey cavity with the chopped apple. Attach the turkey, breast side upwards, to a rotisserie and cook for 3 hours. After the first 30 minutes, brush the skin frequently with the apple juice. When the turkey is cooked through and tender, remove it from the rotisserie. Test by inserting the point of a sharp knife into the thickest part; if the juices run clear, the turkey is cooked. Scoop the apple into a bowl. Place the turkey on a carving dish, tent with foil, and let stand for 10 minutes before carving. Beat the sugar and allspice into the apple and serve with the turkey.

8 servings

Crab-stuffed Turkey Breasts

6 skinless, boneless turkey breast portions

8 ounces drained canned white crabmeat

½ cup/1 stick butter, softened

¼ teaspoon ground nutmeg

¼ cup all-purpose flour

1 teaspoon paprika

salt and pepper

Cut out 6 squares of double-thickness foil. Cut a pocket in each turkey portion with a sharp knife. Combine the crabmeat, 6 tablespoons/½ stick of the butter, and the nutmeg in a bowl and season with salt and pepper. Carefully spoon the mixture into the pockets. Combine the flour and paprika in another bowl. Melt the remaining butter and brush it all over the turkey portions, then coat them in the flour mixture. Place each portion on a foil square, fold up the sides, and crimp to seal. Place the foil packets on the barbecue grid and cook for 30 minutes. Unwrap the packets, place the turkey portions directly on the grid, and grill, turning once, for 5 minutes more, until well browned and cooked through.

6 servings

Spiced Turkey Slices

4 tablespoons olive oil

¼ teaspoon chili powder

pinch of ground mace

pinch of ground cardamom

½ teaspoon pepper

6 turkey scallops

salt

Combine the oil, chili powder, mace, cardamom, pepper, and a pinch of salt in a shallow dish. Add the turkey, turn to coat, and marinate, turning occasionally, for 2 hours. Drain the turkey, reserving the marinade. Grill, turning and brushing with the marinade frequently, for about 5 minutes, until firm and golden.

6 servings

Turkey Surprise

1 pound ground turkey

½ cup parsley and thyme stuffing mix

2 teaspoons Worcestershire sauce

grated zest of 1 lemon

1 egg, beaten

½ cup cream cheese

1 teaspoon chopped sage

sunflower oil, for brushing

salt and pepper

Combine the turkey, stuffing mix, Worcestershire sauce, lemon zest, and egg in a bowl and season with salt and pepper. Combine the cheese and sage in another bowl. Divide the turkey mixture into 8 portions and shape each into a neat round. Divide the cheese mixture among 4 of the patties and top them with the remaining patties. Press the edges firmly together. Grill, occasionally brushing lightly with oil, for 10 minutes on each side, until cooked through.

4 servings

Turkey, Tomato, and Tarragon Burgers

8 sun-dried tomato halves in oil, drained and chopped

1 pound ground turkey

1 tablespoon chopped tarragon

½ red onion, finely chopped

¼ teaspoon paprika

¼ teaspoon salt

4 smoked pancetta slices, halved lengthwise

Place the tomatoes, turkey, and tarragon in a blender or food processor and process until smooth. Spoon the mixture into a bowl and stir in the onion. Season with the paprika and salt. Mix well, then divide the mixture into 4 portions, and shape each into a neat round. Stretch 2 strips of pancetta over each burger and secure with toothpicks. Grill, turning frequently, for 10–15 minutes.

4 servings

Turkey Drummers

¼ cup/½ stick butter

4 turkey drumsticks

1 onion, chopped

4 tablespoons tomato ketchup

2 tablespoons white wine vinegar

2 tablespoons mango chutney, chopped

1 tablespoon Worcestershire sauce

½ teaspoon Dijon mustard

Cut 4 squares of double-thickness foil. Melt half the butter in a skillet, add the drumsticks, and cook until brown all over. Place 1 drumstick on each piece of foil. Add the remaining butter to the skillet and cook the onion until softened but not brown. Add all the remaining ingredients and bring to a boil. Spoon the sauce over the drumsticks, fold up the sides of the foil, and crimp the edges to seal. Place on the barbecue grid and cook, turning 2–3 times, for 30–40 minutes.

4 servings

Turkey Kabobs

6 turkey scallops, total weight about 1½ pounds

½ teaspoon paprika

2 tablespoons olive oil

1 teaspoon dried thyme

6 fatty bacon strips, halved lengthwise

2 small, green eating apples, each cored and cut into 6 wedges

1 red or yellow bell pepper, deseeded and cut into 1 inch squares

1 green bell pepper, deseeded and cut into 1 inch squares

12 cherry tomatoes

salt and pepper

Cut each turkey scallop crosswise into 4 wide strips and place in a shallow dish. Add the paprika, oil, and thyme, season with salt and pepper, and mix well to coat. Cover and marinate for 1 hour. Drain the turkey and fold each strip 2–3 times to form 1 inch squares. Wrap a piece of bacon around half the squares. Thread 1 apple wedge onto each of 6 skewers, then thread them alternately with the bacon-wrapped turkey, plain turkey, bell peppers, and cherry tomatoes. Finally, add an apple wedge to each. Grill, turning the skewers several times, for 8–10 minutes.

6 servings

DUCK AND GOOSE

Wild Duck

2 pound young wild duck

2 large garlic cloves

1 small onion, halved

2 rosemary sprigs

1 orange, halved

⅔ cup olive oil

1 tablespoon juniper berries, crushed

2 French bread slices, cut diagonally

3 tablespoons crab apple or red currant jelly

salt and pepper

orange slices, to garnish

salad greens, to serve

Using a sharp, pointed knife, ease a little of the skin away from the duck breast, then slide a garlic clove under each side. Stuff the duck with the onion halves, pushing them as far into the cavity as they will go, then add the rosemary sprigs. Rub the cut orange all over the duck, squeezing as you do so to release the juice, then put the orange halves into the duck cavity. Rub the duck skin all over with plenty of salt and pepper, then brush lightly with the oil. Stir the juniper berries into the remaining oil. Position a foil or drip tray on the barbecue to prevent any dripping fat from flaring up. Place the duck on the grid, breast side down, and cook for 5 minutes, then brush with oil, and cook the other breast for 5 minutes. Brush with oil again, turn the duck back down, and grill for 5 minutes. Repeat the rotation once more, brushing with oil each time. If the duck is very small, the last turn need be only 5 minutes; if it is slightly larger, cook the breasts for 7 minutes each and the back for 10 minutes. The duck is ready when the leg joints move easily and the breast juices are only slightly pink when the flesh is pierced with the point of a sharp knife. About 15 minutes before the duck is ready, brush the bread slices with the oil on both sides and toast for 2½ minutes on each side. Spread 1 side of each slice with the jelly and place on 2 plates. Carve off 1 duck breast for each serving and place them on the toast. Cut off the legs and place them on a bed of salad greens. Pour off any fat from the drip tray and pour the cooking juices over the duck breasts. Garnish with orange slices to serve.

2 servings

Chinese Duckling

1 duckling

2 egg yolks

2 tablespoons soy sauce

3 tablespoons honey

Depending on the size of the duckling, split it into 2 or 4 portions. Combine the egg yolks, soy sauce, and honey in a bowl and rub the mixture all over the duckling portions. Place on the barbecue grid, cut sides down, and grill, turning occasionally, for 45–60 minutes, until the flesh is tender and the skin is crisp.

2–4 servings

Spit-roast Ducklings with Apricot Glaze

2 ducklings, about 4 pounds each

¾ cup apricot preserve

⅔ cup white vermouth

salt

Sprinkle the ducklings with salt, attach to a rotisserie, and cook for 30 minutes. Combine the apricot preserve and vermouth in a pan and heat gently, stirring until blended. Brush the mixture over the ducklings and cook, brushing frequently with the glaze, for 1–1½ hours more, until tender and cooked through. Test by inserting the point of a sharp knife into the thickest part; if the juices run clear, the ducklings are cooked through.

8 servings

Chinese Orange Duck

4 scallions, finely chopped

pinch of ground ginger

1 teaspoon ground turmeric

2 tablespoons dark soy sauce

4 tablespoons fine-cut marmalade

4–5 pound duck, cut into fourths

1 orange, sliced

salt and pepper

Chinese cabbage, to serve

Combine the scallions, ginger, turmeric, soy sauce, and marmalade in a shallow dish. Season the duck portions with salt and pepper, add to the dish, and turn to coat. Cover and marinate for about 4 hours. Drain the duck, reserving the marinade. Grill, bone side down, for 15 minutes, then turn, brush with the marinade, and grill for 10–15 minutes, taking care not to burn the skin. Turn the duck again and cook for 15–20 minutes more, until the flesh feels firm. Turn over and crisp the skin for 5–10 minutes until a rich golden brown. Brush the orange slices with the remaining marinade and grill for 5 minutes. Serve the duck on a bed of Chinese cabbage, garnished with the orange slices.

4 servings

Duck Breasts with Cumberland Sauce

4 duck breast fillets

1 tablespoon dark soy sauce

2 tablespoons orange juice

1 tablespoon chopped tarragon

1 orange

4 tablespoons lemon juice

¾ cup red currant jelly

6 tablespoons port

1 teaspoon arrowroot or cornstarch

pepper

tarragon sprigs, to garnish

Prick the duck in several places with a large needle and rub well with pepper. Combine the soy sauce, orange juice, and tarragon in a bowl, then rub the mixture over the duck breasts to coat them thoroughly. Place in a dish, cover, and marinate for at least 2 hours. Meanwhile, peel the orange as thinly as possible and cut the zest into very fine strips. Place in a small pan with just enough water to cover and bring to a boil. Boil for 1 minute, then drain and refresh under cold running water. Drain again. Squeeze the juice from the orange into a pan, add the lemon juice and red currant jelly, and bring to a boil over low heat, stirring frequently. Add the port and simmer for 5 minutes. Stir the arrowroot or cornstarch with 1½ tablespoons of water to make a paste and stir into the sauce. Bring back to a boil, stirring constantly, and cook for 1 minute. Stir in the orange zest. Remove the pan from the heat and cover the surface with a disk of damp waxed paper to prevent a skin from forming. Let cool. Drain the duck breasts and place on the barbecue grid, skin side down. Grill for 3–4 minutes on each side for medium or 5–6 minutes on each side for well done. Garnish with tarragon and serve with the sauce.

4 servings

Maple Duck with Apricot Pecan Chutney

1 cup dried apricots

1 large onion, sliced

scant ½ cup raisins

¼ cup brown sugar

1¼ cups white wine vinegar

1 teaspoon yellow mustard seeds

¼ teaspoon ground ginger

¼ teaspoon cayenne pepper

1 tablespoon salt

½ cup chopped pecan nuts

4 duck breasts, about 7–8 ounces each

4 tablespoons maple syrup

1 teaspoon vanilla extract

juice and finely grated zest of 1 orange

juice and finely grated zest of 1 lime

Put the apricots, onion, raisins, sugar, vinegar, mustard seeds, ginger, cayenne, and salt into a large, heavy pan. Bring to a boil, lower the heat, and simmer very gently, stirring frequently, for 45 minutes, until thickened. Stir in the pecans, ladle into sterilized jars, cover, and seal. Cut off any excess fat from the duck breasts and score the skin in a crisscross pattern. Cut the duck breasts into 1½ inch cubes and thread onto skewers. Combine the maple syrup, vanilla, citrus juice, and zest. Seal the duck for 2 minutes on each side, then remove the skewers from the barbecue, and brush with the glaze. Return to the barbecue and grill, turning and brushing with the glaze frequently, for 5–8 minutes, or until cooked through and tender. Serve the duck skewers with the chutney.

4 servings

Spit-roasted Goose

9 pound goose

⅔ cup chopped white mushrooms

2 garlic cloves, minced

15 anchovy fillets, finely chopped

1 cup/2 sticks butter, softened

3 tablespoons chopped parsley

1 goose liver or 3 chicken livers, finely chopped

salt and pepper

Rub the goose inside and out with salt and pepper, then prick the skin all over with a fine skewer or needle. Combine the mushrooms, garlic, anchovies, butter, parsley, and liver in a bowl and season with salt and pepper. Stuff the goose with this mixture, then sew up the opening with fine string. Attach the goose to a rotisserie and cook for 2 hours, until cooked through and tender. Test by inserting the point of a sharp knife into the thickest part; if the juices run clear, the goose is cooked through. Transfer to a carving dish, tent with foil, and let stand for 10 minutes before carving into large slices.

6 servings

Goose with Apples and Calvados

9 pound goose

2 apples, cored and cut into chunks

2 shallots or pearl onions, minced

1 cup/2 sticks butter, softened

3 tablespoons chopped sage

3 tablespoons Calvados, or other apple liqueur

6 cured bacon strips, finely chopped

salt and pepper

Rub the goose inside and out with salt and pepper, then prick the skin all over with a fine skewer or needle. Combine the apples, shallots or pearl onions, butter, sage, Calvados, and bacon in a bowl and season with salt and pepper. Stuff the goose with this mixture, then sew up the opening with fine string. Attach the goose to a rotisserie and cook for 2 hours, until cooked through and tender. Test by inserting the point of a sharp knife into the thickest part; if the juices run clear, the goose is cooked through. Transfer to a carving dish, tent with foil, and let stand for 10 minutes before carving into large slices.

6 servings

chapter 4

Fish and Shellfish

Almond-stuffed Trout

grated zest and juice of 1 lemon

1 cup sliced almonds

pinch of ground cumin

1 tablespoon chopped parsley

4 trout, cleaned

4 bay leaves

sunflower oil, for brushing

salt and pepper

Combine the lemon zest and juice, almonds, cumin, and parsley in a bowl and season with salt and pepper. Pack the mixture into the fish and place a bay leaf on top of each one. Tie up the fish with a little string to prevent them from opening or place in a hinged, wire basket. Brush the fish with oil and grill, brushing with more oil occasionally, for 10 minutes on each side, or until the skin begins to split and the flesh looks pale and firm.

4 servings

Stuffed Trout with Sour Cream and Horseradish Sauce

½ cup sour cream

4 teaspoons grated horseradish

4 tablespoons chopped parsley

2 tablespoons chopped mint

⅔ cup/1¼ sticks butter

1 cup blanched almonds, toasted and chopped

2 cups soft white bread crumbs

finely grated zest and juice of 1 lemon

4 trout, about 12 ounces each, cleaned

salt and pepper

Combine the sour cream, horseradish, parsley, and mint in a blender or food processor and process until smooth. Pour the sauce into a bowl and season with salt and pepper. Melt 1/2 cup/1 stick of the butter in a small pan, stir in the almonds, bread crumbs, lemon zest, and juice, and season with salt and pepper. Spoon the mixture into the cavities of the fish. Cut 4 large squares of double-thickness foil and grease with the remaining butter. Place a trout on each foil square and wrap securely. Cook on the barbecue, turning once, for 20–25 minutes, until tender.

4 servings

Trout with Lemon

4 trout, cleaned

4 bay leaves

4 lemon slices

4 parsley sprigs

1/4 cup/1/2 stick butter

salt and pepper

Cut 4 squares of double-thickness foil. Sprinkle the cavity of the fish with salt and pepper and place a bay leaf, lemon slice, and parsley sprig inside each. Grease the foil squares with the butter and place a fish on each one. Wrap securely and cook on the barbecue for 20–25 minutes, until the flesh feels firm.

4 servings

Bacon-stuffed Trout

3 tablespoons butter

6 bacon strips, chopped

1 onion, chopped

1½ cups sliced mushrooms

2 tablespoons chopped parsley

grated zest of ½ lemon

1½–2 cups soft whole-wheat bread crumbs

1 egg, beaten

3 trout, cleaned

salt and pepper

Melt half the butter in a skillet, add the bacon and onion, and cook over low heat for 3 minutes. Stir in the mushrooms and cook for 2 minutes more. Tip the mixture into a bowl and add the parsley, lemon zest, and bread crumbs. Mix well, season with salt and pepper, and stir in the egg to bind. Divide the mixture among the fish cavities, closing the openings with toothpicks. Melt the remaining butter. Cut 3 squares of double-thickness foil and brush with the butter. Place a fish in the center of each foil square and wrap securely. Cook the packets on the barbecue, turning occasionally, for about 30 minutes, until the flesh flakes easily.

3 servings

Herbed Fish

4 trout or whiting, cleaned

1 teaspoon dried mixed herbs

2 rosemary sprigs

4 tablespoons olive oil

1 tablespoon lemon juice

1 teaspoon garlic paste

salt and pepper

lemon wedges, to garnish

Make 3 cuts across each side of all the fish and sprinkle with salt and pepper. Place the mixed herbs and rosemary in a shallow dish and put the fish on top. Combine the oil, lemon juice, and garlic paste in a bowl and pour the mixture over the fish. Cover and marinate, turning several times, for 2–3 hours. Drain the fish, reserving the marinade. Grill, basting frequently with the marinade, for 5–6 minutes on each side. Serve garnished with lemon wedges.

4 servings

Trout with Fennel Mayonnaise

3 egg yolks

1¼ cups olive oil

1–2 teaspoons tarragon vinegar

1 small fennel bulb

¾ cup/1½ sticks butter, softened

1 teaspoon lemon juice

4 trout, about 8 ounces each, cleaned

finely ground sea salt and pepper

dried fennel stalks, for cooking

lemon wedges, to garnish

Whisk the egg yolks in a bowl, add a generous pinch of sea salt, and whisk again. Gradually whisk in the oil, a few drops at a time to begin with and then in a thin, steady stream. Whisk in ½ teaspoon of the vinegar, then whisk in another ½ teaspoon. Taste the mayonnaise and, if necessary, gradually whisk in the remaining vinegar. Cut off the feathery tops from the fennel bulb, chop finely, and reserve. Trim the bulb and thinly slice in a food processor or coarsely grate into a bowl. Fold the fennel into the mayonnaise, cover, and chill. Mash the butter with the lemon juice and season with pepper. Put 1 teaspoon of the butter mixture inside each fish and secure the cavity with a toothpick. Spread the remaining butter mixture over both sides of each fish. Douse the dried fennel stalks with cold water and place them on the barbecue coals. Grill the fish for 7 minutes on each side, then garnish with some of the reserved fennel tops and the lemon wedges. Garnish the mayonnaise with the remaining fennel tops and serve with the trout.

4 servings

Sea Trout with Orange Dressing

1 sea trout, about 3–3½ pounds, cleaned

4–5 tablespoons orange juice

grated zest and juice of 1 lemon

⅔ cup Mayonnaise (see page 281)

⅔ cup set plain yogurt

salt and pepper

Cut a square of double-thickness foil and place the fish on it. Spoon 3 tablespoons of the orange juice, the lemon zest, and lemon juice over it. Season with salt and pepper and wrap the fish securely. Cook on the barbecue, turning occasionally, for 1–1¼ hours. Meanwhile, combine the mayonnaise, yogurt, and remaining orange juice and season with salt and pepper. Serve the fish with the orange dressing.

6 servings

Stuffed Salmon

1 salmon, about 2½–3 pounds, cleaned

1 onion, chopped

2 celery stalks, chopped

3 bacon strips, chopped and fried until crisp

2 tablespoons chopped parsley

3/4 cup soft white bread crumbs

1/4 cup/1/2 stick butter, melted

salt and pepper

Cut a square of double-thickness foil and grease well. Remove the head from the fish if this hasn't already been done. Place the fish on the foil square. Combine the onion, celery, bacon, parsley, bread crumbs, and butter in a bowl and season with salt and pepper. Fill the cavity of the fish with the stuffing and close the opening with toothpicks. Wrap the fish securely. Cook on the barbecue, turning occasionally, for 1–1 1/4 hours, until the flesh flakes easily.

4–6 servings

Salmon Steaks with Rosemary

4 salmon steaks

4 tablespoons olive oil

1 teaspoon chopped rosemary

rosemary sprigs, for cooking

4 lemon wedges, to serve

Place the salmon steaks in a shallow dish. Combine the oil and chopped rosemary in a bowl and season with salt and pepper. Brush the mixture onto both sides of the steaks. Pour the remaining mixture on top of the steaks and marinate for at least 30 minutes. Drain the fish, reserving the marinade. Place a few rosemary sprigs on the coals and grill the salmon, turning and brushing with the marinade occasionally, for 10–20 minutes. Serve with the lemon wedges.

4 servings

Marinated Salmon with Capers

6 tablespoons capers

4 tablespoons olive oil

4 tablespoons lemon juice

6 shallots, finely chopped

1 teaspoon thyme

2 bay leaves

6 salmon steaks

salt and pepper

Combine the capers, olive oil, lemon juice, shallots, thyme, and bay leaves in a shallow dish and season with salt and pepper. Add the salmon steaks, turning to coat, and marinate for 2 hours. Drain the salmon, reserving the marinade. Grill, turning and brushing with the marinade occasionally, for 10–15 minutes.

6 servings

Japanese Salmon Kabobs

5 scallions

1 inch piece of fresh ginger root, minced

5 tablespoons shoyu

4 tablespoons sugar

4 tablespoons rice wine or dry sherry

2 pounds salmon fillet, skinned and thinly sliced

Finely chop 1 scallion and cut the remainder into 1 inch lengths. Combine the ginger, chopped scallion, shoyu, sugar, and rice wine or sherry in a shallow dish. Add the fish, turning to coat, then cover, and marinate for at least 1 hour. Drain the fish, reserving the marinade. Thread the salmon and scallion pieces onto 4 skewers. Grill, turning and brushing with the marinade, for about 5 minutes, until the fish is tender.

4 servings

Salmon and Asparagus Packets

½ cup/1 stick butter, softened

½ cup pistachio nuts

2 tablespoons chopped basil

1 garlic clove, minced

2 teaspoons lime juice

4 salmon fillets, about 7 ounces each

16 thin asparagus spears, trimmed

salt and pepper

Put the butter, nuts, basil, garlic, and lime juice in a blender or food processor, season with salt and pepper, and process until smooth. Spoon the mixture into a bowl and chill. Cut out 4 squares of double-thickness foil and place a salmon fillet in the center of each. Top each fillet with 4 asparagus spears, then add a heaping tablespoon of the pistachio and basil butter. Wrap the fish securely and cook on the barbecue for 15–20 minutes, until the fish flakes easily.

4 servings

Whole Baked Fish in Banana Leaves

2½–3 pound porgy, cleaned and scaled

1 tablespoon lime juice

1 teaspoon salt

1 small onion, coarsely chopped

1 red or yellow bell pepper, deseeded and coarsely chopped

1 inch piece of fresh ginger root, coarsely chopped

2 red chilies, deseeded and coarsely chopped

1 lemongrass stalk, chopped

½ cup coconut milk

½ teaspoon chili powder

½ cup cilantro

banana leaves or foil, for wrapping

Make 2–3 diagonal slits on each side of the fish. Combine the lime juice and salt in a bowl and rub the mixture well into the slits. Put the onion, bell pepper, ginger, chilies, lemongrass, coconut milk, chili powder, and cilantro into a blender or food processor and process until smooth. Scrape the paste into a bowl. Dip the banana leaves into boiling water and drain. Place the fish on the leaves and rub in one fourth of the spice paste. Turn the fish over and rub in another fourth of the spice paste. Wrap the leaves securely around the fish and tie with string. Alternatively, wrap the fish in foil. Cook on the barbecue for 10–15 minutes on each side, until tender. Heat the remaining spice paste in a pan. To serve the fish, place the packet on a platter and turn back the leaves or foil. Serve with the hot spice paste.

4 servings

Porgy Steaks with Almonds

6 porgy steaks, about 8 ounces each

1 lemon, cut into 6 thin wedges

24 blanched almonds, toasted

1 small onion, finely chopped

6 tablespoons olive oil

2 tablespoons coarsely chopped parsley

1–2 tablespoons drained bottled capers

scant 1 cup Mayonnaise (see page 281)

salt and pepper

Make a small slit in the side of each fish steak and press a lemon wedge into it. Press 4 almonds into the top of each steak. Place the fish steaks in a shallow dish, sprinkle with the onion, oil, and parsley, and season with salt and pepper. Cover and marinate for at least 6 hours. Drain the fish steaks and grill for 5–6 minutes on each side, until cooked through. Stir the capers into the mayonnaise in a bowl and serve with the fish.

6 servings

Porgy with Pesto and Tomato Sauce

4 porgy steaks, about 6 ounces each

6 tablespoons olive oil

4 large tomatoes, skinned, deseeded, and chopped

4 anchovy fillets, chopped

3 tablespoons pesto sauce

salt and pepper

Season the fish on both sides with salt and pepper and brush lightly with 2 tablespoons of the oil. Grill for 4–5 minutes on each side. Meanwhile, heat the remaining oil in a pan. Add the tomatoes and anchovies, season with salt and pepper, and cook gently for 5 minutes. Stir in the pesto sauce. Serve the porgy steaks with the sauce spooned over them.

4 servings

Sea Bass with Fennel

1 sea bass, 3–4 pounds, cleaned

White Wine Marinade (see page 19)

4 fennel sprigs

parsley sprigs, to garnish

lemon wedges, to serve

Cut a large square of double-thickness foil, place the fish on it, and fold up the edges. Pour the marinade over the fish and marinate for 2–4 hours. Place the fennel sprigs inside the fish and place the open foil packet on the barbecue grid. Cook, basting occasionally with the marinade, for 45–60 minutes, until tender. Serve garnished with parsley and with lemon wedges for squeezing.

4–6 servings

Sea Bass with Parsley, Lemon, and Dill

1 sea bass, about 2½ pounds, cleaned

3 tablespoons coarsely chopped parsley

juice and grated zest of 2 lemons

4 tablespoons olive oil

4 dill sprigs

salt and pepper

lemon wedges and dill sprigs, to garnish

Put the fish in a large dish. Combine the parsley, lemon juice and zest, and olive oil in a pitcher and season with salt and pepper. Pour the mixture over the fish, cover, and marinate for 4 hours. Drain the fish, reserving the marinade. Place the dill sprigs in the cavity of the fish. Grill for 10–15 minutes, brush with the marinade, turn over, and brush with the marinade again. Grill for 10 minutes more, until the fish is tender. Serve garnished with lemon wedges and dill sprigs.

4–6 servings

Sea Bass with Lime Aioli

4–6 garlic cloves, minced

2 egg yolks

juice and finely grated zest of 2 limes

1½ cups extra virgin olive oil

4 large potatoes, unpeeled

4 sea bass fillets, 6–8 ounces each

salt and pepper

lime wedges, to garnish

Place the garlic, egg yolks, and lime juice in a blender or food processor and process briefly to mix. With the machine running, gradually add about 1¼ cups of the olive oil in a thin steady stream until the mixture forms a thick cream. Turn into a bowl, and season with salt and pepper. Slice the potatoes thinly and brush with the remaining oil. Grill for 2–3 minutes on each side, until tender. Keep warm on the side of the barbecue. Score the fish fillets, brush with the remaining olive oil, and place skin side down on the barbecue grid. Grill, turning once, for 3–4 minutes, until just cooked. Serve with the potatoes and aioli, garnished with lime wedges.

4 servings

Red Snapper Grilled in Grape Leaves

4 red snapper, about 6 ounces each, cleaned

6 tablespoons olive oil

2 bay leaves, crumbled

1 tablespoon thyme leaves

1 tablespoon chopped chives

1 teaspoon crushed black peppercorns

½ teaspoon salt

2 garlic cloves, finely chopped

2 tablespoons lemon juice

12 large grape leaves, rinsed and soaked in boiling water for 10 minutes, if preserved

Put the fish in a shallow dish. Combine the oil, herbs, peppercorns, salt, garlic, and lemon juice in a pitcher and pour the mixture over the fish. Turn to coat, then cover and marinate for 2 hours. Drain the fish, reserving the marinade. Wrap each snapper in three grape leaves, folding 1 over the head, 1 over the tail, and 1 around the middle. Brush the leaves with the marinade. Grill for 4 minutes on each side.

4 servings

Red Snapper with Almond Paste

6 red snapper, cleaned

2 tablespoons lime juice

2 cups almonds, toasted and ground

generous ½ cup superfine sugar

1 teaspoon ground cinnamon

2 teaspoons orange flower water

7 tablespoons olive oil

½ teaspoon saffron powder

salt and pepper

sliced pickled lemons, to serve

Sprinkle the inside of each fish with lime juice and a little salt and pepper. Combine the almonds, sugar, cinnamon, orange flower water, and 3–4 tablespoons of the oil in a bowl to form a stiff paste. Using half the paste, fill the cavity of each fish. Cut a large square of double-thickness foil, brush with oil, and place all the fish on it, folding up the edges slightly. Spread the remaining paste over the fish and sprinkle with the saffron. Drizzle with the remaining oil and wrap the fish securely. Cook on the barbecue for 15–20 minutes, until tender. Serve with slices of pickled lemons.

6 servings

Red Snapper with Olives, Capers, and Oregano

6 red snapper, about 8 ounces each, cleaned

2 tablespoons chopped oregano

2 tablespoons chopped parsley

¾ cup pitted black olives, sliced

2 tablespoons capers

4 tablespoons olive oil

1 garlic clove, minced

salt and pepper

Cut 6 squares of double-thickness foil and place a fish on each. Season the fish inside and out with salt and pepper. Fill the cavities of the fish with half the oregano and parsley. Combine the remaining oregano and parsley with the olives, capers, olive oil, and garlic in a bowl and spoon the mixture over the fish. Wrap each fish securely. Cook on the barbecue for about 20 minutes, until tender.

6 servings

Tuna Steaks with Mustard

¼ cup/½ stick butter, melted

1 tablespoon Dijon mustard

1 tablespoon lemon juice

4 tuna steaks, about 5 ounces each

salt and pepper

lemon slices, to garnish

Combine the butter, mustard, and lemon juice in a bowl and season with salt and pepper. Brush half this mixture on both sides of each tuna steak. Grill for 10 minutes, turn the tuna over, brush with the remaining butter mixture, and grill for 10 minutes more. Serve garnished with lemon slices.

4 servings

Seared Peppered Tuna

6 tablespoons rice vinegar

1 tablespoon sugar

2 ounce piece of fresh ginger root, thinly sliced

8 ounces rice noodles

1½ tablespoons sesame oil

1½ tablespoons sesame seeds, toasted

2 tablespoons lime juice

5 tablespoons peanut oil

2 garlic cloves, minced

4 tuna steaks, about 6 ounces each

4 tablespoons dried pink peppercorns, crushed

salt

Pour the rice vinegar into a small pan and add the sugar and 1 teaspoon salt. Bring to a boil, add the ginger, lower the heat, and simmer for 1–2 minutes. Transfer the mixture to a bowl and cool. Prepare the noodles according to the packet instructions. Drain, refresh under cold water, and drain again. Tip the noodles into a bowl, add the sesame oil and sesame seeds, and toss lightly. Combine the lime juice, oil, and garlic in a shallow dish and season with salt. Add the fish, turning to coat, and marinate, turning once, for 1 hour. Place the peppercorns on a shallow plate. Drain the tuna and roll the edges of each steak in the peppercorns to coat. Sear for 1 minute on each side. Slice thinly and serve with the ginger and noodles.

4 servings

Tuna with Anchovies and Caper Vinaigrette

½ cup extra virgin olive oil

2 tablespoons white wine vinegar

1 teaspoon Dijon mustard

1 tablespoon chopped tarragon

1 tablespoon chopped Italian parsley

2 tablespoons capers, rinsed and crushed

pinch of sugar

4 thick tuna steaks, about 8 ounces each

12 canned anchovy fillets, drained and halved

4 garlic cloves, cut into thin slivers

salt and pepper

Reserve 2 tablespoons of the oil and combine the remainder with the vinegar and mustard, whisking well to combine. Stir in the tarragon, parsley, and capers and season with salt, pepper, and a pinch of sugar. Cover and set aside. Make 6 small incisions in each tuna steak. Using the point of the knife to help, insert 1 piece of anchovy and 1 garlic sliver into each incision. Brush the steaks all over with the reserved olive oil and season with salt and pepper. Grill for 3–4 minutes on each side, until just cooked. Serve with the caper vinaigrette.

4 servings

Simple Steaks

6 swordfish steaks

¼ cup/½ stick butter, melted

1 tablespoon lime juice

1 tablespoon chopped cilantro

salt and pepper

Season the fish with salt and pepper. Combine the butter, lime juice, and cilantro in a bowl and brush this mixture over the fish steaks. Grill, turning once and basting occasionally with the butter mixture, for 10–15 minutes.

6 servings

Swordfish with Black Olive Butter

½ cup/1 stick butter, softened

¼ cup pitted black olives, very finely chopped

½ teaspoon anchovy paste

1 garlic clove, minced

1 tablespoon capers, finely chopped

juice and finely grated zest of ½ lemon

4 swordfish steaks, about 6 ounces each

3 tablespoons olive oil

salt and pepper

Combine the butter, olives, anchovy paste, garlic, capers, lemon juice, and zest in a bowl, beating well until thoroughly mixed. Season with salt and pepper. Alternatively, mix in a food processor. Place a piece of waxed paper on the counter and spread the olive butter down the middle. Roll the paper over and twist the ends to make a neat cylinder. Chill until firm. Brush the swordfish steaks with oil and grill for 3–4 minutes on each side, until just cooked. Unroll the olive butter and slice. Serve the steaks topped with slices of the butter.

4 servings

Swordfish with Toasted Almond and Parsley Pesto

1 cup unblanched whole almonds

1 garlic clove, minced

2 tablespoons finely grated Parmesan cheese

2 cups coarsely chopped parsley

scant 1 cup extra virgin olive oil

2 tablespoons ricotta cheese

4 swordfish steaks, about 6 ounces each

olive oil, for brushing

salt and pepper

lemon wedges, to serve

Spread out the almonds on a cookie sheet and place under a preheated broiler. Broil, turning frequently, for 2–3 minutes, until golden. Place half the almonds, the garlic, Parmesan, parsley, extra virgin olive oil, and ricotta in a blender or food processor, season with salt and pepper, and process until smooth, scraping down the sides of the bowl if necessary. Transfer the pesto to a bowl. Coarsely chop the remaining almonds and stir them into the pesto. Brush the fish steaks with olive oil and grill for 2–3 minutes on each side, until cooked through. Serve with the pesto and the lemon wedges.

4 servings

Swordfish with Fennel Seeds

4 swordfish steaks, 7–8 ounces each

2 teaspoons fennel seeds, crushed

finely grated zest and juice of 1 lemon

1 tablespoon drained bottled capers, chopped

2 tablespoons chopped dill

1 teaspoon paprika

1–2 garlic cloves, minced

⅔ cup olive oil

Place the swordfish steaks in a shallow dish. Combine the fennel, lemon zest and juice, capers, dill, paprika, garlic, and olive oil in a jug. Pour the mixture over the fish, turning to coat. Cover and marinate for 2–3 hours. Drain the fish, reserving the marinade. Grill, basting frequently with the marinade, for 5–7 minutes.

4 servings

Mackerel with Plum Sauce

1 pound tart red plums, halved and pitted

2 tablespoons sugar

1 teaspoon coriander seeds, crushed

1 garlic clove, minced

pinch of paprika

1 teaspoon finely grated lemon zest

4 tablespoons water

4 mackerel, about 12 ounces each, cleaned

salt and pepper

Cut the plum halves into wedges and place in a pan with the sugar, coriander seeds, garlic, paprika, and lemon zest. Add the measured water and bring to a boil, then lower the heat, cover, and simmer for 10 minutes, until softened. Spoon the plum mixture into a blender or food processor and process until smooth. Push the mixture through a wire strainer into a clean pan, bring back to a boil, and cook, stirring constantly, for 5 minutes, until thickened and reduced. Transfer the pan to the side of the barbecue to keep warm. Make 3 diagonal slashes on both sides of each fish. Season with salt and pepper and grill for 6–7 minutes on each side. Serve the fish with the plum sauce.

4 servings

Baked Stuffed Mackerel

4 mackerel, cleaned

2 tablespoons/¼ stick butter

2 tart apples, peeled, cored, and diced

4 celery stalks, diced

scant 1/2 cup golden raisins

1/2 cup soft white bread crumbs

2 tablespoons lemon juice

salt and pepper

Cut 4 squares of double-thickness foil. Remove the heads from the fish if this hasn't already been done and place the fish on the foil squares. Melt the butter in a large skillet, add the apple and celery, and cook for 5 minutes, until softened. Transfer to a bowl, stir in the golden raisins and bread crumbs, and season with salt and pepper. Sprinkle the insides of the fish with the lemon juice and season with salt and pepper. Spoon the stuffing mixture into the cavities. Wrap the fish securely and cook on the barbecue for about 20 minutes.

4 servings

Deviled Mackerel

4 mackerel, cleaned

1 1/2 cups sliced mushrooms

1/4 cup/1/2 stick butter, softened

1 tablespoon Worcestershire sauce

1 tablespoon mustard powder

Cut 4 squares of double-thickness foil and grease well. Cut off the fish heads if this hasn't already been done and place a fish on each foil square. Divide the mushrooms equally among the cavities in the mackerel. Combine the butter, Worcestershire sauce, and mustard in a bowl, then divide the mixture among the cavities. Wrap the fish securely. Grill, turning occasionally, for 20–25 minutes.

4 servings

Apple Mackerel

4 mackerel, cleaned

3 tablespoons butter

1 apple, peeled, cored, and diced

2 celery stalks, chopped

1 small onion, chopped

2 cups cooked long grain rice

1 teaspoon lemon juice

salt and pepper

Cut 4 squares of double-thickness foil and grease well. Open the fish, press flat, and lift out the backbones. Place each fish on a foil square. Melt the butter in a skillet and cook the apple, celery, and onion until soft. Stir in the rice and lemon juice, sprinkle with salt and pepper, and mix well. Stuff the mackerel with the mixture. Wrap the fish securely and cook on the barbecue, turning once, for 20 minutes.

4 servings

Mackerel with Orange and Walnut

4 mackerel, cleaned

4 small oranges, peeled and chopped

½ cup chopped walnuts

½ cup soft white bread crumbs

2 tablespoons lemon juice

salt and pepper

Cut 4 squares of double-thickness foil. Remove the heads from the fish if this hasn't already been done and place the fish on the foil squares. Combine the oranges, walnuts, and breadcrumbs in a bowl and season with salt and pepper. Sprinkle the insides of the fish with the lemon juice and season with salt and pepper. Spoon the stuffing mixture into the cavities. Wrap the fish securely and cook on the barbecue for about 20 minutes.

4 servings

Mackerel with Fennel

1 tablespoon butter, melted

1 teaspoon dried fennel

1 teaspoon finely chopped onion

2 tablespoons lemon juice

⅔ cup plain yogurt

4 mackerel, cleaned

1 tablespoon sunflower oil

salt and pepper

Combine the butter, fennel, onion, lemon juice, and yogurt in a bowl and season with salt and pepper. Brush a little of the mixture inside each fish and brush the outside with oil. Place the fish on a double sheet of foil on the barbecue grid. Cook, turning and brushing the outsides with oil and the insides with the yogurt mixture, for 20–30 minutes, until cooked. Gently heat the remaining yogurt mixture in a pan on the side of the barbecue and serve as a sauce with the fish.

4 servings

Mackerel Kabobs

2 pounds mackerel fillets, cut into 1 inch pieces

6 pearl onions, halved

8–12 white mushrooms

1 green bell pepper, deseeded and cut into squares

4 tablespoons hard cider

4 tablespoons olive oil

2 teaspoons oregano

salt and pepper

Thread the mackerel, onions, mushrooms, and bell pepper squares alternately onto oiled skewers and place them in a shallow dish. Combine the hard cider, olive oil, and oregano in a pitcher and season with salt and pepper. Pour the mixture over the kabobs and marinate for 1 hour. Drain the kabobs, reserving the marinade. Grill, turning once and basting frequently with the marinade, for 8–10 minutes.

4 servings

Spicy Fish Sate

1 pound mackerel fillets

2 garlic cloves, minced

1 inch piece of fresh ginger root, minced

2 teaspoons light soy sauce

2 tablespoons lime or lemon juice

1 small red chili, very finely chopped

2 tablespoons peanut oil

1 shallot, finely chopped

1¾ cups water

1 tablespoon dark brown sugar

½ teaspoon chili powder

1 cup unsalted roasted peanuts, finely ground

½ papaya, peeled, deseeded, and cut into chunks

salt and pepper

Cut each fish fillet into 1 inch diagonal strips and place in a bowl. Combine half the garlic, the ginger, soy sauce, half the lime or lemon juice, and the chili in a pitcher. Pour the mixture over the mackerel, turning to coat, cover, and marinate for 30–60 minutes. Heat the oil in a small pan. Add the remaining garlic and the shallot and cook for 3–4 minutes, until lightly golden. Pour in 1¾ cups water, add the sugar, chili powder, and peanuts, stir well, and bring to a boil. Lower the heat and simmer, stirring occasionally, for 10–15 minutes, until thickened. Remove the pan from the heat, stir in the remaining lime or lemon juice, and season with salt and pepper. Place the pan on the side of the barbecue to keep warm. Drain the fish and thread 3 pieces onto each skewer, adding a piece of papaya to the ends. Grill for 3–4 minutes on each side. Serve with the sate sauce.

4 servings

Japanese-style Fish

6 tablespoons shoyu

1 garlic clove, minced

2 tablespoons sesame oil

2 tablespoons brown sugar

pinch of ground ginger

3 sole, cleaned

1 scallion, chopped

Combine the shoyu, garlic, sesame oil, sugar, and ginger in a shallow dish. Add the fish, turning to coat, and marinate for 1 hour. Drain the fish, place on a sheet of greased foil, and grill for 4–5 minutes on each side. Slice into fillets and serve sprinkled with the scallion.

6 servings

Marinated Baby Sole

6 sole, about 8 ounces each, dark skin removed

2/3 cup lime juice

2/3 cup dry white wine

1 tablespoon honey

1/2 cup peanut oil

pinch of ground allspice

2 teaspoons soy sauce

salt and pepper

lime wedges and cilantro sprigs, to garnish

Put the sole in a shallow dish. Combine the lime juice, wine, honey, oil, allspice, and soy sauce in a jug and season with salt and pepper. Pour the mixture over the fish, turning to coat. Cover and marinate, turning 2–3 times, for 3 hours. Drain the fish, reserving the marinade. Grill, basting frequently with the marinade, for 5 minutes on each side. Garnish with lime wedges and cilantro before serving.

6 servings

Sole Flambéed with Pernod

4 large oranges

8 ounces black grapes, halved and deseeded

4 sole, about 1 pound each, cleaned

sunflower oil, for brushing

4 tablespoons Pernod or pastis

salt and pepper

Using a zester, remove the zest from 2 of the oranges and place in a bowl. Add the grapes. Cut a thin slice from the top and bottom of each orange. Place the oranges, cut side down, on a board and cut off the rind in strips from the top down. Take care not to remove any flesh, but remove all the pith. Hold each orange over a bowl to catch any juice and remove the segments. Place in the bowl with the grapes. Cut 3 diagonal slashes in both sides of each fish, brush with oil, and season with salt and pepper. Grill, turning once, for 5–6 minutes. Transfer the fish to a platter and divide the fruit and juice among them. Heat the Pernod in a soup ladle, pour 1 tablespoon on each portion, and ignite. Serve when the flames die down.

4 servings

Cornmeal-crusted Fish with Lemon and Sesame Mayonnaise

1 egg yolk

2 tablespoons lemon juice

½ teaspoon Dijon mustard

⅔ cup sunflower oil

1 teaspoon sesame oil

finely grated zest of 1 small lemon

2 tablespoons olive oil

4 sole or John Dory fillets, about 6 ounces each

scant ½ cup cornmeal mush

salt and pepper

Put the egg yolk, lemon juice, and mustard in a blender or food processor and process until thoroughly mixed. Combine the sunflower oil and sesame oil in a pitcher. With the motor running, gradually add the oil mixture in a thin stream. Transfer to a bowl, stir in the lemon zest, and season with salt and pepper. Brush the olive oil all over the fish. Place the fillets on a plate and sprinkle generously with the cornmeal. Season with salt and pepper. Oil a large sheet of foil and place it on the barbecue.

Place the fish, flesh side down, on the foil and cook for 3 minutes, then turn over, and cook for 3 minutes more. Serve with the lemon and sesame mayonnaise.

4 servings

Skewered Flounder

12 fatty bacon strips

1 pound flounder fillets, skinned

2/3 cup Hard Cider and Honey Marinade (see page 23)

Lemon Sauce (see page 273)

Place the bacon strips on a board and stretch with the back of a knife, then cut in half. Cut the fish fillets into 24 pieces. Place each piece of fish on a piece of bacon, roll up, and secure with a toothpick. Place the rolls in a shallow dish, pour the marinade over them, and marinate for 2 hours. Drain the fish rolls, reserving the marinade. Remove the toothpicks and thread the rolls onto 4 skewers. Grill, turning and brushing with the marinade, for 8–10 minutes. Serve with the lemon sauce.

4 servings

Fish Kabobs with Herb Butter

6 tablespoons/3/4 stick butter

1 tablespoon finely chopped dill

1 tablespoon finely chopped tarragon

1 tablespoon finely chopped chives

1 tablespoon lemon juice

8 bacon strips

1 1/2 cups white mushrooms

1 pound cod steaks, skinned and cut into 2 inch cubes

4 tomatoes, cut into fourths

2 green bell peppers, deseeded and cut into chunks

8 ounces flounder fillet, skinned and cut into squares

salt and pepper

Melt the butter in a small pan, then stir in the herbs and lemon juice, and season with salt and pepper. Roll up each bacon strip. Thread the bacon rolls, mushrooms, cubes of cod, tomatoes, bell peppers, and squares of flounder alternately onto 3–4 skewers. Brush the kabobs with the herb butter and grill, turning and basting with the herb butter several times, for 8–10 minutes. Serve the kabobs with the remaining butter spooned over them.

3–4 servings

Flounder and Anchovy Roll-ups

12 small flounder fillets

anchovy paste, for spreading

olive oil, for brushing

⅔ cup Mayonnaise (see page 281)

3 tablespoons sour cream

3 tablespoons finely chopped parsley

sea salt and pepper

Cut each fish fillet in half crosswise. Thinly spread the anchovy paste on 1 side of each piece and roll up. Thread 6 fish rolls onto each of 4 skewers and brush lightly with olive oil. Grill for 2–3 minutes on each side. Season lightly with salt and pepper. Combine the mayonnaise, sour cream, and parsley in a bowl. Serve the fish roll-ups with the parsley mayonnaise.

4 servings

Cod Flamenco

2 tablespoons/¼ stick butter

1 tablespoon olive oil

1 onion, sliced

8 ounces green beans

2 tomatoes, skinned and sliced

2 tablespoons tomato paste

1 green bell pepper, deseeded and sliced

4 cod steaks, about 8 ounces each

salt and pepper

Cut 4 squares of double-thickness foil and grease well. Melt the butter with the oil in a skillet and cook the onion until softened. Add the beans, tomatoes, tomato paste, and bell pepper and cook for 5 minutes more. Season with salt and pepper. Place a cod steak in the center of each foil square and top with the vegetable mixture. Wrap the fish securely and cook the packets on the barbecue for about 20 minutes.

4 servings

Spicy Cod Packets

4 cod steaks, about 8 ounces each

6 tablespoons olive oil

1 onion, thinly sliced into rings

2 tomatoes, thinly sliced

2 tablespoons finely chopped cilantro

½ teaspoon medium curry powder

2 tablespoons lemon juice

salt and pepper

cilantro sprigs, to garnish

Cut 4 large squares of double-thickness foil and brush lightly with oil. Place a cod steak in the center of each piece. Put a few onion rings on top of each steak, then a few tomato slices on top of the onion, and sprinkle with chopped cilantro. Combine the remaining oil, curry powder, and lemon juice and pour a little of the mixture over each steak. Season with salt and pepper then wrap the fish securely. Cook on the barbecue for 20 minutes. Remove from the foil packets before serving either hot or cold, garnished with cilantro sprigs.

4 servings

Cod with Black Beans and Ginger

4 cod steaks, about 6 ounces each

1 red chili, deseeded and finely chopped

1½ tablespoons fermented black beans, finely chopped

1 inch piece of fresh ginger root, finely chopped

finely grated zest and juice of 1 lime

1-2 tablespoons light soy sauce

2 garlic cloves, minced

2 tablespoons Chinese rice wine or dry sherry

2 teaspoons sesame oil

2 scallions, thinly sliced

Place the fish in a shallow dish. Combine the chili, black beans, ginger, lime zest and juice, soy sauce, garlic, rice wine or sherry, sesame oil, and scallions in a bowl. Pour the mixture over the fish, turning to coat, then cover, and marinate for 30 minutes. Cut 4 squares of double-thickness foil. Place a cod steak in the center of each foil square and turn up the edges slightly. Divide the marinade among them and crimp the foil to seal the packets. Grill the packets for 10–15 minutes until tender.

4 servings

Cod in Nut Coating with Banana Coconut Salsa

3/4 cup unsalted roasted peanuts, finely chopped

1/4 teaspoon chili powder

6 allspice berries, finely crushed

4 cod fillets, 6–8 ounces each

6 tablespoons/3/4 stick butter, melted

3/4 cup grated coconut

1 small garlic clove, minced

finely grated zest and juice of 1 lime

1/2 small red onion, finely chopped

2 tablespoons chopped cilantro

3 bananas

salt and pepper

Combine the peanuts, chili powder, crushed allspice, and 1/2 teaspoon salt in a bowl, then sprinkle onto a large plate. Dip each cod fillet into the melted butter and then into the peanut mixture, shaking off any excess. Combine the coconut, garlic, lime zest and juice, onion, and cilantro in a bowl. Grill the cod fillets for 2–3 minutes on each side. Meanwhile, peel and finely dice the bananas, then gently stir into the coconut mixture. Serve the cod fillets with the banana coconut salsa.

4 servings

Fish Parcels

4 cod or haddock steaks

4 white mushrooms, sliced

½ small onion, finely chopped

4 tomatoes, chopped

¼ cup peas

2 tablespoons/¼ stick butter

1 tablespoon lemon juice

salt and pepper

Cut 4 squares of double-thickness foil and place a fish steak on each. Season with salt and pepper. Divide the mushrooms, onion, tomatoes, and peas among the fish steaks. Dot with the butter and sprinkle with the lemon juice. Wrap the fish securely and cook on the barbecue for 20–30 minutes.

4 servings

Fish Burgers with Yogurt Mayo

1 pound skinless cod or haddock fillet

4 scallions, coarsely chopped

1 egg white

1 cup soft bread crumbs

2 tablespoons sunflower oil

3 tablespoons strained plain yogurt

3 tablespoons Mayonnaise (see page 281)

salt and pepper

Check the fish for bones, then cut it into pieces. Put it into a blender or food processor with the scallions and process briefly until finely chopped. Add the egg white and bread crumbs and season with salt and pepper. Process briefly until the ingredients are combined. Divide the mixture into 4 portions and shape each into a neat round. Chill for at least 1 hour. Brush the burgers with oil and grill for about 3 minutes on each side, until firm. Meanwhile, combine the yogurt and mayonnaise in a bowl and season with salt and pepper. Serve the burgers with the yogurt mayo.

4 servings

Cod and Pineapple Kabobs

15 ounce can pineapple chunks in syrup

½ cup soy sauce

4 tablespoons Chinese rice wine or dry sherry

2 tablespoons brown sugar

1 tablespoon minced fresh ginger root

1 teaspoon mustard powder

1 garlic clove, minced

2 pounds cod fillet, cut into 1 inch cubes

1 green bell pepper, deseeded and cut into 1 inch squares

Drain the pineapple, reserving 4 tablespoons of the syrup. Combine the reserved syrup, the soy sauce, rice wine or sherry, sugar, ginger, mustard, and garlic in a shallow dish. Add the fish cubes, turning to coat. Cover and marinate for at least 1 hour. Drain the fish cubes, reserving the marinade. Thread the fish cubes, pineapple chunks, and bell pepper squares alternately onto 6 skewers. Grill, turning and brushing with the marinade frequently, for 8–10 minutes.

6 servings

Orange Grilled Fish

2 pounds cod fillets, skinned and cut into 1 inch cubes

4 tablespoons soy sauce

2 tablespoons tomato ketchup

2 tablespoons chopped parsley

⅔ cup orange juice

grated zest of ½ orange

salt and pepper

Place the fish cubes in a shallow dish. Combine the soy sauce, ketchup, parsley, orange juice, and zest in a bowl and season with salt and pepper. Pour the mixture over the fish and marinate for 1 hour. Drain the fish, reserving the marinade. Thread the fish cubes onto 6 skewers and grill, basting frequently with the marinade, for about 8 minutes. Turn the skewers and grill, basting frequently, for 7 minutes more.

6 servings

Fish Kabobs with Garlic Butter

3 pounds cod or other firm white fish fillet, cut into 1 inch cubes

2 onions, sliced into rings

4 garlic cloves, minced

½ cup sunflower oil

4 tablespoons lime or lemon juice

1 tablespoon French mustard

generous 1 cup/2 sticks butter

3 tablespoons chopped parsley

3 red bell peppers, deseeded and cut into 1 inch pieces

8 pita breads

2 tomatoes, sliced

salt and pepper

Place the fish cubes and 1 of the onions in a shallow dish. Combine half the garlic with the oil, lime or lemon juice, and mustard in a bowl and spoon the mixture over the fish. Cover and marinate for 6 hours. Soften the butter in a bowl, beat in the remaining garlic and the parsley, and season with salt and pepper. Drain the fish, reserving the marinade. Thread the fish cubes and bell pepper pieces alternately onto 8 skewers, brush with the marinade, and grill, turning once, for 10–15 minutes. Split the pita breads and spread the insides with the garlic butter. Place a hot kabob down the center of each one, remove the skewer, and garnish with the remaining onion rings and the tomato slices.

8 servings

Haddock and Ham Skewers

3 cured ham steaks

12 ounces haddock fillet, skinned

3 tablespoons olive oil

6 tablespoons white wine

2 garlic cloves, minced

2 teaspoons chopped parsley

2 teaspoons chopped tarragon

pepper

Place the ham steaks in a pan and add water to cover. Bring to a boil, then reduce the heat, and simmer for 3 minutes. Drain and cool. Cut the ham and haddock into cubes and place in a shallow dish. Combine the oil, wine, garlic, parsley, and tarragon and season with pepper. Pour the mixture over the meat and fish, cover, and marinate for at least 2 hours. Drain the meat and fish, reserving the marinade. Thread the ham and haddock alternately onto 4 oiled skewers. Grill, turning and basting with the marinade frequently, for 10–15 minutes.

4 servings

Fish Cakes

12 ounces smoked haddock fillet

12 ounces potatoes, boiled and peeled

1 tablespoon butter

2 tablespoons parsley

1 egg, beaten

sunflower oil, for brushing

salt and pepper

lemon wedges and Tomato Sauce (see page 280), to serve

Place the fish in a large pan, pour in water to cover, and bring to a boil. Lower the heat and poach gently for 10 minutes, until the flesh flakes easily. Drain well, remove and discard the skin, and flake the flesh. Mash the potatoes and add the butter. Combine the fish, potatoes, and parsley and season with salt and pepper. Stir in the beaten egg to bind, then shape the mixture into a rectangle on a floured board. Cut into 10 portions and shape each into a neat round. Chill for 30 minutes. Brush the fish cakes with oil and grill for 5 minutes on each side. Serve with lemon wedges and tomato sauce.

5 servings

Piri Piri Fish Kabobs

1 onion

1½ pounds monkfish fillet, skinned and cut into 1 inch pieces

1 small red bell pepper, deseeded and cut into 1 inch squares

1 small yellow bell pepper, deseeded and cut into 1 inch squares

1 teaspoon hot chili sauce

3 tablespoons corn oil

1 garlic clove, minced

2 teaspoons brown sugar

Cut the onion into wedges and separate the leaves. Thread the fish, onion, and bell peppers alternately onto metal skewers. Combine the chili sauce, corn oil, garlic, and sugar in a bowl. Brush the mixture over the kabobs. Grill, turning and brushing with the chili mixture occasionally, for 10 minutes.

6 servings

Monkfish with Garlic and Rosemary

1 pound ripe tomatoes, skinned

1 tablespoon balsamic vinegar

2 monkfish fillets, about 12 ounces each, skinned

4 garlic cloves, cut into thin slivers

2 long rosemary sprigs

5 tablespoons olive oil

1 tablespoon lemon juice

salt and pepper

Put the tomatoes in a blender or food processor and process until smooth. Push through a metal strainer into a bowl, stir in the vinegar, and season with salt and pepper. Cover and set aside. Slice each fish fillet lengthwise without cutting all the way through, to make a pocket. Lay the garlic slivers along the length of each pocket and top each with a rosemary sprig. Season with salt and pepper. Re-form the fillets and tie them with string at 3/4 inch intervals. Combine the olive oil and lemon juice in a shallow dish. Add the fish fillets, spoon the mixture over them, cover, and marinate, turning occasionally, for 1 hour. Drain the fish, reserving the marinade. Grill, basting frequently with the marinade, for 15–20 minutes, until tender. Meanwhile, heat the tomato sauce. To serve, remove the string from the fish and thinly slice the fillets. Serve with the tomato sauce.

4 servings

Seafood Brochettes with Saffron Sauce

pinch of saffron threads

1 tablespoon boiling water

2 egg yolks

1 tablespoon lemon juice

1/4 teaspoon ground coriander

1/4 teaspoon ground cumin

scant 1 cup olive oil

12 ounces monkfish fillet, skinned and cut into 1 inch cubes

12 scallops, halved crosswise if large

1 1/2 teaspoons lime juice

3 tablespoons sunflower oil

salt and pepper

To make the sauce, place the saffron in a small bowl, pour the boiling water over, and steep for 10 minutes. Combine the egg yolks and lemon juice in another bowl, add the saffron and its soaking liquid, coriander, and cumin, and whisk until the mixture is slightly thickened. Gradually whisk in the olive oil in a thin stream until the mixture forms a thick, creamy mayonnaise. Cover and set aside. Put the monkfish cubes and scallops in a shallow dish. Combine the lime juice and sunflower oil in a pitcher and season with salt and pepper. Pour the mixture over the seafood and marinate for 30–40 minutes. Drain the seafood, reserving the marinade. Thread the fish cubes and scallops alternately onto 8 skewers. Grill, turning and brushing with the marinade frequently, for 3–4 minutes. Serve with the saffron sauce.

4 servings

Peppered Monkfish Kabobs

1¼ pounds monkfish fillet, skinned and cut into 1 inch cubes

⅔ cup plain yogurt

1 tablespoon black peppercorns, lightly crushed

3 tablespoons olive oil

sea salt

lemon slices, to garnish

Put the monkfish cubes into a shallow dish. Add the yogurt, peppercorns, and olive oil and season with sea salt. Stir to coat, then cover and marinate for 1 hour. Drain the fish cubes, reserving the marinade. Thread the monkfish onto 4 skewers. Grill the kabobs, turning and basting with the marinade frequently, for 10–15 minutes until the fish is tender and golden. Serve garnished with the lemon slices.

4 servings

Halibut Steaks with Avocado

4 halibut steaks

¼ cup/½ stick butter, melted

4 teaspoons lemon juice

1 teaspoon finely chopped chervil

1 ripe avocado, peeled and pitted

3 tablespoons sour cream

salt and pepper

Sprinkle the fish with salt and pepper. Combine the butter, 3 teaspoons of the lemon juice, and the chervil in a bowl and brush the mixture all over the fish. Grill, turning and brushing with the melted butter mixture frequently, for 10–15 minutes. Meanwhile, mash the avocado with a fork, then blend in the sour cream and remaining lemon juice. To serve, place a spoonful of the mixture on each fish steak.

4 servings

Fish Brochettes with Herbs

1½ pounds halibut fillets, skinned and cut into 1 inch cubes

3 tablespoons olive oil

1 tablespoon lemon juice

1 tablespoon chopped tarragon

1 tablespoon chopped dill

1 tablespoon chopped parsley

lemon wedges, to serve

Put the fish cubes into a shallow dish. Pour the olive oil and lemon juice over them and sprinkle with the chopped herbs. Marinate for 3–4 hours. Drain the fish cubes, reserving the marinade. Thread the fish cubes onto 4 skewers. Grill, turning and brushing with the marinade frequently, for 8–10 minutes. Serve with lemon wedges.

4 servings

Whiting with Almonds

¼ cup all-purpose flour

4 whiting, cleaned

½ cup/1 stick butter, melted

½ cup sliced almonds, toasted

4 tablespoons lemon juice

salt and pepper

Place the flour in a shallow dish and season with salt and pepper. Coat the fish evenly in the flour. Grill, brushing frequently with the melted butter, for 20 minutes, until the flesh flakes easily when tested with a fork. Combine the almonds and lemon juice with the remaining butter and pour the mixture over the fish to serve.

4 servings

Sardines in Grape Leaves

24 small sardines, cleaned

¾ cup olive oil

4 tablespoons lemon juice

3 garlic cloves, minced

6 thyme sprigs, finely chopped

2 shallots, finely chopped

½ teaspoon dried oregano

24 large grape leaves, rinsed and soaked in boiling water for 10 minutes, if preserved

salt and pepper

lemon wedges, to serve

Put the sardines in a shallow dish and pour the oil and lemon juice over them. Add the garlic, thyme, shallots, and oregano, cover, and marinate for 1 hour. Drain the sardines, reserving the marinade. Season the fish with salt and pepper. Brush the vein side of each grape leaf with a little of the marinade, then roll each around a sardine with the fish head at the stem end. Press the leaves gently to seal. Brush the leaves with a little more marinade. Grill in a hinged basket, basting frequently with the marinade, for 3–4 minutes on each side. Serve with lemon wedges.

4–6 servings

Marinated Sardines

12 sardines, cleaned

2 tablespoons lemon juice

3 tablespoons white wine vinegar

1 tablespoon honey

1 tablespoon sunflower oil

⅔ cup hard cider

Place the sardines in a shallow dish. Combine the lemon juice, vinegar, honey, oil, and hard cider in a bowl, whisking well. Pour the mixture over the sardines, cover, and marinate, turning occasionally, for 2–3 hours. Drain the sardines, reserving the marinade. Grill, turning once and basting with the marinade, for 8–10 minutes.

4 servings

Sardines with Horseradish Cream

2 tablespoons sunflower oil

1 tablespoon Worcestershire sauce

1 tablespoon lemon juice

12 sardines, cleaned

$^{2}/_{3}$ cup thick Mayonnaise (see page 281)

1 tablespoon creamy horseradish sauce

1 tablespoon chopped parsley

salt and pepper

Combine the oil, Worcestershire sauce, and lemon juice in a bowl and season with salt and pepper. Brush the fish, inside and out, with this mixture and sprinkle with salt and pepper. Grill, turning once and basting occasionally with the oil mixture, for 8–10 minutes. Combine the mayonnaise, horseradish sauce, and parsley in a bowl and serve with the sardines.

4 servings

Sardines with Herb Oil

2 garlic cloves, minced

6 tablespoons olive oil

1 tablespoon chopped oregano

1 tablespoon chopped thyme

1 tablespoon chopped parsley

1 tablespoon lemon juice

1 tablespoon fennel seeds, crushed

12 sardines, cleaned

coarse sea salt

Combine the garlic, oil, herbs, lemon juice, and fennel seeds in a bowl. Brush the sardines with a little of the herb oil, sprinkle with sea salt, and grill, turning once, for 6–8 minutes, until just cooked.

4 servings

Spanish Sprats

2 tablespoons sunflower oil

4 tablespoons lemon juice

1 garlic clove, minced

1½ pounds sprats, cleaned

salt and pepper

4 lemon wedges, to serve

Combine the oil, lemon juice, and garlic in a shallow dish and season with salt and pepper. Add the sprats and marinate for 30 minutes. Drain the fish and thread onto 4–6 skewers. Grill, turning occasionally, for 10 minutes. Serve with lemon wedges.

4–6 servings

Spicy Herrings

4–6 small herrings, cleaned

1¼ cups fish or chicken broth

⅔ cup tomato ketchup

2 tablespoons Worcestershire sauce

2 tablespoons wine vinegar

2 tablespoons brown sugar

dash of Tabasco sauce

2 tablespoons tomato paste

3 small onions, cut into fourths

4 tomatoes, halved

1 tablespoon cornstarch

salt and pepper

Cut off the heads, tails, and fins of the fish if this has not already been done, then cut each crosswise into 4 pieces, and place in a shallow dish. Combine the broth, ketchup, Worcestershire sauce, vinegar, sugar, Tabasco, and tomato paste in a pitcher. Pour the mixture over the fish, cover, and marinate for 1 hour. Drain the fish, reserving the marinade. Thread the fish, onions, and tomatoes alternately onto oiled skewers and season with salt and pepper. Grill, turning and brushing with the marinade frequently, for 10 minutes. Stir the cornstarch with a little water to make a smooth paste and add to the remaining marinade. Pour the mixture into a pan and bring to a boil, stirring constantly. Serve the fish accompanied by the sauce.

4–6 servings

Shrimp Poona

18 raw jumbo shrimp

6 tablespoons hot chutney

Slit the backs of the shrimp, de-vein, and open out into butterflies. Grill, shell-side uppermost, for 3 minutes. Turn the shrimp over and place a little of the chutney in each one. Grill for 5 minutes more.

6 servings

Shrimp with Basil Butter

24 raw large shrimp

olive oil, for brushing

¾ cup/1½ sticks butter

24 large basil leaves, coarsely chopped

2 large garlic cloves, minced

salt and pepper

basil sprigs, to garnish

Split each shrimp by cutting along the underside and through the head and tail, leaving the back shell intact. Open out each shrimp so that it lies flat. Season the cut surfaces with salt and pepper and brush both sides generously with oil. Grill, shell side downward, for 2 minutes. Turn the shrimp over and grill for 2 minutes more. Meanwhile, melt the butter and stir in the basil and garlic. Arrange the shrimp, flesh side uppermost, on a serving platter. Spoon the hot basil butter over them and garnish with basil sprigs.

4 servings

Coconut Butterfly Shrimp

12 raw jumbo shrimp

2 garlic cloves, minced

½ inch piece of fresh ginger root, very finely shredded

2 tablespoons lime juice

1–2 red chilies, deseeded and finely chopped

⅔ cup coconut cream

Pull off the heads and legs of the shrimp, then cut along the back of each without cutting right through. Remove the dark vein that runs along the back. Gently press down on each shrimp to flatten out and make a butterfly shape, then rinse, and pat dry with paper towels. Place the shrimp in a large, shallow dish. Combine the garlic, ginger, lime juice, chilies, and coconut cream in a pitcher. Pour the mixture over the shrimp, turning to coat, then cover and marinate for 1–2 hours. Drain the shrimp and thread onto 4 skewers. Grill, turning once, for 5–6 minutes, until just cooked.

4 servings

Shrimp and Mango Kabobs

16 raw jumbo shrimp, peeled and de-veined

1 tablespoon sunflower oil

4 tablespoons lemon juice

2 garlic cloves, minced

1 teaspoon minced fresh ginger root

1 teaspoon chili powder

1 tablespoon honey

1 teaspoon sea salt

1 large mango, peeled, pitted, and cut into bite-size pieces

Put the shrimp in a shallow dish and add the oil, lemon juice, garlic, ginger, chili powder, honey, and salt. Mix well and marinate for about 10 minutes. Drain the shrimp, reserving the marinade. Thread the shrimp and mango pieces alternately onto 8 skewers. Grill, brushing frequently with the remaining marinade, for 2 minutes on each side, until the shrimp have changed color and are just cooked.

4 servings

Garlic-buttered Shrimp

2 tablespoons olive oil

2 tablespoons/¼ stick butter, melted

1 garlic clove, minced

1 tablespoon lemon juice

1 tablespoon chopped parsley

12 ounces raw large shrimp

Combine the oil, butter, garlic, lemon juice, and parsley in a shallow dish. Add the shrimp, stir well to coat, and marinate for 2 hours. Thread the shrimp onto skewers and grill for 3–5 minutes on each side until they change color.

4 servings

Shrimp in Balsamic Marinade

12 raw jumbo shrimp

5 tablespoons olive oil

2 tablespoons balsamic vinegar

2 tablespoons chopped oregano or marjoram

2 garlic cloves, minced

pepper

Remove the legs from the shrimp and cut off the heads. One at a time, holding the shrimp with the back uppermost, slice along its length from the thickest part toward the tail, cutting almost through it. Remove the dark vein that runs down the back. Gently press the shrimp to flatten and make a butterfly shape. Rinse under cold running water, pat dry with paper towels, and place in a shallow dish. Combine the oil, vinegar, oregano or marjoram, and garlic in a pitcher and season with pepper. Pour the mixture over the shrimp, turning to coat, cover, and marinate for 1 hour. Drain the shrimp, reserving the marinade. Thread 3 shrimp onto each of 4 skewers. Grill, turning once and basting frequently with the marinade, for 3–4 minutes, or until just cooked.

4 servings

Spicy Skewered Shrimp

1 teaspoon chili powder

1 tablespoon white wine vinegar

1 garlic clove, minced

1 teaspoon chopped parsley

6 tablespoons sunflower oil

1 pound shrimp, peeled and de–veined

salt and pepper

Combine the chili powder, vinegar, garlic, parsley, and oil in a shallow dish and season with salt and pepper. Add the shrimp, stir to coat, and marinate for 2 hours. Drain the shrimp, reserving the marinade. Thread the shrimp onto 4 skewers. Grill, turning and basting with the marinade occasionally, for 5–8 minutes.

4 servings

Brandied Lobster

1 freshly boiled lobster, about 1½ pounds

¼ cup/½ stick butter

2 tablespoons brandy

4 tablespoons heavy cream

salt and pepper

shredded lettuce, to serve

Split the lobster in half down the back. Remove the bag in the head, the feathery gills, and the intestine, a thin gray or black line running down through the tail meat. Crack the large claws with a hammer or a large sharp knife. Loosen the body and tail meat slightly by lifting the edges so that the butter mixture can seep down the sides. Heat the butter, brandy, and cream in a pan, whisking constantly until the butter has melted. Brush the lobster flesh with some of the mixture and place on the barbecue grid shell side down. Grill, basting every 2 minutes, for 10 minutes. Baste again, then turn the lobster halves over, and grill for 3 minutes more. Heat the remaining butter mixture until it is bubbling. Place the lobsters on a bed of shredded lettuce, pour the butter over them, and season well with salt and pepper.

2 servings

Lobster with Saffron Mayonnaise

pinch of saffron threads

1 tablespoon boiling water

2 egg yolks

1 tablespoon lemon juice

scant 1 cup sunflower oil

2 live lobsters, 1½ pounds each

2 tablespoons/¼ stick butter, melted

salt and pepper

To make the mayonnaise, place the saffron threads in a small bowl, pour the boiling water over them, and steep for 10 minutes. Combine the egg yolks and lemon juice in another bowl, add the saffron and its soaking liquid, and whisk until the mixture is slightly thickened. Gradually whisk in the oil in a thin stream until the mixture forms a thick, creamy mayonnaise. To kill the lobsters, drive the point of a sharp knife right through the natural cross on the head into the brain, then split in half down the back. Remove the bag in the head, the feathery gills, and the intestine, a thin gray or black line running down through the tail meat. Brush the flesh with melted butter and season with salt and pepper. Grill the lobster halves, shell side down, for 15 minutes, then turn them over, and grill for 5 minutes more, until the flesh is firm. Serve with the saffron mayonnaise.

4 servings

Scallop Kabobs

⅔ cup white wine

2 tablespoons lemon juice

1 onion, sliced

1 carrot, sliced

1 celery stalk, chopped

1 parsley sprig

1 thyme sprig

1 bay leaf

6 black peppercorns, lightly crushed

4 tablespoons sunflower oil

12 scallops

4 cherry tomatoes

2 tablespoons/1/4 stick butter, melted

lemon wedges, to serve

Combine the wine, lemon juice, onion, carrot, celery, parsley, thyme, bay leaf, peppercorns, and oil in a shallow dish and let stand for 1 hour. Add the scallops and marinate for 2–3 hours. Drain the scallops, thread onto 4 skewers with the tomatoes, and brush with melted butter. Grill, turning and brushing with melted butter frequently, for 5–6 minutes, until just cooked. Serve with lemon wedges.

4 servings

Scallop and Monkfish Skewers with Fennel Sauce

4 dried fennel stalks, about 8 inches long

1 pound monkfish fillet

8 large scallops

8–10 tablespoons olive oil

1 garlic clove, minced

3 tablespoons chopped fennel

pinch of dried chili flakes

2 teaspoons lemon juice

1 fennel bulb

salt and pepper

Pull off any leaves still attached to the fennel stalks, leaving just a clump at 1 end. Soak the stalks in cold water for 30 minutes. Cut the monkfish into 12 chunks about the same size as the scallops and place in a shallow dish. Add the scallops, 2 tablespoons of the olive oil, and the garlic, season with pepper, and stir well to mix. Cover and marinate for at least 30 minutes. Meanwhile, combine the chopped fennel, chili flakes, lemon juice, and remaining oil in a bowl. Cover and set aside to steep. Drain the monkfish and scallops, reserving the marinade, and thread them alternately onto the fennel stalks. Grill the skewers, turning once and basting frequently with the marinade, for 5–6 minutes, until lightly charred and tender. Meanwhile, thinly slice the fennel bulb and toss with the sauce. Serve the skewers with the fennel sauce.

4 servings

Mussels and Clams Marinière with Orange

1½ pounds fresh mussels, scrubbed and beards removed

1½ pounds fresh clams, scrubbed

2 bay leaves

2 thyme sprigs

2 shallots, finely chopped

1 garlic clove, finely chopped

2 tablespoons/¼ stick butter, melted

½ teaspoon lightly crushed peppercorns

juice and finely grated zest of 2 oranges

scant 1 cup dry white wine

2 tablespoons chopped parsley

Discard any mussels or clams that do not close immediately when sharply tapped. Cut out 2 large squares of double-thickness foil, place them on the counter, and bring up the edges slightly. Put the mussels on 1 foil square and the clams on the other. Add 1 bay leaf and 1 thyme sprig to each. Combine the shallots, garlic, butter, peppercorns, orange juice and zest, and wine in a bowl and pour the mixture equally over the shellfish. Bring up the sides of the foil and crimp to seal. Cook the packets on the barbecue, shaking occasionally, for 5–10 minutes, until the shellfish have opened. Discard any that remain shut. Tip the contents of the parcels into a large colander set over a bowl, then strain the cooking liquid through a cheesecloth-lined strainer into another boil. Serve the shellfish with the cooking liquid poured over it and sprinkled with the parsley.

4 servings

Mussel and Bacon Kabobs

3–4 pounds fresh mussels, scrubbed and beards removed

1¼ cups water

1 egg, beaten

fine white bread crumbs, for coating

8 ounces fatty bacon strips

sunflower oil, for brushing

salt and pepper

lemon wedges, to garnish

Tangy Tartar Sauce (see page 283), to serve

Discard any mussels that do not close immediately when sharply tapped. Place the mussels in a large pan and pour in the measured water. Cover tightly, bring to a boil, and cook, shaking the pan occasionally, for about 5 minutes, until the mussels have opened. Drain and discard any mussels that remain shut. Remove the mussels from their shells, then dip first into the beaten egg, and then into the bread crumbs. Stretch the bacons strips with the back of a knife, cut in half crosswise, and roll up. Thread the mussels and bacon rolls alternately onto skewers, brush with oil, and season with salt and pepper. Grill, turning frequently, for 3–5 minutes. Garnish with lemon wedges and serve with tartar sauce.

6 servings

Baby Squid with Chili and Cilantro Stuffing

1 pound prepared baby squid

3 scallions, thinly sliced

2 garlic cloves, minced

1–2 red chilies, deseeded and chopped

2 tablespoons chopped cilantro

1 lime

1½ cups ground almonds

2 tablespoons peanut oil, plus extra for brushing

Finely chop the squid tentacles place in a bowl and add the scallions, garlic, chilies, and cilantro. Grate the lime zest into a bowl and squeeze the juice. Stir about 1 tablespoon of the juice into the mixture with the almonds and oil. Stuff the squid with this mixture, securing the open end of each with a toothpick. Lightly brush the squid with oil. Grill, turning frequently, for 3–4 minutes, until just cooked.

4 servings

Stuffed Baby Squid with Olives, Capers, and Tomatoes

1 pound prepared baby squid

½ cup pitted black olives, chopped

2 tablespoons drained bottled capers, chopped

1–2 garlic cloves, minced

4 tomatoes, skinned, deseeded, and chopped

4 tablespoons chopped oregano

2 cups soft white bread crumbs

1½ tablespoons lemon juice

4 tablespoons olive oil, plus extra for brushing

Finely chop the squid tentacles, place in a bowl, and add the olives, capers, garlic, tomatoes, oregano, bread crumbs, lemon juice, and oil. Mix well. Stuff the squid with this mixture, securing the open end of each with a toothpick. Lightly brush the squid with oil. Grill, turning frequently, for 3–4 minutes, until just cooked.

4 servings

Squid and Shrimp Skewers

2 red bell peppers

2 red chilies

1 tablespoon sherry vinegar

12 ounces prepared squid

12 raw jumbo shrimp

3 tablespoons chopped oregano

5 tablespoons olive oil

2 shallots, finely chopped

1 tablespoon lemon juice

salt and pepper

Place the bell peppers and chilies on a cookie sheet under a preheated broiler. Broil the bell peppers for 10–15 minutes and the chilies for 5–6 minutes, turning them occasionally until the skins are charred and blistered. Transfer to a plastic bag, seal the top, and let cool. Rub off the skins, then halve, and deseed. Pat dry with paper towels, then place in a blender or food processor. Add the vinegar and process until smooth. Season with salt and pepper. Cut the squid into 1 inch squares and score in a crisscross fashion. Place the squid and shrimp in a shallow dish. Combine the oregano, olive oil, shallots, and lemon juice in a pitcher, then pour the mixture over the squid and shrimp. Toss to coat, cover, and marinate for 30–40 minutes. Drain the seafood, reserving the marinade. Thread the squid and shrimp alternately onto skewers. Grill, turning once and brushing frequently with the marinade, for 6–8 minutes. Serve with the bell pepper and chili sauce poured over them.

4 servings

chapter 5
Vegetarian

Baked Stuffed Acorn Squash

generous pinch of saffron threads

$1\frac{3}{4}$ cups boiling water

$1\frac{1}{3}$ cups quick-cook couscous

2 large eggplants

6 tablespoons olive oil

$\frac{1}{2}$ teaspoon ground cinnamon

1 cup pecan nuts, toasted and chopped

2 small acorn squash, cut in half lengthwise and deseeded

2 tablespoons/$\frac{1}{4}$ stick butter

12 medjool dates, threaded onto 4 small skewers

salt and pepper

Place the saffron in a heatproof bowl, pour in the boiling water, and let steep for 10 minutes. Add the couscous, stir well, and let stand for 6–8 minutes, until the grains swell and the water is absorbed. Fluff up the grains with a fork. Slice the eggplants lengthwise into $\frac{1}{2}$ inch slices. Using 3 tablespoons of the olive oil, brush the eggplant slices on both sides. Grill for 5–6 minutes on each side, until tender. Cool slightly, then cut into $\frac{1}{2}$ strips, and add to the couscous. Add the cinnamon and pecans, season with salt and pepper, and toss well. Brush the squash with the remaining oil and fill with the couscous mixture. Dot with butter. Cut 4 large squares of double-thickness foil and wrap each squash half. Place in the embers of the barbecue and cook for 30 minutes, until tender. Grill the dates, turning frequently, for 3–4 minutes, until golden. To serve, unwrap the squash and serve with the date kabobs.

4 servings

Zucchini and Tomato Skewers

1 pound zucchini, cut into ¾ inch slices

1 tablespoon lemon juice

8 small tomatoes

1 small onion, sliced into rings

1 tablespoon sunflower oil

salt and pepper

Blanch the zucchini slices in boiling water for 1 minute. Drain well and sprinkle with lemon juice and pepper. Thread the tomatoes, zucchini, and onion onto 4 skewers and brush with oil. Grill, turning occasionally, for 5–10 minutes. Season with salt before serving.

4 servings

Vegetable Kabobs with Peanut Sauce

5 tablespoons peanut oil

3 tablespoons lemon juice

3 zucchini, cut into 1 inch slices

8 canned baby corn cobs, drained

8 white mushrooms

1 small onion, chopped

8 ounces flat mushrooms, chopped

1 cup roast salted peanuts

⅔ cup water

2 tablespoons soy sauce

dash of Tabasco sauce

2 tomatoes, cut into fourths

salt and pepper

Combine 3 tablespoons of the oil and the lemon juice in a dish and season with salt and pepper. Add the zucchini, corn, and whole mushrooms, mix well, and let stand, stirring occasionally, for at least 2 hours. Heat the remaining oil in a pan, add the onion and chopped mushrooms, and cook for 8 minutes. Transfer the mixture to a blender and process for 30 seconds. Add the peanuts and process for 30 seconds more. Return the mixture to the pan, stir in the measured water, soy sauce, and Tabasco, and simmer for 10 minutes. Transfer the pan to the side of the barbecue to keep warm. Drain the vegetables and thread them, with the tomatoes, alternately onto 4 skewers. Grill, turning occasionally, for about 10 minutes. Serve with the sauce.

4 servings

Spiced Vegetable Kabobs

4 tablespoons tomato ketchup

4 tablespoons vegetarian Worcestershire sauce

1 tablespoon white wine vinegar

1 tablespoon raw sugar

4 tablespoons sunflower oil

1 teaspoon prepared hot mustard

selection of vegetables (such as small tomatoes, small mushrooms, par-boiled

pearl onions, deseeded red and green bell pepper chunks, and zucchini chunks)

salt and pepper

Combine the ketchup, Worcestershire sauce, vinegar, sugar, oil, and mustard in a bowl. Thread your choice of vegetables alternately onto 6 skewers and brush them all over with the mixture. Grill, turning and brushing with the basting mixture occasionally, for 10–12 minutes, until the vegetables are tender.

6 servings

Hot and Spicy Vegetable Kabobs

8 ounces eggplant, cut into 1 inch cubes

8 ounces zucchini, cut into 1 inch chunks

1½ cups white mushrooms

1 small green bell pepper, halved, deseeded, and cut into 1 inch squares

1 small red bell pepper, halved, deseeded, and cut into 1 inch squares

4 cherry tomatoes

Barbecue Sauce (see page 270)

Steam the eggplant, zucchini, mushrooms, and bell peppers for 5 minutes or blanch them in boiling water for 3 minutes, then drain. When the vegetables are cool enough to handle, thread them alternately onto 4 oiled skewers and place in a shallow dish. Pour the barbecue sauce over the skewers, turning to coat, and let stand for 5 minutes. Drain the skewers, reserving the sauce, and grill for 5 minutes. Add a tomato to the end of each skewer, turn them over, brush with the sauce, and grill for 5 minutes more. Serve with the remaining sauce spooned over.

4 servings

Zucchini with Herbs

1 pound zucchini

1½ tablespoons salt

1 tablespoon chopped thyme

1 teaspoon coriander seeds, crushed

½ teaspoon black peppercorns, crushed

1 tablespoon lemon juice

4 large tomatoes, skinned, deseeded, and chopped

1 large garlic clove, finely chopped

⅔ cup olive oil

Cut each zucchini lengthwise into slices about ¼ inch thick. Put the slices in a colander and sprinkle with the salt. Let drain for 1 hour, then rinse the slices, and pat dry with paper towels. Cut out a large square of double-thickness foil and pile the zucchini on it. Add the thyme, coriander, black pepper, and lemon juice and sprinkle with the tomatoes and garlic. Drizzle a little olive oil over the top, fold up the sides of the foil, and crimp to seal. Cook on the barbecue for 15 minutes. To serve, spoon into a large dish and pour the remaining olive oil over the top.

4 servings

Baby Eggplants with Herbed Yogurt

2 tablespoons chopped parsley

2 tablespoons chopped dill

2 tablespoons chopped mint

1 small red onion, finely chopped

2 garlic cloves, minced

¾ cup Kalamata or other olives, pitted and sliced

2 teaspoons fennel seeds, crushed

1 tablespoon capers, chopped

1 gherkin, chopped

finely grated zest and juice of 1 lime

2/3 cup strained plain yogurt

12 baby eggplants

3 tablespoons olive oil

salt and pepper

Combine the parsley, dill, mint, onion, garlic, olives, fennel seeds, capers, gherkin, lime zest and juice, and yogurt in a bowl. Halve the eggplants lengthwise, leaving them still attached at the stalk. Brush the eggplants with olive oil and grill for 2–3 minutes on each side. Serve with the herbed yogurt.

4 servings

Baked Beets with Mustard and Walnut Sauce

3/4 cup walnut halves

3/4 cup crème fraîche

1 1/2 tablespoons whole-grain mustard

3 tablespoons chopped chives, plus extra to garnish

8 raw beets

salt and pepper

Cut 8 squares of double-thickness foil. Spread out the walnuts on a cookie sheet and roast in a preheated oven, 350°F, for 8–10 minutes, until golden. Let cool, then chop coarsely. Reserve 3 tablespoons for the garnish and put the rest in a bowl. Stir in the crème fraîche, mustard, and chives and season with salt and pepper. Wrap each beet in a foil square, place in the embers of the barbecue, and cook for 40–50 minutes, until tender. To serve, unwrap the foil, split open the beets, and top with the sauce, reserved walnuts, and extra chives.

4 servings

Ratatouille

2 tablespoons/1/4 stick butter

3 tablespoons olive oil

1 garlic clove, minced

2 small eggplants, sliced

1 green bell pepper, halved, deseeded, and sliced

1 red bell pepper, halved, deseeded, and sliced

5 zucchini, sliced

14 ounce can tomatoes

1 teaspoon dried basil

2 bay leaves

salt and pepper

Cut a large square of double-thickness foil, place on a counter, and turn up the edges of the square. Heat the butter and oil in a large skillet. Add the garlic and eggplant and cook for 3–4 minutes, until the eggplant has softened. Add the bell peppers, zucchini, tomatoes, basil, and bay leaves, season to taste with salt and pepper, and bring to a boil. Mix well, then turn the mixture onto the foil square. Bring up the sides of the foil and crimp to seal. Cook on the barbecue for 15–20 minutes, until all the vegetables are tender.

6–8 servings

Bell Peppers and Goat Cheese with Chili Relish

6 large red chilies

2 tablespoons lime juice

2 garlic cloves, minced

3 tablespoons chopped Italian parsley or cilantro

2 red bell peppers

2 yellow bell peppers

2 individual goat cheeses

1 tablespoon thyme leaves

2 tablespoons extra virgin olive oil

¼ cup pitted black olives, finely chopped

sea salt and cracked black pepper

Put the chilies on a cookie sheet and a place under a preheated broiler. Broil, turning occasionally, for 5–10 minutes, until charred and blistered all over. Place in a plastic bag, seal the top, and let cool. Remove the stalks, cut the chilies in half, and deseeded. Coarsely chop the flesh. Place the chilies in a mortar and pound with a pestle. Stir in the lime juice, garlic, and parsley or cilantro, and season with salt. Set aside. Halve the bell peppers lengthwise, leaving the stalk intact, and deseed. Grill, cut side down, for 8–10 minutes, until well charred. Cut the cheeses into 4 slices. Turn the bell pepper halves over, place a piece of cheese in the center of each, sprinkle with the thyme and olive oil, and grill for 10 minutes more, until the peppers have softened and the cheese has melted. Serve sprinkled with the chopped olives and cracked black pepper, accompanied by the chili relish.

4 servings

Bell Pepper Kabobs

2 green bell peppers, halved, deseeded, and cut into 1 inch squares

2 red bell peppers, halved, deseeded, and cut into 1 inch squares

2 yellow bell peppers, halved, deseeded, and cut into 1 inch squares

½ cup olive oil

2 garlic cloves, finely chopped

1 tablespoon crushed black peppercorns

3 tablespoons lemon juice

coarsely ground sea salt

Thread alternate colored bell pepper squares onto 8 skewers. Brush generously all over with oil. Grill, turning and brushing with oil frequently, for 7–10 minutes, until just beginning to char. Brush with oil again, then place on serving plates. Sprinkle with garlic and peppercorns, season with salt, and drizzle with lemon juice to serve.

4 servings

Marinated Vegetable Kabobs

1 small onion, minced

2 garlic cloves, minced

6 tablespoons corn oil

1 teaspoon dried mixed herbs

grated zest of 1 orange

2 zucchini, cut into 1 inch slices

1 small red bell pepper, halved, deseeded, and cut into 1 inch squares

1 small green bell pepper, halved, deseeded, and cut into 1 inch squares

1 small eggplant, cut into 1 inch cubes

1½ cups white mushrooms

1 can artichoke hearts, drained and cut into fourths

salt and pepper

Combine the onion, garlic, oil, herbs, and orange zest in a large, shallow dish and season with salt and pepper. Add all the vegetables, stir to coat, and marinate for 1 hour. Drain the vegetables, reserving the marinade. Thread the vegetables alternately onto skewers. Grill, turning and basting with the marinade frequently, for 10–15 minutes, until the vegetables are browned.

6 servings

Mediterranean Vegetables

2 large Bermuda onions

2 green bell peppers

2 red bell peppers

2 large firm ripe tomatoes

1 large eggplant

about 1 cup olive oil

2 garlic cloves, minced

2 tablespoons chopped parsley

3 firm zucchini, halved lengthwise

12 large firm mushrooms

salt and pepper

Remove the outer skin from the onion, leaving the point intact, then cut in half horizontally. Trim the stalks of the bell peppers. Cut the tomatoes in half horizontally. Cut the eggplant in half lengthwise, score the flesh, without cutting through the skin, and sprinkle generously with salt. Let drain upside down on a wire rack for 30 minutes. Brush the cut surface of the onion with oil and place, cut side down, on the barbecue grid. Brush the bell peppers with oil and grill, turning frequently, until charred. Remove the bell peppers and cool slightly. Peel the bell peppers and cut into strips, discarding the seeds. Place the strips in a bowl, add 4 tablespoons of the olive oil, and season with salt and pepper. Stir in the garlic and parsley. When the cut surfaces of the onion are charred, turn them over, move to the side of the barbecue, and grill until tender. Cut the onion into chunks and add to the bowl of bell peppers, with a little extra oil. Brush the tomatoes with oil and grill, cut side down, until slightly charred, then turn over. Rinse the eggplant halves and pat dry with paper towels. Brush with oil and grill, skin side down, until the skin is dark brown. Brush with oil again, turn them over, and grill until the center flesh is creamy and tender. Dip the zucchini halves in oil and grill, cut side down, for 4–5 minutes, then turn them over. Dip the mushrooms in oil and grill for 3 minutes. When the mushrooms, zucchini, and eggplant are all cooked, transfer to a serving dish and serve with the onion and bell pepper mixture.

6 servings

Mixed Vegetables with Green Olive and Walnut Paste

3/4 cup pitted green olives

3/4 cup walnut pieces

1/4 cup drained bottled pickled walnuts

2 garlic cloves, minced

1 cup parsley

1/2 cup extra virgin olive oil

1 large eggplant

4 bell peppers

2 zucchini

8 baby leeks

6 tablespoons olive oil

4 large slices of crusty rustic bread

salt and pepper

Put the olives, walnut pieces, pickled walnuts, garlic, and parsley in a blender or food processor and process until finely chopped. With the machine running, gradually add the extra virgin olive oil until the mixture forms a stiff paste. Scrape into a bowl, season with salt and pepper, and set aside. Cut the eggplant into 1/2 inch thick slices. Halve the bell peppers. Remove the seeds but leave the stalks intact. Slice the zucchini lengthwise. Brush the eggplant slices, zucchini, and leeks with olive oil. Grill the eggplant and bell peppers for 6–8 minutes and the zucchini and leeks for 3 minutes, turning all the vegetables frequently. Brush the bread with the remaining olive oil and grill on both sides until golden. Spread the toast with the olive and walnut paste and top with the vegetables.

4 servings

Potato and Bell Pepper Kabobs

6 small potatoes

6 small onions

12 mushrooms

2 green bell peppers, halved, deseeded, and cut into 12 pieces

1/4 cup/1/2 stick butter, melted

1/2 teaspoon garlic salt

1/4 teaspoon black pepper

6 small tomatoes

salt

Par-boil the potatoes and onions in lightly salted, boiling water, for about 10 minutes, until barely tender, then drain. Thread the potatoes, onions, mushrooms, and bell pepper pieces alternately onto 6 skewers. Combine the butter, garlic salt, and black pepper and brush the mixture generously over the kabobs. Grill for 5 minutes, then add a tomato to each skewer. Turn, brush with the butter mixture, and grill for 5 minutes more.

6 servings

Garbanzo Bean Burgers

28 ounces canned garbanzo beans, drained and rinsed

1 onion, finely chopped

1 teaspoon salt

½ teaspoon pepper

2 tablespoons chopped cilantro or parsley

¼ teaspoon cayenne pepper

½ teaspoon ground coriander

1 cup soft bread crumbs

all-purpose flour, for coating

sunflower oil, for brushing

Tomato Sauce (see page 280), to serve

Place the beans in a bowl and mash well with a potato masher. Add the onion, salt, pepper, cilantro or parsley, cayenne, coriander, and bread crumbs and knead together. Shape the mixture into 2 inch rounds, about ½ inch thick. Coat the burgers with flour and chill until firm. Brush the burgers with oil and place on a sheet of foil on the barbecue grid. Grill for 4–5 minutes on each side. Serve with tomato sauce.

4 servings

Black Bean Kabobs with Mango Relish

⅔ cup dried black beans, soaked overnight in cold water and drained

1 ripe mango, peeled and pitted

2 onions

2 red chilies, deseeded and finely chopped

½ inch piece of fresh ginger root, minced

3 tablespoons olive oil

1 garlic clove, minced

½ teaspoon ground cumin

½ teaspoon ground coriander

1 tablespoon chopped cilantro

2 zucchini

24 mixed red and yellow cherry tomatoes

salt and pepper

Rinse the beans under cold running water, then transfer to a pan, add cold water to cover, and bring to a boil. Boil vigorously for 10 minutes, then lower the heat, and simmer for 40–50 minutes, until tender. Drain well and set aside. Place the mango flesh in a bowl and mash with a fork. Mince 1 onion and finely chop the other. Add the minced onion, half the chilies, and the ginger to the bowl and mix well. Season with salt and pepper and set aside. Heat 2 tablespoons of the oil in a frying pan. Add the remaining onion, the chili and the garlic and cook gently for 5–10 minutes, until softened. Stir in the cumin and coriander and cook for 2 minutes more. Turn the onion and spice mixture into a bowl, add the drained beans and cilantro, and mash well. Divide the mixture into 24 portions and roll into balls. Using a potato peeler, cut the zucchini lengthwise into strips. Brush with the remaining oil. Thread the bean balls onto metal skewers, alternating with the tomatoes and weaving the zucchini strips in between. Grill for 4 minutes on each side. Serve with mango relish.

4 servings

Lentil Sausages

3/4 cup brown lentils

2/3 cup bulgar wheat

5 tablespoons sunflower oil, plus extra for brushing

1 onion, very finely chopped

2 scallions, very finely chopped

2 tablespoons very finely chopped parsley

1/2 teaspoon paprika

1 egg, lightly beaten

salt and pepper

Place the lentils in a pan, add 3 3/4 cups water, and bring to a boil. Lower the heat and simmer for 30 minutes, until tender. Stir in the bulgar wheat and the oil. Simmer for 3–4 minutes more, then turn off the heat, cover, and let stand for 15 minutes, until the water has been absorbed. Stir in the onion, scallions, parsley, paprika, and egg and season with salt and pepper. Mash well until smooth. With damp hands, roll the mixture into "sausage" shapes about 3 inches long, then chill until firm. Brush with oil, then grill for about 3 minutes on each side.

4 servings

Red Bean and Rice Patties

3/4 cup dried red kidney beans, soaked overnight and drained

generous 1/2 cup brown rice

1 tablespoon peanut oil, plus extra for brushing

1 onion, finely chopped

1 garlic clove, minced

3 green chilies, deseeded and finely chopped

1 teaspoon cumin seeds

1 teaspoon ground coriander

½ teaspoon ground turmeric

2 eggs, beaten

3 tablespoons chopped cilantro

¼ cup pistachio nuts, chopped

½ cup strained plain yogurt

salt and pepper

Rinse the beans, place in a pan, and pour in cold water to cover. Bring to a boil. Boil vigorously for 10 minutes, then lower the heat, and simmer for 50–60 minutes, until tender. Drain, let cool, then mash. Bring a small pan of lightly salted water to a boil, add the rice, lower the heat, and simmer for 20–25 minutes, until the grains are just cooked. Drain, refresh under cold running water, then drain again. Heat the oil in a skillet, add the onion, garlic, and 1 chili, and cook for 5 minutes. Add the cumin seeds, coriander, and turmeric and cook for 1–2 minutes more. Add the contents of the skillet to the mashed beans, stir in the rice, and mix well. Add the eggs, season with salt and pepper, and mix to combine. Set aside. Place the cilantro, pistachios, and remaining chilies in a blender or food processor and process until smooth. Scrape the mixture into a bowl, stir in the yogurt, and season to taste. Divide the bean and rice mixture into 4 portions and shape each into a flat round. Brush each patty with oil and grill for 4–5 minutes on each side. Serve with yogurt sauce.

4 servings

Mushrooms in Grape Leaves

20 large white mushrooms

⅔ cup olive oil

2 large garlic cloves, finely chopped

3 tablespoons finely chopped parsley

24 grape leaves, rinsed and soaked in boiling water for 10 minutes, if preserved

salt and pepper

parsley sprigs, to garnish

Trim the mushroom stalks so that they are level with the caps. Pour the oil into a pitcher. Spear the mushrooms, 1 at a time, and dip in the oil for a few seconds, then remove, and shake off the excess. Place, stalk side up, on a plate. Press 2–3 pieces of garlic into the stalk of each mushroom, then sprinkle with a little parsley, pressing it down with the back of a spoon. Season with salt and pepper. Place the grape leaves, vein side up, on a counter and brush each with a little oil. Place a mushroom in the center of each vine leaf (4 extra are allowed in case of tearing). Carefully fold over the leaves to enclose the mushrooms. Brush the leaf packets with a little more oil and place on a plate, rounded side upward. Arrange in a hinged basket and grill for 2½ minutes on each side. Garnish with parsley sprigs.

4–6 servings

Mushrooms with Parsley and Garlic Butter

½ cup/1 stick sweet butter, softened

2 large garlic cloves, crushed

1 teaspoon lemon juice

4 tablespoons finely chopped parsley

3¼ cups white mushrooms

2–3 tablespoons brandy

salt and pepper

Combine the butter, garlic, lemon juice, and parsley and season with salt and pepper, beating until blended. Divide the mixture in 2 and roll half into a cylinder. Wrap in foil and chill. Melt the remaining butter mixture. Arrange the mushrooms on a large piece of double-thickness foil and spoon the butter over them. Fold up the sides and crimp the edges to seal. Cook the packet on the barbecue for 10 minutes, until the mushrooms are tender. Open the foil and spoon the brandy over them. Cut the chilled butter into slices and place on top of the mushrooms.

4–6 servings

Goat Cheese in Grape Leaves

1 tablespoon chopped thyme

1 tablespoon chopped Italian parsley

1 tablespoon chopped oregano

1 teaspoon crushed mixed peppercorns

1 tablespoon lemon juice

4 individual goat cheeses

2 tablespoons olive oil

4–8 grape leaves, rinsed and soaked in boiling water for 10 minutes, if preserved

Combine the thyme, parsley, oregano, peppercorns, and lemon juice in a shallow bowl. Brush the cheeses with the oil and roll them in the herb mixture. Wrap the coated cheeses in the grape leaves, then brush them with any remaining oil. Grill, turning once, for 8 minutes, until the cheeses are just soft.

4 servings

Baby Brioche Florentine with Hollandaise Sauce

scant 1 cup /2 sticks butter

3 egg yolks

2 tablespoons water

1 tablespoon lemon juice

1 pound young leaf spinach

pinch of grated nutmeg

8 baby brioche rolls

8 quail eggs

salt and pepper

Cut 8 squares of double-thickness foil. Melt 3/4 cup/1 1/2 sticks butter in a small pan over low heat. Remove from the heat and cool slightly. Put the egg yolks into a large heatproof bowl, add the measured water, set the bowl over a pan of barely simmering water, and whisk until light, creamy, and pale in color. Gradually whisk in the melted butter, adding it in a thin stream, leaving the white, milky residue in the base of the pan. Continue to whisk until the mixture is thick and foamy. Remove from the heat, stir in the lemon juice and season with salt and pepper. Keep the sauce warm. Melt the remaining butter in a large pan and add the spinach with just the water clinging to its leaves after washing. Cover and cook, stirring once, for 3–4 minutes, until just wilted. Drain well, transfer to a bowl, and season with nutmeg, salt, and pepper. Cut a neat slice off the top of each brioche. Remove some of the crumb from the center of the rolls to make a hollow. Place a spoonful of spinach in each hollow and carefully crack a quail egg over the top. Replace the brioche "lids." Wrap each brioche in a foil square, place right side up on the barbecue grid, and cook for 30–40 minutes, until the eggs are just set. Serve with hollandaise sauce.

4 servings

Haloumi Packets

1 tablespoon chopped thyme

1 tablespoon chopped basil

1 tablespoon chopped marjoram

1 teaspoon crushed mixed peppercorns

1 tablespoon lemon juice

8 ounces haloumi cheese

2 tablespoons olive oil

4–8 grape leaves, rinsed and soaked in boiling water for 10 minutes, if preserved

Combine the thyme, basil, marjoram, peppercorns, and lemon juice in a shallow bowl. Cut the cheese into fourths, brush with the oil and roll them in the herb mixture. Wrap the coated cheese in the grape leaves, then brush them with any remaining oil. Grill, turning once, for 8 minutes, until the cheese is just soft.

4 servings

Haloumi Wrapped in Radicchio

1½ tablespoons chopped oregano

2 tablespoons extra virgin olive oil

1 garlic clove, minced

2 tablespoons lemon juice

8 ounces haloumi cheese, cubed

1 large head of radicchio

salt and pepper

Combine the oregano, olive oil, garlic, and lemon juice in a bowl, add the haloumi, and toss to coat. Remove any stalk and core from the radicchio and gently pull the leaves apart. Lay 3–4 leaves on a counter and place a fourth of the haloumi mixture in the center. Wrap the radicchio around and then wrap the whole packet in a double thickness of foil. Repeat with the remaining radicchio and cheese mixture. Cook on the barbecue for 3–4 minutes on each side.

4 servings

Grilled Radicchio with Pears and Roquefort

4 ripe pears, cut into fourths and cored

finely grated zest and juice of 2 oranges

4 tablespoons honey

4 small radicchio, cut into fourths

1 tablespoon walnut oil

1 cup crumbled Roquefort cheese

pepper

Cut a large square of double-thickness foil. Place the pears in a single layer on the foil square and turn up the edges slightly. Combine the orange zest, orange juice, and honey in a pitcher and pour the mixture over the pears. Bring up the sides of the foil and crimp to seal. Cook on the barbecue for 15–20 minutes, until the pears are tender. About 6 minutes before the pears are ready, brush the radicchio with the walnut oil, and grill for 2–3 minutes on each side. To serve, divide the pears and their cooking juices among 4 plates, add 4 radicchio pieces to each plate, and sprinkle with the cheese and pepper.

4 servings

Polenta and Vegetable Kabobs

6½ cups water

2 cups cornmeal mush

4 ounces baby carrots

2 red onions, cut into wedges

3½ cups mushrooms

1 red bell pepper, halved, deseeded, and cut into squares

4 ounces baby zucchini, thickly sliced

olive oil, for brushing

salt and pepper

grated Parmesan cheese, to serve

Bring the measured water to a boil in a large pan and add a pinch of salt. Pour in the cornmeal in a thin, steady stream, beating constantly. Cook, stirring constantly, for 20–30 minutes, until the mixture leaves the sides of the pan. Remove from the heat, pour onto a board or cookie sheet, and let cool. Blanch the carrots in a small pan of lightly salted, boiling water for a few minutes until crisp and tender, then drain. When the polenta is set, cut it into 1 inch cubes. Thread the polenta cubes, onion wedges, mushrooms, bell pepper, zucchini, and carrots alternately onto 6–8 skewers. Brush with olive oil and grill for 5–6 minutes on each side, until the vegetables are tender and the polenta is golden. Serve with grated Parmesan.

6–8 servings

Red Chili Polenta Wedges and Garlic Skewers

3 cups water

1 teaspoon salt

1⅔ cups cornmeal mush

⅔ cup finely grated Parmesan cheese

8 sun-dried tomato halves in oil, drained and finely chopped

4 large red chilies, broiled, peeled, deseeded, and chopped

12 garlic cloves, unpeeled

6 tablespoons olive oil

Pour the water into a large pan, add the salt, and bring to a boil. Reduce the heat slightly and add the cornmeal mush in a thin stream, beating constantly. Cook, stirring constantly, for 20–30 minutes, until the mixture comes away from the sides of the pan. Immediately stir in the Parmesan, sun-dried tomatoes, and chilies. Tip the polenta out onto a board or cookie sheet. Let cool, then cut into long, chunky wedges. Bring a small pan of water to a boil. Add the garlic, lower the heat, and simmer for 10 minutes. Drain and when cool, thread 3 cloves onto each of 4 skewers. Brush the polenta wedges and garlic skewers with the oil and grill for 3 minutes on each side, until the garlic is soft and the polenta is charred and golden.

4 servings

Polenta and Vegetable Terrine with Roasted Tomatoes

4 tablespoons olive oil, plus extra for brushing

1 red bell pepper

3½ cups mushrooms, cut into fourths

2 red onions, cut into small wedges

4 ounces baby zucchini, cut in half lengthwise

4 ounces baby carrots

4 ounces green beans

4 ounces broccoli, cut into flowerets

6½ cups water

2 cups cornmeal mush

⅔ cup grated Parmesan cheese, plus extra for sprinkling

2 garlic cloves, minced

8 ripe plum tomatoes, cut in half lengthwise

salt and pepper

black olives, to garnish

Brush a 2½ pound loaf pan with olive oil. Place the bell pepper under a preheated boiler and broil, turning frequently, for 10 minutes, until blistered and charred. Place in a plastic bag, seal the top, and cool. Peel off the charred skin, halve, and deseed. Cut the flesh into 1 inch wide strips. Heat half the oil in a skillet, add the mushrooms and onion, cover, and cook for 2–3 minutes. Remove with a slotted spoon and drain on paper towels. Blanch the zucchini, carrots, beans, and broccoli in separate pans of boiling water until crisp and tender. Drain, refresh under cold water, and drain again. Bring the measured water to a boil in a large pan and add a pinch of salt. Pour in the cornmeal in a thin, steady stream, beating constantly. Cook, stirring constantly, for 20–30 minutes, until the mixture leaves the sides of the pan. Remove from the heat, add the mushroom and onion mixture, zucchini, carrots, beans, broccoli, bell pepper strips and Parmesan, and mix well. Pour the mixture into the loaf pan. Level the surface and cool. When the polenta has set, turn it out, and cut into ¾ inch slices. Brush both sides of each slice with a little of the remaining oil. Combine the remaining oil with the garlic, brush the mixture over the tomatoes, and season with salt and pepper. Grill the polenta slices and tomatoes, cut side down at first, for 6–8 minutes, turning once. Serve the slices topped with the tomato halves, garnished with olives. Hand extra grated Parmesan separately.

6–8 servings

Chinese Cabbage Steamed with Shiitake Mushrooms

12 ounces Chinese cabbage

1½ cups shiitake mushrooms, thinly sliced

½ inch piece of fresh ginger root, finely shredded

1 garlic clove, minced

1½ teaspoons light soy sauce

2 teaspoons light brown sugar

1 green chili, deseeded and finely chopped

1 teaspoon sesame oil

3 scallions, finely chopped

Shred the cabbage leaves into 1/2 inch strips and place in a large bowl. Combine all the remaining ingredients in another bowl, then add to the Chinese cabbage, and toss lightly. Cut a large square of double-thickness foil and pile the mixture into the center. Wrap securely and grill, shaking the packet occasionally, for 5–10 minutes, until the vegetables are tender.

4 servings

Fennel, Lemon, and Black Olive Kabobs

2 tablespoons lemon juice

1 garlic clove, minced

1/2 cup extra virgin olive oil

3/4 cup pitted black olives, finely chopped

2 fennel bulbs

1 lemon

sea salt and pepper

Combine the lemon juice, garlic, and 6 tablespoons of the olive oil in a bowl, whisking well. Stir in the olives and season with sea salt and pepper. Cut the fennel bulbs lengthwise into 8 wedges, making sure that each wedge is attached to a little of the core. Cut the lemon into 8 wedges. Thread the fennel and lemon wedges alternately onto 4 skewers and brush all over with the remaining olive oil. Grill for 4 minutes on each side. Serve drizzled with the lemon and olive dressing.

4 servings

Leeks Provençal

1½ pounds leeks, cut into 2 inch lengths

4 tablespoons olive oil

4 large tomatoes, skinned, deseeded, and chopped

grated zest of ½ lemon

3 tablespoons lemon juice

10 black olives, pitted and halved

salt and pepper

Par-boil the leeks for 2 minutes in a large pan of lightly salted, boiling water. Drain well, pat dry with paper towels, and brush with a little olive oil. Grill, turning once or twice, for 3–4 minutes. Meanwhile, heat the remaining oil in a pan on the side of the barbecue and add the tomatoes. Season with salt and pepper and cook gently for 5 minutes, until thickened. Add the lemon zest, juice, and olives and cook for a few more minutes. Serve the leeks with the sauce poured over them.

4–6 servings

Whole Baked Corn with Skorthalia

1 cup soft white bread crumbs

¾ cup ground almonds

4 garlic cloves, minced

2 tablespoons lemon juice

⅔ cup extra virgin olive oil

4 whole corn cobs, with husks

salt and pepper

Put the bread crumbs in a bowl and pour in water to cover. Soak for 5 minutes, then squeeze out the excess liquid, and place the bread crumbs in a blender or food processor. Add the almonds, garlic, and 1 tablespoon of the lemon juice and process until mixed. With the machine running, gradually add the olive oil in a thin steady stream until the mixture resembles mayonnaise. Transfer the mixture to a bowl, season with salt and pepper, and add more lemon juice if required. Pull down the outer leaves of the corn husks and remove the inner silks. Pull the leaves back into position. Grill, turning occasionally, for 30–40 minutes, until the kernels are juicy and tender. To serve, pull back the leaves of the cobs and spread with skorthalia.

4 servings

chapter 6

Dips, Relishes, and Salsas

Japanese Dipping Sauce

½ cup shoyu

4 tablespoons rice wine or dry sherry

2 scallions, finely chopped

2 teaspoons chopped fresh ginger root

1 teaspoon lemon juice

Combine all the ingredients in a bowl. Pour into individual small bowls.

Makes ¾ cup

Chili Dipping Sauce

¼ cup rice vinegar

¼ cup superfine sugar

2 tablespoons water

2 red chilies, finely chopped

Put the vinegar, sugar, and measured water in a small pan and heat gently, stirring constantly, until the sugar has dissolved. Bring to a boil and boil vigorously until syrupy. Stir in the chilies and let cool.

Makes ½ cup

Middle Eastern Yogurt Dip

1½ cups plain yogurt

3 tomatoes, skinned, deseeded, and chopped

1 tablespoon chopped mint

pinch of cayenne pepper

salt

Combine the yogurt, tomatoes, and mint in a bowl and season with cayenne and salt to taste. Cover and chill until required.

Makes about 2 cups

Yellow Bell Pepper Dip

2 yellow bell peppers

4 tablespoons plain yogurt

1 tablespoon dark soy sauce

1 tablespoon chopped cilantro (optional)

pepper

Place the bell peppers on a cookie sheet under a preheated broiler and broil, turning frequently, for about 10 minutes, until well charred and blistered. Place in a plastic bag and tie the top. When cool enough to handle, peel off the skins, deseed, and place the flesh in a blender or food processor with the yogurt. Process until smooth. Transfer to a bowl, stir in the soy sauce and cilantro, if using, and season with pepper.

Makes about 1 cup

Guacamole

2 large avocados

3 tablespoons lemon or lime juice

2 garlic cloves, minced

2 scallions, chopped

1–2 tablespoons chopped mild green chilies

2 tablespoons chopped cilantro

2 tomatoes, skinned, deseeded, and chopped

salt and pepper

Halve and pit the avocados, then scoop the flesh into a bowl. Add the lemon or lime juice and mash coarsely. Stir in the garlic, scallions, chilies, and cilantro and season with salt and pepper. Stir in the chopped tomatoes. Cover and chill for 1 hour.

6 servings

Basic Barbecue Sauce

4 tablespoons tomato ketchup

4 tablespoons brown fruity sauce

1 teaspoon prepared hot mustard

1 tablespoon Worcestershire sauce

1 tablespoon brown sugar

Combine all the ingredients in a small pan and bring to a boil. Use hot or cold.

4 servings

Classic Barbecue Sauce

¼ cup/½ stick butter

1 large onion, chopped

2 tablespoons tomato paste

2 tablespoons white wine vinegar

1 tablespoon lemon juice

2 tablespoons raw sugar

2 teaspoons prepared hot mustard

2 tablespoons Worcestershire sauce

1 teaspoon clear honey

pinch of dried mixed herbs

1 teaspoon chili seasoning

⅔ cup water

salt and pepper

Melt the butter in a pan. Add the onion and cook over low heat for 5 minutes, until soft. Increase the heat slightly, add all the remaining ingredients, and stir well. Bring to a boil, then lower the heat, and simmer for about 10 minutes, until thoroughly combined and syrupy. Serve immediately.

4–6 servings

Spicy Barbecue Sauce

2 tablespoons/¼ stick butter

1 small onion, finely chopped

1 garlic clove, minced

1 teaspoon chili powder

1 teaspoon mustard powder

2 tablespoons molasses

3 tablespoons malt vinegar

⅔ cup water

3 tablespoons Worcestershire sauce

2 tablespoons tomato paste

½ teaspoon Tabasco sauce

salt and pepper

Melt the butter in a skillet. Add the onion and garlic and cook for 2–3 minutes, until soft. Add all the remaining ingredients, stir well, and bring to a boil. Lower the heat and simmer for 30 minutes.

4 servings

Smoky Barbecue Sauce

2 tablespoons/¼ stick butter

1 onion, finely chopped

1 garlic clove, minced

2 tablespoons wine vinegar

⅔ cup water

1 tablespoon prepared hot mustard

2 tablespoons raw sugar

1 lemon slice

1 bay leaf

pinch of cayenne pepper

2 tablespoons Worcestershire sauce

6 tablespoons tomato ketchup

2 tablespoons tomato paste

salt and pepper

Melt the butter in a pan, add the onion and garlic, and cook until soft. Add the vinegar, water, mustard, sugar, lemon slice, bay leaf, and cayenne. Gradually bring to a boil and simmer for 15 minutes. Add the Worcestershire sauce, ketchup, and tomato paste and season with salt and pepper. Simmer for 5–10 minutes more. Discard the lemon slice and bay leaf before serving.

4–6 servings

Spiced Orange Sauce

6 tablespoons light brown sugar

4 tablespoons soy sauce

2/3 cup orange juice

2/3 cup dry white wine

4 tablespoons water

1/2 teaspoon paprika

1/2 teaspoon mustard powder

pinch of ground cinnamon

dash of Tabasco sauce

Combine all the ingredients in a pan. Bring to a boil, lower the heat, and simmer for 5 minutes.

Makes about 2 cups

Lemon Sauce

1/4 cup/1/2 stick butter

2 shallots, finely chopped

1 tablespoon all-purpose flour

1¼ cups dry white wine

4 tablespoons lemon juice

1 lemon, thinly sliced

1 tablespoon finely chopped parsley

salt and pepper

Melt the butter in a pan, add the shallots, and cook for about 3 minutes, until softened but not brown. Add the flour and cook, stirring constantly, for 1 minute. Remove the pan from the heat and gradually stir in the wine. Return the pan to the heat, bring to a boil, stirring, then lower the heat, and simmer for 5 minutes. Season with salt and pepper, stir in the lemon juice, and add the sliced lemon and parsley.

4 servings

Orange and Lemon Barbecue Sauce

2–3 tablespoons olive oil

2 garlic cloves, minced

1 large onion, chopped

2 teaspoons cornstarch

2 tablespoons tomato paste

4 tablespoons raw sugar

grated zest and juice of 1 orange

½ cup lemon juice

2 tablespoons Worcestershire sauce

⅔ cup red wine

salt and pepper

Heat the oil in a pan, add the garlic and onion, and cook until golden in color. Combine the cornstarch, tomato paste, sugar, orange zest and juice, lemon juice, Worcestershire sauce, and red wine in a pitcher and season with salt and pepper. Gradually add the mixture to the onions, stirring constantly until the sauce thickens. Cover and simmer gently for about 20 minutes. Strain before serving.

6–8 servings

Gooseberry Herb Sauce

2 cups gooseberries

2 tablespoons superfine sugar

2 tablespoons/¼ stick butter

1 tablespoon chopped fennel

1 tablespoon chopped parsley

4½ tablespoons water

Place the gooseberries, sugar, butter, and most of the fennel and parsley in a pan and add the measured water. Bring to a boil, lower the heat, and simmer for 10 minutes. Remove from the heat, pour into a bowl, and sprinkle with the remaining fennel and parsley.

4 servings

Red Currant and Mustard Sauce

4 tablespoons red currant sauce

2 tablespoons prepared mild mustard

1 tablespoon lemon juice

Heat all the ingredients in a small pan, stirring until smooth and blended.

4 servings

Mustard Sauce

3 tablespoons butter

¼ cup all-purpose flour

scant 2 cups milk

1 tablespoon mustard powder

1 tablespoon wine vinegar

1 teaspoon superfine sugar

salt

Melt 2 tablespoons of the butter in a pan, stir in the flour, and cook for 1 minute. Gradually add the milk, whisking constantly until the sauce is smooth. Bring to a boil and simmer for 2–3 minutes. Season to taste. Stir the mustard powder with the vinegar in a small bowl, then stir the mixture into the sauce. Add the sugar and the remaining butter.

4–6 servings

Creole Sauce

2 tablespoons sunflower oil

1 large onion, finely chopped

1 green bell pepper, halved, deseeded, and finely chopped

14 ounce can tomatoes

1 small can pimientos, drained and chopped

1 teaspoon sugar

large pinch of mustard powder

pinch of chili powder

1 tablespoon lemon juice

1 tablespoon chopped parsley

salt and pepper

Heat the oil in a pan, add the onion and bell pepper, and cook until soft. Stir in the tomatoes, with their can juice, the pimientos, sugar, mustard, chili powder, and lemon juice and season with salt and pepper. Stir well and bring to a boil. Lower the heat and simmer for 20 minutes. Stir in the parsley just before serving.

4 servings

Sweet and Sour Sauce

14 ounce can tomatoes

2 green bell peppers, halved, deseeded, and diced

2 tablespoons cornstarch

4 tablespoons white wine vinegar

2 tablespoons sugar

⅔ cup tomato juice

1 tablespoon soy sauce

salt and pepper

Put the tomatoes, with their can juice, and the bell peppers in a pan, bring to a boil, then simmer for 5 minutes. Stir the cornstarch and vinegar in a small bowl to make a paste, then stir into the tomato mixture. Add the sugar, tomato juice, and soy sauce and season with salt and pepper. Stir well and simmer for 10 minutes.

4–6 servings

Curry Spice Sauce

4 cloves

2 teaspoons coriander seeds

1 teaspoon cumin seeds

½ teaspoon ground ginger

1 teaspoon ground turmeric

¼ teaspoon chili powder

2 tablespoons sunflower oil

8 ounces onions, sliced

2 garlic cloves, minced

2 tablespoons all-purpose flour

6 tomatoes, skinned, deseeded, and chopped

1 chicken bouillon cube

1¼ cups boiling water

1 teaspoon sugar

salt

Put the cloves, coriander, and cumin seeds in a mortar and grind with a pestle. Combine the ginger, turmeric, chili powder, and the clove mixture in a bowl. Heat the oil in pan, add the spice mixture and cook for 2 minutes. Add the onions and garlic and cook for about 5 minutes, until soft. Stir in the flour and tomatoes and cook for 2 minutes. Dissolve the bouillon cube in the boiling water, then stir into the sauce. Bring to a boil, cover, and simmer for 1 hour, or until the tomatoes have broken down and the sauce is thick. Stir in the sugar and season with salt.

4 servings

Mushroom Sauce

2 tablespoons/¼ stick butter

1 onion, chopped

2½ cups sliced mushrooms

1 tablespoon all-purpose flour

1¼ cups beef broth

dash of Worcestershire sauce

½ teaspoon soy sauce

Melt the butter in a pan, add the onion, and cook for 5 minutes, until soft. Add the mushrooms and cook for 2 minutes. Stir in the flour and cook for 1 minute. Remove the pan from the heat and gradually stir in the beef broth. Return the pan to the heat and bring to a boil, stirring constantly. Add the Worcestershire sauce and soy sauce and season with salt and pepper. Simmer gently for 3–4 minutes.

Makes about 1¼ cups

Tomato Barbecue Sauce

1 tablespoon red wine vinegar

1½ tablespoons light brown sugar

1½ teaspoons prepared hot mustard

pinch of cayenne pepper

pinch of grated lemon zest

1 teaspoon lemon juice

1 small onion, finely chopped

2 tablespoons/¼ stick butter

4 tablespoons tomato ketchup

1 tablespoon Worcestershire sauce

4 tablespoons water

8 stuffed olives, chopped

salt and pepper

Put the vinegar, sugar, mustard, cayenne, lemon zest and juice, onion, butter, ketchup, Worcestershire sauce, and water in a pan and season with salt and pepper. Bring to a boil, cover, and simmer, stirring occasionally, for 15 minutes, until reduced and well combined. Stir in the olives.

4 servings

French Dressing

1 tablespoon wine vinegar

3 tablespoons olive oil

pinch of mustard powder

1 tablespoon chopped herbs

Combine all the ingredients in a screw-topped jar, cover, and shake vigorously.

Makes about 1/4 cup

Tomato Sauce

4 large tomatoes, skinned and coarsely chopped

4 tablespoons tomato ketchup

1 tablespoon red wine vinegar

2 tablespoons olive oil

dash of Tabasco sauce

pinch of mustard powder

salt and pepper

Combine the tomatoes, ketchup, vinegar, oil, Tabasco, and mustard powder in a bowl and season with salt and pepper.

4 servings

Mayonnaise

1 egg yolk

large pinch of mustard power

⅔–1¼ cups sunflower oil, olive oil, or a mixture of both

1 tablespoon white wine vinegar or lemon juice

salt and pepper

Whisk the egg yolk with the mustard powder and salt and pepper to taste. Gradually whisk in the oil, drop by drop to begin with and then in a thin steady stream. When the mixture becomes thick, add a little of the vinegar or lemon juice. When the mixture has the consistency of heavy cream, add the remaining vinegar or lemon juice. Taste and adjust the seasoning.

Makes ⅔–1¼ cups

Yogurt Sauce

⅔ cup plain yogurt

4 mint leaves, chopped

¼ teaspoon honey

1 garlic clove, minced

1 teaspoon dried fenugreek leaves

½ teaspoon ground coriander or 1 teaspoon chopped cilantro

1 tablespoon sunflower oil

½ teaspoon paprika

salt and pepper

Combine the yogurt, mint, honey, garlic, fenugreek leaves, coriander or cilantro, and sunflower oil in a bowl and season with salt and pepper. Sprinkle the paprika over the surface and serve with Indian-style dishes.

Makes ⅔ cup

Cucumber and Yogurt Sauce

1¼ cups plain yogurt

½ large cucumber, peeled and diced

dash of Tabasco sauce

salt and pepper

Beat the yogurt in a bowl with a wooden spoon until quite smooth. Stir in the cucumber and season with salt, pepper, and Tabasco sauce. Chill before serving.

4 servings

Marsala Aioli

2 garlic cloves, minced

2 teaspoons Dijon mustard

1 teaspoon lemon juice

2 egg yolks

scant 1 cup olive oil

2 tablespoons Marsala

salt and pepper

Combine the garlic, mustard, and lemon juice in a bowl and season with salt and pepper. Beat in the egg yolks, then whisk in the olive oil, drop by drop. Finally, stir in the Marsala. Pour into a covered container and chill for 8 hours before using.

Makes about 1 cup

Tangy Tartar Sauce

⅔ cup Mayonnaise (see page 281)

½ teaspoon minced onion

1 tablespoon chopped capers

1 teaspoon chopped parsley

salt and pepper

Combine all the ingredients in a bowl and let stand for 1 hour before serving.

4–6 servings

Seafood Sauce

⅔ cup Mayonnaise (see page 281)

1 tablespoon tomato paste

1 teaspoon grated lemon zest

2 tablespoons lemon juice

1 teaspoon Worcestershire sauce

dash of Tabasco sauce

1 teaspoon minced onion

1 tablespoon chopped parsley

salt and pepper

Combine all the ingredients in a bowl and season with salt and pepper.

Makes about 2/3 cup

Spicy Horseradish Sauce

2/3 cup heavy cream

1 tablespoon lemon juice

2 teaspoons grated horseradish

2 teaspoons Worcestershire sauce

2 scallions, finely chopped

Lightly whip the cream, then stir in all the remaining ingredients. Chill for 4 hours.

4–6 servings

Mustard Butter

1/4 cup/1/2 stick butter, softened

2 teaspoons whole-grain mustard

salt and pepper

Put the butter and mustard in a bowl and season to taste with salt and pepper. Beat until smooth and well blended. Cover and chill until required.

Makes 1/4 cup

Garlic and Herb Butter

2 garlic cloves

2 teaspoons salt

2 tablespoons finely chopped herbs, such as parsley, chervil, oregano or dill

1 cup/2 sticks butter, softened

Using the flat of a knife blade, crush the garlic with the salt to a pulp, then scrape into a bowl. Add the herbs and butter and beat until smooth and blended. Cover and chill until required.

Makes 1 cup

Ginger and Mint Butter

½ cup/1 stick butter, softened

1 tablespoon minced fresh ginger root

2 tablespoons chopped mint

salt and pepper

Put the butter, ginger, and mint in a bowl and season with salt and pepper. Beat until smooth and well blended. Chill until required.

Makes ½ cup

Green Butter

2 tarragon sprigs

2 chervil sprigs

2 parsley sprigs

2 small spinach leaves

1/4 cup/1/2 stick butter, softened

1 teaspoon minced onion

salt and pepper

Put the herbs and spinach in a bowl, pour in boiling water to cover, and let stand for 5 minutes. Drain, rinse in cold water, pat dry with paper towels, and chop finely, then place in another bowl. Add the butter and onion and season with salt and pepper. Beat until smooth and well blended. Cover and chill until required.

Makes 1/4 cup

Citrus Butter

1 cup/2 sticks butter, softened

grated zest of 2 lemons or 2 oranges

Put the ingredients in a bowl and beat until smooth and well blended. Cover and chill until required.

Makes 1 cup

Corn Relish

2 1/2 cups white wine vinegar

scant 1/2 cup sugar

1 tablespoon mustard seeds or 1 teaspoon hot mustard powder

1 teaspoon salt

1 pound fresh or frozen corn kernels

1 green bell pepper, halved, deseeded, and finely chopped

1 red bell pepper, halved, deseeded, and finely chopped

1 onion, finely chopped

4 celery stalks, thinly sliced

Combine a little of the vinegar with the sugar, mustard, and salt to make a smooth paste, then stir in the remaining vinegar. Pour the mixture into a large pan and bring to a boil over low heat. Add all the remaining ingredients and simmer for 20 minutes, until the vegetables are just tender. Pour into a clean, warm jar or bottle and seal with a vinegar-proof cover.

Makes about 2 pounds

Hamburger Tomato Relish

2 pounds tomatoes, skinned and coarsely chopped

2 pounds red bell peppers, halved, deseeded, and finely chopped

1 pound onions, chopped

2 red chilies, very finely chopped

2 cups red wine vinegar

¾ cup light brown sugar

4 tablespoons mustard seeds

2 tablespoons celery seeds

2 tablespoons paprika

2 teaspoons salt

2 teaspoons pepper

Place all the ingredients in a large pan and bring to a boil. Simmer, stirring frequently, for 30 minutes, until thickened and pulpy. Pour into clean, warm jars and seal with vinegar-proof tops.

Makes about 3 pounds

Avocado Relish

2 avocados

2½ tablespoons lemon juice

2 tomatoes, peeled, deseeded, and chopped

1 bunch of scallions, finely chopped

2 tablespoons sunflower oil

1½ teaspoons lime juice

pepper

Peel, halve, and pit the avocados, then dice the flesh and place in a bowl. Sprinkle 2 tablespoons of the lemon juice over the avocado, then add the tomatoes and scallions, and season with black pepper. Mix well. Combine the oil with the remaining lemon juice and the lime juice in a small bowl. Pour the mixture over the avocado relish. Chill before serving with chicken or fish.

4 servings

Cucumber Relish

2 large cucumbers, cut into short lengths

1 head of celery, coarsely chopped

1 large red bell pepper, halved, deseeded, and cut into squares

1 pound onions, cut into wedges

2 scallions, coarsely chopped

3¾ cups white malt vinegar

1 teaspoon curry powder

1 teaspoon mustard powder

½ teaspoon cayenne pepper

½ teaspoon paprika

½ teaspoon ground ginger

2 cups sugar

Pass the cucumbers, celery, bell pepper, onions, and scallions through a grinder. Pour the vinegar into a pan, add the spices, and bring to a boil. Add the vegetables and the sugar, bring back to a boil, then lower the heat, and simmer for 20–30 minutes, until thickened. Cool, spoon into clean jars, and cover with vinegar-proof tops.

Makes 4½ pounds

Mint Relish

2 pounds tart apples, peeled, cored, and coarsely chopped

1 pound onions, coarsely chopped

8 ounces tomatoes, skinned, deseeded, and coarsely chopped

8 cups mint leaves, finely chopped

generous ¾ cup raisins, finely chopped

1 teaspoon mustard powder

2 teaspoons salt

½ teaspoon cayenne pepper

2½ cups brown malt vinegar

1 cup brown sugar

Place all the ingredients in a heavy pan and bring to a boil, stirring constantly. Lower the heat and simmer for 20–30 minutes, until thickened. Cool, spoon into clean jars, and cover with vinegar-proof tops.

Makes 5 pounds

Instant Chutney

1 apple, peeled, cored, and finely chopped

1 onion, finely chopped

3 tomatoes, skinned and chopped

2 celery stalks, finely chopped

1 red bell pepper, halved, deseeded and finely chopped

1 tablespoon chopped mint

1 tablespoon horseradish sauce

1 garlic clove, minced

2 tablespoons sugar

2 tablespoons vinegar

1 teaspoon salt

pepper

Place all the ingredients in a pan and bring to a boil. Lower the heat, cover, and simmer for 5 minutes. Serve hot or cold.

Makes 1 pound

chapter 7
Salads

Sour Cream Potato Salad

1 pound new potatoes

2 tablespoons olive oil

1 teaspoon white wine vinegar

4 tablespoons sour cream

salt and pepper

1 tablespoon chopped chives, to garnish

Cook the potatoes in lightly salted, boiling water for 15–20 minutes, until just tender. Drain, cool slightly, then cut into 1/2 inch pieces, and place in a salad bowl. Combine the oil and vinegar in a pitcher and pour the mixture over the potatoes while they are still warm. Whisk the sour cream with a fork, then gently fold it into the potatoes. Season with salt and pepper and sprinkle with the chives.

4 servings

Hot Potato Salad with Feta and Caper Vinaigrette

1 1/2 pounds small, red-skinned potatoes

1 tablespoon sherry vinegar

1 1/2 teaspoons Dijon mustard

2 tablespoons drained capers, coarsely chopped

1 tablespoon chopped tarragon

6 tablespoons extra virgin olive oil

1 cup crumbled feta cheese

salt and pepper

Cook the potatoes in lightly salted, boiling water for 10–15 minutes, until just tender. Drain, cut in half if large, and place in a bowl. Combine the vinegar, mustard, capers, and tarragon in another bowl, gradually whisk in the olive oil, and season with salt and pepper. Pour the dressing over the potatoes, toss lightly, and sprinkle with the feta.

4 servings

Classic Potato Salad

1 pound cooked potatoes, peeled and sliced

6 tablespoons Mayonnaise (see page 281)

1 tablespoon lemon juice

1 tablespoon olive oil

2 tablespoons finely chopped chives

4 tablespoons finely chopped leeks

salt and pepper

Place three-quarters of the potatoes in a bowl. Pour the mayonnaise over them and sprinkle with the lemon juice, oil, and halve the chives. Season with salt and pepper and toss gently until the potatoes are well coated. Spoon the mixture into a serving dish, arrange the remaining potato slices on top, and sprinkle with the remaining chives. Sprinkle the leeks around the edge of the dish. Cover and chill for 30 minutes before serving.

4 servings

Sweet Potato and Walnut Salad

1 pound sweet potatoes, peeled and halved lengthwise

5 tablespoons walnut oil

1 tablespoon white wine vinegar

1 shallot, finely chopped

1 garlic clove, minced

½ cup walnuts, chopped

scant ½ cup raisins

salt and pepper

Cut the sweet potato halves crosswise into ½ inch thick slices. Bring a pan of lightly salted water to a boil, add the sweet potato slices and cook for 5 minutes, until just tender. Drain well. Combine the oil, vinegar, shallot, and garlic in a large bowl, add the sweet potatoes, walnuts, and raisins, and toss well. Season with salt and pepper. Serve warm or chilled.

4 servings

Caesar Salad

3 tablespoons olive oil

1 garlic clove, minced

2 slices of bread, crusts removed and cubed

1 romaine lettuce, torn into pieces

2 x quantity French Dressing (see page 280)

1 egg, beaten

⅔ cup grated Parmesan cheese

Heat the oil and garlic in a skillet. Add the bread cubes and cook, stirring constantly, for 3–4 minutes, until crisp. Drain on paper towels. Place the lettuce in a large salad bowl. Pour the dressing and egg over it, sprinkle with the Parmesan and bread cubes, and toss well. Serve immediately.

4–6 servings

Cucumber, Radish, and Dill Salad

2 cucumbers

6 tablespoons sea salt

1 bunch of radishes, thinly sliced

1 egg yolk

1 tablespoon whole-grain mustard

1 tablespoon honey

2 tablespoons lemon juice

3 tablespoons olive oil

3 tablespoons chopped dill

pepper

Cut the cucumbers in half lengthwise and scoop out the seeds. Slice thinly, then layer the slices in a colander, and sprinkle with the salt. Let stand for 1–1½ hours, then rinse well, and pat dry with paper towels. Place the cucumber and radishes in a salad bowl. Combine the egg yolk, mustard, honey, and lemon juice in a bowl, whisking well, and season with pepper. Gradually whisk in the olive oil, then stir in the dill. Pour the dressing over the cucumber and radishes and toss.

4–6 servings

Cucumber Salad with Mint

2½ cups plain yogurt

1–2 garlic cloves, minced

½ cucumber, peeled and sliced

½ teaspoon dried mint

salt and pepper

Beat the yogurt in a bowl until smooth. Stir in the garlic and cucumber and season with salt and pepper. Spoon the mixture into a serving bowl and sprinkle the mint on top. Chill for 2 hours before serving.

6 servings

Salad Mimosa

4 lettuce hearts, shredded

½ bunch of watercress, coarsely chopped

2 celery stalks, chopped

4½ tablespoons French Dressing (see page 280)

2 hard-cooked eggs, chopped

2 oranges, peeled and segmented

2 teaspoons olive oil

1 teaspoon white wine vinegar

1 banana, peeled and thinly sliced

1 tablespoon lemon juice

10 green grapes, halved and deseeded

1 tablespoon light cream

Combine the lettuce, watercress, celery, dressing, and eggs in a bowl, tossing until well blended. Transfer to a glass serving dish. Combine the orange segments, oil, and vinegar in a small bowl. Combine the banana and lemon juice in another bowl. Combine the grape halves and cream in a third bowl. Arrange the fruit and their dressings decoratively on top of the salad and serve immediately.

4 servings

Artichoke Salad

1 head of crisp lettuce

2 celery stalks, sliced

¾ cup stuffed olives

14 ounce can artichoke hearts, drained

2 tablespoons olive oil

1 tablespoon lemon juice

salt and pepper

Tear the lettuce into pieces and place in a salad bowl with the celery and olives. Cut the artichoke hearts in half lengthwise and add to the salad. Combine the oil and lemon juice in a screw-top jar, season with salt and pepper, close the lid, and shake vigorously. Just before serving, toss the salad with the dressing.

4–6 servings

Tomato and Avocado Salad

4 tomatoes, skinned and cut into fourths

1 avocado, peeled, halved, pitted, and sliced

7 ounce can red kidney beans, drained and rinsed

4 tablespoons sunflower oil

2 tablespoons white wine vinegar

1 teaspoon mustard powder

1 teaspoon sugar

2 teaspoons chopped marjoram

salt and pepper

Place the tomatoes, avocado, and beans in a salad bowl. Combine the oil, vinegar, mustard, sugar, and marjoram in a screw-top jar and season with salt and pepper. Close the lid and shake vigorously. Pour the dressing over the salad and toss well.

4 servings

Tomato and Onion Salad

4–6 tomatoes, skinned and thinly sliced

2 onions, thinly sliced

French Dressing (see page 280)

½ teaspoon dried basil

2 tablespoons chopped parsley

Arrange the tomato and onion slices in a dish and pour the dressing over them. Sprinkle the herbs on top.

4–6 servings

Red Cabbage and Pineapple Coleslaw

8 ounce can pineapple rings, drained and syrup reserved

6 scallions, sliced

3 tablespoons golden raisins

2 cups shredded red cabbage

2 tablespoons French Dressing (see page 280)

salt and pepper

2 chopped scallions, to garnish

Reserve 1 pineapple ring for the garnish and chop the remainder. Place the chopped pineapple, sliced scallions, golden raisins, and cabbage in a salad bowl. Combine 1 tablespoon of the reserved syrup with the French dressing in a pitcher, season with salt and pepper, and pour the mixture over the salad. Toss well and garnish with the pineapple ring and chopped scallions.

4 servings

Honey-Lemon Slaw

2 tablespoons Mayonnaise (see page 281)

1 tablespoon honey

½ teaspoon grated lemon zest

1 tablespoon lemon juice

½ teaspoon ground ginger

2½ cups shredded red cabbage

2½ cups shredded white cabbage

salt and pepper

Combine the mayonnaise, honey, lemon zest and juice, and ginger in a large bowl. Stir in the red and white cabbage until evenly coated. Season with salt and pepper and chill before serving.

4–6 servings

Italian Coleslaw

7½ cups shredded white cabbage

4 carrots, grated

1 garlic clove, minced

6 tablespoons olive oil

2 tablespoons white wine vinegar

1 teaspoon finely chopped oregano

¼ teaspoon crushed fennel seeds

celery salt and freshly ground white pepper

Put the cabbage and carrots in a bowl. Combine the garlic, oil, vinegar, oregano, and fennel seeds in a screw-top jar and season with celery salt and pepper. Close the lid and shake vigorously. Pour the dressing over the vegetables and toss well.

6 servings

Walnut, Orange, and Belgian Endive Salad

4 oranges, peeled and thinly sliced

4 heads of Belgian endive, sliced

1 cup walnuts, chopped

4½ teaspoons honey

3 tablespoons lemon juice

4½ tablespoons olive oil

¼ teaspoon French mustard

salt and pepper

Put the orange slices, Belgian endive, and walnuts in a bowl. Combine the honey, lemon juice, oil, and mustard in a screw-top jar and season with salt and pepper. Close the lid and shake vigorously. Pour the dressing over the salad and toss well.

4 servings

Beet and Pink Grapefruit Salad

1½ pounds raw young beets

2 pink grapefruit

½ cup peeled hazelnuts, chopped

1 tablespoon raspberry vinegar

3 tablespoons hazelnut oil

1 garlic clove, minced

1 head of radicchio, leaves separated

8 ounces young spinach leaves

salt and pepper

Peel the beets, cut into fine julienne strips, and place in a salad bowl. Cut a thin slice off the base of the grapefruit and place them, cut side down, on a board. Cut off the rind in strips, taking care to remove all the white pith. Holding the grapefruit over the salad bowl to catch any juice, cut out the segments with a sharp knife. Add them to the salad bowl, stir in the hazelnuts, and toss lightly. Combine the vinegar, oil, and garlic in a small bowl, whisking well. Pour the dressing over the salad, season with salt and pepper, and toss well. Arrange the radicchio and spinach leaves on serving plates and spoon the salad mixture on top.

4–6 servings

Bell Pepper, Anchovy, and Tomato Salad

2 large red bell peppers

3 large tomatoes, skinned, deseeded, and sliced

4 ounces canned anchovy fillets, drained

4 tablespoons olive oil

2 tablespoons lemon juice

1 garlic clove, minced

salt and pepper

Place the bell peppers under a preheated broiler and cook, turning occasionally, for 10–15 minutes, until blistered and charred. Transfer to a plastic bag, seal the top, and cool. Peel off the skin, halve and deseed, then cut the flesh into wide strips. Arrange the bell pepper strips and tomato slices on a flat serving dish. Rinse the anchovy fillets under cold water and lay in a lattice pattern on top of the salad. Combine the oil, lemon juice, and garlic in a bowl and season with salt and pepper. Pour the dressing over the salad and chill for 30 minutes before serving.

4 servings

Fennel Salad

1 cup sliced zucchini

1 large fennel bulb, sliced

1 cup thinly sliced cucumber

1 cup sliced green beans

⅔ cup sour cream

1 teaspoon whole-grain mustard

salt

6 stuffed green olives, to garnish

Spread out the zucchini slices on a plate and sprinkle with salt. Let stand for 15 minutes, then rinse and pat dry with paper towels. Place the zucchini slices in the base of a salad bowl, place the fennel slices on top, then the cucumber, and finally, the beans. Combine the sour cream and mustard in a bowl and pour the mixture over the salad. Garnish with the olives and chill before serving.

4–6 servings

Celery and Fennel Salad with Blue Cheese Dressing

3 ounces Roquefort or Gorgonzola cheese

¼ cup crème fraîche or sour cream

1 tablespoon red wine vinegar

3 scallions, thinly sliced

¾ cup pecan nuts, finely chopped

2 pears, halved, cored, and chopped

1½ teaspoons lemon juice

1 fennel bulb, thinly sliced

4 celery stalks, thinly sliced

pepper

salad greens, to serve

Put the blue cheese, crème fraîche or sour cream, and vinegar in a blender or food processor and process until smooth. Transfer to a bowl and stir in the scallions and two-thirds of the nuts, and season with pepper. Toss the pears with the lemon juice in a bowl, then add the fennel and celery. To serve, arrange a bed of salad greens, top with the fennel mixture, spoon the blue cheese dressing over it, and sprinkle with the remaining pecans.

4–6 servings

Midsummer Salad

¼ cup/½ stick butter

2 large slices of bread, crusts removed and cut into ½ inch cubes

1 garlic clove, halved

1 large romaine lettuce, leaves separated and torn into pieces

1 small onion, sliced into thin rings

⅓ cup grated Parmesan cheese

1 cup sliced white mushrooms

2 ounces canned anchovy fillets, drained

6 tablespoons French Dressing (see page 280)

Melt the butter in a skillet. Add the bread cubes and cook until golden brown all over. Remove with a slotted spoon and drain on paper towels. Rub a large salad bowl with the cut sides of the garlic. Combine the lettuce, onion, cheese, mushrooms, and anchovies in the bowl. Pour the dressing over the salad and toss well, then sprinkle with the bread cubes, and serve.

6 servings

Carrot and Celery Root Salad

8 ounces carrots, cut into julienne strips

8 ounces celery root, cut into julienne strips

6 scallions, thinly sliced

2 tablespoons sesame oil

2 teaspoons yellow mustard seeds

1 tablespoon light soy sauce

2 tablespoons lime juice

pepper

Place the carrots and celery root in a bowl with the scallions. Heat the oil in a small skillet and add the mustard seeds. When they start to pop, remove the skillet from the heat, and add the seeds to the salad. Combine the soy sauce and lime juice in a small bowl and season with pepper. Pour the dressing over the salad and toss well together before serving.

4–6 servings

Spinach, Bacon, and Mushroom Salad

4 fatty bacon strips, chopped

8 ounces young spinach leaves

2½ cups sliced mushrooms

3 tablespoons olive oil

1 tablespoon lemon juice

1 garlic clove, minced

1 teaspoon chopped chives

pinch of mustard powder

salt and pepper

Cook the bacon in a dry skillet, stirring occasionally, for about 5 minutes, until crisp and golden. Remove with a slotted spoon and drain on paper towels. Discard any tough stalks and shred the spinach leaves. Put the spinach, bacon, and mushrooms into a salad bowl. Combine the oil, lemon juice, garlic, chives, and mustard powder in a screw-top jar and season with salt and pepper. Cover with the lid and shake vigorously. Pour the dressing over the salad and toss well.

4–6 servings

Kohlrabi and Bean Sprout Salad

¾ cup unsalted cashew nuts

8 ounces kohlrabi

1 cup shredded coconut

2 cups bean sprouts, rinsed and dried

3 scallions, finely chopped

1 tablespoon chopped mint

1 garlic clove, minced

2 tablespoons lime juice

2 tablespoons honey

Spread out the cashews on a cookie sheet and roast in a preheated oven, 350°F, for 10–15 minutes, until golden. Let cool, then chop coarsely. Coarsely grate the kohlrabi into a bowl and add the coconut, bean sprouts, scallions, and mint. Combine the garlic, lime juice, and honey in a pitcher and pour the mixture over the salad. Toss lightly and sprinkle with the cashews.

4–6 servings

Puy Lentil and Bell Pepper Salad

1½ cups Puy lentils

1 small onion, studded with 2 cloves

2 bay leaves

5 cups water

3 red bell peppers

1½ teaspoons coriander seeds, crushed

5 tablespoons olive oil

2–3 tablespoons lemon juice

2 garlic cloves, crushed

salt and pepper

Place the lentils, onion, bay leaves, and measured water in a pan and bring to a boil. Boil for 10 minutes, then lower the heat, cover, and simmer for 15 minutes, until the lentils are just tender. Drain well. Remove and discard the onion and bay leaf. Place the bell peppers on a cookie sheet under a preheated broiler, turning frequently, for 10–12 minutes, until blistered and charred. Place in a plastic bag, seal the top, and let cool. Peel, halve, deseed, and cut the flesh into strips. Combine the coriander seeds, olive oil, lemon juice, and garlic in a bowl. Add the drained lentils and bell pepper strips, toss together, and season with salt and pepper.

6–8 servings

Black and White Chili Bean Salad

⅔ cup dried black kidney beans, soaked overnight and drained

⅔ cup navy beans, soaked overnight and drained

1 red onion, finely chopped

4 tomatoes, skinned and chopped

2 red chilies, deseeded and finely chopped

1 bunch of cilantro, finely chopped

2 garlic cloves, minced

¼ cup olive oil

finely grated zest and juice of 2 limes

salt and pepper

Place the kidney beans and navy beans in 2 separate pans, add water to cover, and bring to a boil. Boil vigorously for 10 minutes, then reduce the heat, and simmer the kidney beans for 50–60 minutes, and the navy beans for 45–50 minutes. Drain, refresh under cold running water, and drain again. Combine the beans in a salad bowl and add the onion, tomatoes, chilies, cilantro, and garlic, stirring gently to mix. Whisk the oil, zest, and juice in a pitcher and pour the mixture over the salad. Season with salt and pepper and toss well.

6 servings

Three Bean Salad

4 ounces frozen green beans, cut into ½ inch pieces

15½ ounce can lima beans, drained and rinsed

15½ can red kidney beans, drained and rinsed

1 onion, chopped

3 tomatoes, cut into fourths

4 tablespoons sunflower oil

2 tablespoons white wine vinegar

1 teaspoon French mustard

pinch of sugar

salt and pepper

Cook the green beans in lightly salted, boiling water for 5 minutes, then drain, and cool. Combine the green beans, lima beans, kidney beans, onion, and tomatoes in a salad bowl. Combine the oil, vinegar, mustard, and sugar in a screw-top jar and season with salt and pepper. Close the lid and shake vigorously. Pour the dressing over the beans and toss lightly.

4 servings

Greek Salad

1 romaine lettuce, shredded

½ cucumber, cut into chunks

8 ounces feta cheese, cut into cubes

4 tomatoes, skinned and sliced

6 anchovy fillets, finely chopped

6 large black olives, halved and pitted

pinch of dried marjoram

1 tablespoon finely chopped parsley

4 tablespoons olive oil

4 teaspoons white wine vinegar

1 tablespoon chopped mixed herbs

4 scallions, chopped

1 teaspoon sugar

salt and pepper

Place the lettuce on a serving platter and arrange the cucumber, feta, tomatoes, anchovies, and olives on top. Sprinkle with marjoram and parsley and season with pepper. Combine the oil, vinegar, mixed herbs, scallions, and sugar in a screw-top jar and season with salt and pepper. Close the lid and shake vigorously. Pour the dressing over the salad just before serving.

4–6 servings

Shrimp, Grape, and Cottage Cheese Salad

1 head of Belgian endive, leaves separated

1¼ cups cottage cheese

4 ounces green grapes, deseeded

8 ounces cooked peeled shrimp

4 tablespoons thick Mayonnaise (see page 281)

4 tablespoons lemon juice

2 tablespoons finely chopped parsley

salt and pepper

lemon slices, to garnish

Line a salad bowl with the Belgian endive. Combine the cottage cheese, grapes, and shrimp in another bowl and season with salt and pepper. Pile the mixture into the center of the salad bowl. Combine the mayonnaise, lemon juice, and parsley in another bowl and spoon the dressing over the salad. Garnish with lemon slices.

4 servings

Tropical Cheese Salad

1 pineapple

1½ cups grated Cheddar cheese

1 apple, cored and sliced

¼ cup walnuts, coarsely chopped

3 tablespoons raisins

4 tablespoons heavy cream

dash of Worcestershire sauce

dash of lemon juice

1 tablespoon chopped chives

1 tablespoon chopped parsley

salt and pepper

1 head of lettuce, to serve

Cut the pineapple in half lengthwise without removing the leafy top. Scoop out the flesh with a sharp knife and cut into bite-size pieces. Combine the pineapple, cheese, apple, walnuts, raisins, cream, Worcestershire sauce, lemon juice, chives, and parsley in a bowl and season with salt and pepper. Pile the mixture back into the pineapple shells and serve on a bed of lettuce.

6 servings

Tabbouleh and Fennel Salad

1⅓ cups bulgar wheat

1 fennel bulb, very thinly sliced

1 red onion, thinly sliced

5 tablespoons chopped mint

5 tablespoon chopped parsley

2 teaspoons fennel seeds, crushed

2 tablespoons olive oil

finely grated zest and juice of 2 lemons

salt and pepper

Place the bulgar wheat in a bowl, pour in enough cold water to cover, and let stand for 30 minutes, until all the water has been absorbed. Line a colander with cheesecloth, drain the wheat in the colander, then gather up the sides of the cheesecloth and squeeze to extract as much liquid as possible. Tip the wheat into a salad bowl. Stir in the fennel, onion, mint, parsley, fennel seeds, oil, lemon zest, and half the lemon juice. Season with salt and pepper. Cover and let stand for 30 minutes, then taste, and add more lemon juice if necessary.

6 servings

Macaroni and Frankfurter Salad

generous 1 cup short-cut macaroni

5–6 tablespoons French Dressing (see page 280)

12 frankfurter sausages, freshly cooked

1 small green bell pepper, halved, deseeded, and chopped

3–4 scallions, sliced

2 tomatoes, coarsely chopped

½ cup raisins

salt and pepper

chopped parsley, to garnish

Cook the macaroni in a pan of lightly salted, boiling water for 8–10 minutes, until tender. Drain, rinse under hot water, and drain again. Tip into a bowl, add the dressing, and toss. Cut the frankfurters into ½ inch slices and add to the bowl with the bell pepper, scallions, tomatoes, and raisins. Season with salt and pepper and mix well. Garnish with parsley and serve hot or cold.

4–6 servings

Orechiette, Fava Bean, and Romano Salad

8 ounces frozen fava beans, thawed

4 cups orechiette or other small pasta shapes

5 tablespoons extra virgin olive oil

1 cup grated Romano cheese

½ cup pitted black olives

5 tablespoons chopped Italian parsley

1 tablespoon balsamic vinegar

salt and pepper

Blanch the beans in lightly salted, boiling water for 1 minute. Drain, refresh under cold water, and drain again. Pop the beans out of their skins and place in a salad bowl. Cook the pasta in a large pan of lightly salted, boiling water for 8–10 minutes, until tender. Drain, refresh under cold water, and drain again. Tip the pasta into the salad bowl, add all the remaining ingredients and toss well.

4 servings

Spicy Rice Salad

1 tablespoon sunflower oil

1 small onion, chopped

2 teaspoons curry powder

1 teaspoon tomato paste

5 tablespoons water

dash of lemon juice

$^{2}/_{3}$ cup Mayonnaise (see page 281)

1$^{1}/_{3}$ cups freshly cooked long grain rice

1 green bell pepper, deseeded, and sliced into rings

salt

Heat the oil in a small pan and cook the onion for about 5 minutes, until softened. Add the curry powder and cook for 2–3 minutes. Add the tomato paste, water, and lemon juice and season with salt. Cook for 5 minutes, then strain, and cool. Combine the curry mixture with the mayonnaise, then mix gently with the hot rice. Transfer to a serving dish, top with the bell pepper rings, and serve warm or cold.

4 servings

chapter 8
Side Dishes

Baked Potatoes with Avocado Filling

4 potatoes

1 avocado, halved and pitted

½ cup cream cheese

salt and pepper

Par-boil the potatoes for 15–20 minutes, then drain, pat dry with paper towels, and wrap in foil. Tuck them into the hot coals and cook for 40–50 minutes. Scoop the avocado flesh into a bowl, add the cheese, season with salt and pepper, and beat until combined. Unwrap the cooked potatoes, cut them in half, and scoop some of the flesh into the bowl. Mix thoroughly, then pile the mixture back into the skins and heat through on the barbecue.

4 servings

Baked Potatoes with Sour Cream and Chives

4 potatoes

1 tablespoon chopped chives

⅔ cup sour cream

salt and pepper

Par-boil the potatoes for 15–20 minutes, then drain, pat dry with paper towels, and wrap in foil. Tuck them into the hot coals and cook for 40–50 minutes. Combine the chives and sour cream in a bowl and season with salt and pepper. Unwrap the cooked potatoes, split them open, and divide the topping among them.

4 servings

Baked Potatoes with Blue Cheese

4 potatoes

2 ounces blue cheese

2 tablespoons light cream

3 tablespoons milk

¼ cup chopped walnuts

4 walnut halves, to garnish

Par-boil the potatoes for 15–20 minutes, then drain, pat dry with paper towels, and wrap in foil. Tuck them into the hot coals and cook for 40–50 minutes. Place the cheese in a bowl and mash with a fork. Stir in the cream and milk until thoroughly combined, then add the chopped walnuts. Unwrap the cooked potatoes, split them open, and divide the topping among them. Garnish each with a walnut half.

4 servings

Baked Potatoes with Curry Mayonnaise

4 potatoes

1 teaspoon mild curry paste

2 tablespoons mango chutney

4 tablespoons Mayonnaise (see page 281)

Par-boil the potatoes for 15–20 minutes, then drain, pat dry with paper towels, and wrap in foil. Tuck them into the hot coals and cook for 40–50 minutes. Combine the curry paste, chutney, and mayonnaise in a bowl. Unwrap the cooked potatoes, split them open, and divide the topping among them.

4 servings

Hasselback Potatoes

16 small new potatoes

3 tablespoons olive oil

sea salt flakes

Thread the potatoes onto 4 skewers. Using a sharp knife, make as many thin slashes as possible right the way around each one. Brush with oil and sprinkle with sea salt. Grill, turning frequently, for 20–25 minutes.

4 servings

Cheese and Potato Hash

2 pounds potatoes, cut into ½ inch cubes

8 ounces Cheddar or Monterey Jack cheese, cut into ½ inch cubes

1 onion, finely chopped

salt and pepper

Cut 4 squares of double-thickness foil. Par-boil the potatoes in lightly salted, boiling water for 3 minutes, then drain well. Divide the potatoes, cheese, and onion among the foil squares and season with salt and pepper. Wrap securely and cook on the barbecue for 20 minutes, until tender.

4 servings

Potatoes Lyonnaise

2 pounds potatoes

2 tablespoons/¼ stick butter

3 tablespoons sunflower oil

2 large onions, thinly sliced

1 tablespoon chopped parsley

salt and pepper

Cut out 2 large squares of double-thickness foil. Par-boil the potatoes in lightly salted, boiling water for 10 minutes. Drain and cool, then slice thinly. Heat the butter and oil in a large skillet, add the onions, and cook for 2–3 minutes, until translucent. Add the potatoes and parsley and season with salt and pepper. Stir well, then divide the mixture between the foil squares. Wrap securely and cook on the barbecue for 45–50 minutes, until tender.

6–8 servings

Rosemary Potatoes

1 pound new potatoes

4 long rosemary sprigs

1–2 tablespoons olive oil

1 tablespoon sea salt flakes

Par-boil the unpeeled potatoes for 10 minutes, drain and cool slightly. Thread the potatoes onto the rosemary sprigs, brush with oil, and sprinkle with sea salt flakes. Grill, turning occasionally, for 10 minutes.

4 servings

Potato Wedges with Sun-dried Tomato Aioli

4 large potatoes

4–6 large garlic cloves, minced

2 egg yolks

2 tablespoons lemon juice

1½ cups olive oil

8 sun-dried tomato halves in oil, drained and finely chopped

paprika, for sprinkling

sea salt flakes

Place the unpeeled potatoes in a pan, pour in water to cover, and bring to a boil. Lower the heat and simmer for 15–20 minutes, until just tender. Drain and cool slightly. Meanwhile, place the garlic, egg yolks, and lemon juice in a blender or food processor and process briefly to mix. With the machine running, gradually add 1¼ cups of the oil in a thin stream until the mixture forms a thick cream. Scrape into a bowl, stir in the sun-dried tomatoes, and season with salt and pepper. Cut the potatoes into wedges, brush with the remaining oil and sprinkle with paprika. Thread each wedge onto a skewer to make them easier to turn, if you like, or place them directly on the barbecue grid. Grill, turning frequently, for 5–6 minutes, until golden brown all over. Sprinkle with sea salt and serve with the aioli.

4 servings

Sweet Potatoes and Aioli

4–6 garlic cloves, minced

2 egg yolks

2 tablespoons lemon juice

1½ cups olive oil

1 pound sweet potatoes

salt and pepper

Put the garlic, egg yolks, and lemon juice in a blender or food processor and process briefly to mix. With the machine running, gradually add 1¼ cups of the oil until the mixture forms a thick cream. Scrape into a bowl and season with salt and pepper. Cut the unpeeled sweet potatoes into ¼ inch thick slices and brush with the remaining oil. Grill for 5 minutes on each side, until tender. Serve with the aioli.

4 servings

Stuffed Tomatoes

4 tomatoes

1 garlic clove, finely chopped

½ cup soft bread crumbs

2 ounces Gorgonzola

2 rosemary sprigs

1 tablespoon sunflower oil

Cut 4 squares of double-thickness foil. Cut the tops off the tomatoes and scoop out the core and seeds. Combine the garlic and bread crumbs in a bowl and crumble in the blue cheese. Snip the rosemary leaves into small pieces directly into the bowl and stir in the oil. Spoon the filling into the tomatoes and replace the "lids." Place each tomato on a foil square, wrap securely, and cook on the barbecue for 10–15 minutes, until tender.

4 servings

Tomatoes and Onions

2 beefsteak tomatoes, thickly sliced

2 Bermuda onions, thickly sliced

2 tablespoons olive oil

6 thyme sprigs

salt and pepper

Arrange the tomato and onion slices in a hinged basket, brush with oil, season with salt and pepper, and top with the thyme sprigs. Grill for 3 minutes, then brush with a little more oil, turn the basket over, and grill for 3 minutes more.

6 servings

Cheese-topped Tomatoes

8 medium tomatoes

sunflower oil, for brushing

1 onion, finely chopped

4 tablespoons finely chopped parsley

1½ cups soft white bread crumbs

16 small cheese slices

salt and pepper

Cut the tomatoes in half and scoop out the seeds. Brush the insides with oil. Combine the onion, parsley, and bread crumbs in a bowl and season with salt and pepper. Spoon the filling into the hollow tomatoes. Grill for 5 minutes, then top each tomato half with a slice of cheese, and grill for 5 minutes more.

4 servings

Grilled Corn

4 fresh or frozen corn cobs

¼ cup Garlic and Herb Butter (see page 285) or butter, melted

salt and pepper

If using fresh corn, turn back the husks and remove the silks from inside. Brush fresh or frozen corn with melted garlic or plain butter and season with salt and pepper. Smooth the husks of fresh corn back into place or wrap frozen corn in a double thickness of foil. Grill fresh corn, turning occasionally, for 30–40 minutes, and frozen corn for 15–20 minutes. Use potholders to remove the husks and serve the corn with any remaining butter poured over.

4 servings

Golden Glow Corn

½ cup/1 stick butter, softened

2 tablespoons sieved pimiento

½ teaspoon onion powder (optional)

½ teaspoon paprika

4 fresh corn cobs

salt and pepper

Combine the butter, pimiento, onion powder, if using, and paprika in a bowl, beating well with a wooden spoon. Turn back the husks of the corn cobs and remove the silks from inside. Spread with the butter and season with salt and pepper. Smooth the husks back into place and grill for 30–40 minutes. Serve with any remaining golden glow butter.

4 servings

Grilled Baby Corn

1 pound drained canned or fresh baby corn cobs

½ cup/1 stick butter

1 tablespoon lemon juice

1 garlic clove, minced

salt and pepper

If using canned corn, pat it dry with paper towels. Season the cobs with salt and pepper and thread onto skewers. Combine the butter, lemon juice, and garlic in a pan and heat—on the stovetop or the barbecue—until melted and bubbling. Brush the corn cobs with the butter mixture. Grill, turning and brushing with the butter mixture frequently, for 6–7 minutes, until golden brown. To serve, push the corn off the skewers into a dish and pour any remaining butter over it.

Serves 4–6

Hot Asparagus with Balsamic Vinegar and Tomato Dressing

2 tablespoons balsamic vinegar

1–2 garlic cloves, minced

12 ounces tomatoes, skinned, deseeded, and chopped

7 tablespoons olive oil

1 pound young asparagus spears

½ cup pine nuts, toasted

1 ounce Parmesan cheese, thinly shaved

sea salt flakes and pepper

Combine the vinegar, garlic, tomatoes, and 5 tablespoons of the oil in a bowl. Trim the asparagus spears, brush with the remaining oil, and grill for 5–6 minutes, until tender. Transfer to a dish, spoon the dressing over them, sprinkle with pine nuts and Parmesan, and season with sea salt and pepper.

4 servings

Parsley Mushrooms

6 large round mushroom caps

sunflower oil, for brushing

2 garlic cloves, finely chopped

1 onion, finely chopped

4 tablespoons chopped parsley

salt and pepper

Remove the mushroom stalks and brush the caps with oil. Grill for 15 minutes. Meanwhile, combine the garlic, onion, and parsley in a bowl and season with salt and pepper. Put a spoonful of the filling into the center of each mushroom cap and grill for 5 minutes more.

6 servings

Garlic-stuffed Mushrooms

2 tablespoons olive oil

2 tablespoons lemon juice

6 large round mushroom caps

¼ cup/½ stick butter

1 large onion, chopped

2 garlic cloves, minced

1 cup soft bread crumbs

1 tablespoon chopped thyme

salt and pepper

Combine the oil and lemon juice in a large bowl and season with salt and pepper. Add the mushrooms, toss to coat, and marinate for 2–3 hours. Melt the butter in a small pan, add the onion and garlic, and cook for 5 minutes. Remove the pan from the heat and stir in the bread crumbs and thyme. Drain the mushroom marinade into the bread crumb mixture and mix well. Pack the filling into the mushroom caps. Grill for 8–10 minutes.

6 servings

Herb and Tomato Mushrooms

6 large round mushroom caps

2 tablespoons soft white bread crumbs

1 small onion, very finely chopped

1 teaspoon mixed dried herbs

1 tomato, skinned and chopped

1 tablespoon sunflower oil

Remove the stalks from the mushrooms and chop finely, reserving the caps. Combine the chopped stalks, bread crumbs, onion, herbs, and tomato in a bowl. Brush the mushroom caps with oil and place on a sheet of foil. Spread each cap with the filling and cook on the barbecue for about 20 minutes.

6 servings

Italian-style Zucchini

4 zucchini

4 tablespoons bottled tomato relish

4 tablespoons grated Parmesan cheese

salt and pepper

Par-boil the zucchini in lightly salted, boiling water for 4 minutes. Drain and cut in half lengthwise. Grill, cut side down, for 4–5 minutes. Turn them over and spread each with tomato relish. Sprinkle with Parmesan and pepper and grill for 5–10 minutes more, until tender.

4 servings

Eggplant Fans

2 eggplants

2 ripe tomatoes, thinly sliced

1 garlic clove, finely chopped

1 onion, chopped

2 tablespoons sunflower oil

4 canned artichoke hearts, drained and cut into fourths

12 black olives, pitted and sliced

1/2 teaspoon dried mixed herbs

salt and pepper

Cut the eggplants in half lengthwise. Place the halves, cut side down, on a cutting board and slit each lengthwise at 1/2 inch intervals, but leaving the stem intact. Place the tomato slices in the slits. Cut 4 squares of double-thickness foil. Reserve a little garlic and sprinkle the remainder, with the onion, over each foil square. Place the eggplant halves on top. Coat the artichoke hearts in 1 tablespoon of the oil and arrange them, with the olives, in the "fans." Brush each eggplant half with the remaining oil and sprinkle with the remaining garlic, the mixed herbs, and salt and pepper to taste. Wrap securely and cook on the barbecue for 40 minutes.

4 servings

Foil-wrapped Onions

4 large onions, peeled

2 tablespoons/1/4 stick butter, melted

2 teaspoons Worcestershire sauce

salt and pepper

Cut 4 squares of double-thickness foil and place an onion on each. Brush with the melted butter and Worcestershire sauce and season with salt and pepper. Wrap the foil halfway up the sides of the onions. Grill, turning every 10 minutes, for 45–60 minutes, until softened. Remove the foil and blackened skin before serving.

4 servings

Creamy Cabbage

5 cups shredded red, white, or green cabbage

6 tablespoons heavy cream

3 tablespoons butter

salt and pepper

Line a heavy casserole with foil. Put the cabbage in the base and add the cream and butter. Season with salt and pepper. Cover and cook on the barbecue for 30 minutes.

4 servings

Mozzarella and Salami Bread

1 large French bread stick

4 ounces mozzarella cheese, thinly sliced

4–6 black olives, pitted and thinly sliced

2 ounces sliced salami

Cut a large square of double-thickness foil and grease with butter. Using a sharp knife, cut the bread into thick slices without cutting all the way through. Insert a slice each of mozzarella, olive, and salami in between the bread slices. Place the loaf on the foil and wrap securely. Cook on the barbecue for 10 minutes on each side. Unwrap and cut between the slices to serve.

4–8 servings

Garlic Bread

1 French bread stick

2 garlic cloves, minced

6 tablespoons/¾ stick butter, softened

1 teaspoon dried rosemary

2 tablespoons chopped parsley

pepper

Cut a large square of double-thickness foil and grease with butter. Using a sharp knife, cut the bread into thick slices without cutting all the way through. Combine the garlic, butter, rosemary, parsley, and pepper to taste in a bowl, beating well until thoroughly mixed. Spread the garlic butter between the bread slices. Place the loaf on the foil and wrap securely. Cook on the barbecue for 10 minutes on each side. Unwrap and cut through the base of the slices to serve.

4 servings

Hot Garlic and Sausage Loaf

1 small French bread stick

¼ cup/½ stick butter, softened

2 garlic cloves, minced

8 thin pork sausage links

sunflower oil, for brushing

salt and pepper

Cut out a large square of double-thickness foil. Make 8 equally spaced cuts into the bread without cutting through completely. Combine the butter and garlic in a bowl, beating until smooth. Season with salt and pepper. Divide the mixture between the bread slices. Place the loaf on the foil square and wrap securely. Cook on the barbecue, turning once, for about 15 minutes. Meanwhile, brush the sausage links with oil and grill, turning occasionally, for 10 minutes. Unwrap the bread and place a sausage link between each slice.

4 servings

Savory Cheese

8 ounces firm cheese, such as Gouda, Edam, or Swiss

1 tablespoon olive oil

2 teaspoons wine vinegar

pinch of mustard powder

½ teaspoon dried mixed herbs

salt and pepper

crusty bread, to serve

Cut the cheese into 1 inch cubes and thread onto skewers. Combine the oil, vinegar, mustard powder, and herbs in a bowl and season with salt and pepper. Brush the mixture all over the cheese. Grill for about 1 minute, then turn over with a metal spatula, and grill for 1 minute more. Serve with crusty bread.

8 servings

chapter 9
Desserts

Golden Baked Apples

4 large tart apples, cored

1/4 cup brown sugar

2 teaspoons cinnamon

1/2 cup walnuts, chopped

1/4 cup/1/2 stick butter

Cut 4 squares of double-thickness foil and place an apple on each. Combine the sugar, cinnamon, and walnuts in a bowl and fill the apple cavities with the mixture. Dot the apples with butter and wrap securely. Cook on the barbecue, turning occasionally, for 20–30 minutes, until tender.

4 servings

Crunchy Baked Apples with Chocolate Sauce

4 tart apples, cored

3/4 cup granola

4 tablespoons light corn syrup

4 tablespoons lemon juice

2 tablespoons/1/4 stick butter

6 ounces semisweet chocolate, broken into pieces

2/3 cup orange juice

Cut 4 squares of double-thickness foil. Score the skin around the circumference of each apple and place each on a foil square. Combine the granola, half the syrup, and the lemon juice in a bowl, then fill the cavities in the apples with this mixture, pressing it down well. Dot with butter and wrap each apple securely. Cook on the barbecue, turning occasionally, for 20–30 minutes. Meanwhile, place the chocolate and 3 tablespoons of the orange juice in a small pan and heat gently until melted. Stir in the remaining syrup and orange juice. Bring to a boil, stirring constantly, then simmer, stirring occasionally, for 10 minutes. Let cool slightly. To serve, unwrap the apples, place on plates, and pour the warm sauce over them.

4 servings

Mulled Pears

4 small ripe pears, peeled, halved, and cored

4 teaspoons raw sugar

4 tablespoons red currant jelly

grated zest of 1 orange

16 cloves

Cut 4 squares of double-thickness foil and place 2 pear halves on each. Combine the sugar, jelly, and orange zest in a bowl and divide the mixture evenly among the pears. Spike each pear half with 2 cloves, then wrap securely. Cook on the barbecue for about 30 minutes.

4 servings

Baked Pears with Lemon Cream

4 pears, halved and cored

4 teaspoons brown sugar

3 tablespoons butter

2 egg yolks

½ teaspoon vanilla extract

¼ cup superfine sugar

½ teaspoon grated lemon zest

1 tablespoon cornstarch

1 cup light cream

Cut 4 squares of double-thickness foil and place 2 pear halves on each. Sprinkle each with brown sugar and dot with butter. Wrap the pears securely. Cook on the barbecue, turning occasionally, for 20–30 minutes. Meanwhile, beat the egg yolks with the vanilla in a bowl. Combine the superfine sugar, lemon zest, and cornstarch in a small pan. Gradually stir in the cream, then heat gently, stirring constantly, until thickened. Stir a little of the thickened sauce into the egg yolk mixture, then stir the egg yolk mixture into the pan. Cook over low heat for 2–3 minutes, then let cool slightly. Serve the hot baked pears with the warm lemon cream.

4 servings

Almond-stuffed Apricots

5 tablespoons ground almonds

3 tablespoons superfine sugar

1 tablespoon Amaretto liqueur

14 ounce can apricot halves in fruit juice, drain and juice reserved

2 tablespoons candied cherries

2 tablespoons red currant jelly

Combine the almonds, sugar, and liqueur in a bowl to make a soft paste. Spoon a little of the almond mixture into the hollow side of each apricot half and top with a cherry. Place the apricots on a sheet of foil and cook on the barbecue for 15 minutes. Meanwhile, pour the reserved juice into a pan and stir in the red currant jelly. Stand directly on top of the coals until hot. Serve the apricots with a little of the juice mixture spooned over.

6 servings

Apricot and Nut Fruit Bread

1 cup dried apricots

generous 3/4 cup chopped preserved ginger

1/4 cup/1/2 stick sweet butter

1/4 cup sliced almonds

2 fruit loaves

Cut 2 large squares of double-thickness foil. Place the apricots, ginger, and butter in a blender or food processor and process until the mixture is almost smooth. Transfer to a bowl and stir in the almonds. Slice the loaves at 3/4 inch intervals, cutting about three-quarters of the way through each time. Spread the apricot mixture between the slices. Wrap each loaf securely in a foil square, shiny side inward. Cook, turning occasionally, for 20 minutes. Unwrap and slice to serve.

8–10 servings

Toffee Cakes

4 teacakes or 4 slices of fruit bread, cut into 1 inch cubes

1/4 cup/1/2 stick butter, melted

3 tablespoons light corn syrup

1 tablespoon lemon juice

Thread the teacake or bread cubes onto 4 skewers. Combine the butter, syrup, and lemon juice in a bowl and brush the mixture all over the cubes. Grill, turning frequently, for 5–10 minutes, until crisp and golden.

4 servings

Peach Packets

6 large peaches, peeled, halved, and pitted

6 tablespoons/¾ stick butter, diced

6 tablespoons dry vermouth

6 tablespoons orange flower water

6 tablespoons brown sugar

¾ cup heavy cream, chilled, to serve

Cut 6 pieces of double-thickness foil and grease lightly. Place 2 peach halves on each foil square and dot with butter. Pour 1 tablespoon vermouth, then 1 teaspoon orange flower water over each peach. Sprinkle 1 tablespoon sugar over each peach, then bring up the sides of the foil and crimp the edges to seal. Cook on the barbecue for 20–30 minutes. To serve, unwrap the parcels, transfer the peaches to a platter, pour the juices from the packets over them, and serve with cream.

6 servings

Honeyed Peaches

1¼ cups Marsala

4 tablespoons honey

1 strip of orange zest

4 peaches, peeled, halved, and pitted

2 tablespoons/¼ stick butter, melted

4 amaretti

vanilla ice cream, to serve

Place the Marsala, honey, and orange zest in a pan, bring to a boil, then simmer for 2 minutes. Add the peach halves and simmer for 3–4 minutes, until just tender. Remove from the heat and leave the peaches to cool in the syrup. Remove the peaches with a slotted spoon. Bring the syrup to a boil and cook until reduced by half. Brush the peach halves with melted butter and grill, turning once, for 5–7 minutes. Transfer the peaches to serving plates, spoon a little of the syrup over them, and crumble the amaretti on top. Serve with vanilla ice cream.

4 servings

Figs and Blackberries on Toast

12 ripe figs

1 cup blackberries

pared zest and juice of 2 oranges

2 tablespoons crème de cassis

1 tablespoon superfine sugar

½ teaspoon ground cinnamon

2 tablespoons/¼ stick butter, melted

4 brioche or white bread slices

strained plain yogurt, to serve

Cut 4 squares of double-thickness foil. Cut the figs into fourths without cutting all the way through, so that they open out like flowers. Divide the figs and blackberries evenly among the foil squares. Cut the orange zest into thin julienne strips and place them in a bowl. Add the orange juice and crème de cassis, then divide the mixture among the fruit. Bring up the sides of the foil and crimp the edges to seal. Combine the sugar, cinnamon, and butter in a bowl and brush the mixture over 1 side of each brioche or bread slice. Cook the fruit packets on the barbecue for 8–10 minutes. Shortly before the end of the cooking time, grill the brioche or bread slices, buttered side up, until golden. Serve the cinnamon toast on individual plates, topped with the figs and blackberries and a spoonful of yogurt.

4 servings

Satsumas with Rum and Raisins

6 large satsumas

scant ½ cup raisins

2 tablespoons brown sugar

3 tablespoons rum

heavy cream, to serve

Cut 6 squares of double-thickness foil. Using a sharp knife, carefully cut around the circumference of each satsuma, cutting only the zest and not the fruit. Ease away the top half of the zest and discard. Remove the white pith, but leave the fruit intact in its "cup." Combine the raisins and sugar in a bowl, then push the mixture into the center of each satsuma. Place each satsuma on a square of foil and drizzle with a little rum, then wrap securely. Place the foil packets among the coals and cook for 15 minutes. Unwrap and serve with cream.

6 servings

Spicy Oranges

4 large oranges, peeled and segmented

4 tablespoons brown sugar

pinch of ground cinnamon

4 tablespoons rum

¼ cup/½ stick butter

Cut 4 squares of double-thickness foil and place 1 orange on each. Turn up the sides of the foil. Sprinkle each orange with sugar, cinnamon, and rum and dot with butter. Wrap securely and grill, turning once, for 15 minutes.

4 servings

Chocolate Gone Bananas

4 ripe bananas

6 ounces semisweet chocolate, broken into pieces

Cut 4 squares of double-thickness foil. Make a small slit in the skin of each banana and insert 1–2 pieces of the chocolate. Wrap securely in foil and cook on the barbecue for about 10 minutes.

4 servings

South Sea Banana Bubbles

4 bananas, peeled and thickly sliced

1/4 cup/1/2 stick butter

2 tablespoons orange syrup

2 tablespoons dark rum

1 orange, peeled and sliced

Cut 4 squares of double-thickness foil and place 1 sliced banana on each. Dot with the butter, spoon over the syrup and rum, and cover with the orange slices. Wrap securely and cook on the barbecue for about 10 minutes.

4 servings

Baked Bananas with Coffee and Rum Cream

3/4 cup whipping cream

2 tablespoons strong brewed coffee

1/2 cup confectioner's sugar

2 tablespoons dark rum

6 large ripe bananas

Whisk the cream until soft peaks form, then add the coffee, and whisk again. Fold in the confectioner's sugar, followed by the rum. Transfer to a small bowl and chill until required. Cook the unpeeled bananas on the barbecue, turning occasionally, for 10–15 minutes, until blackened on the outside and very soft. Serve with the coffee and rum cream.

6 servings

Honeyed Bananas

8 under-ripe bananas

2 tablespoons/¼ stick butter, melted

4 tablespoons honey

2 tablespoons brandy

1 tablespoon lemon juice

½ cup sliced almonds and ⅔ cup whipped cream, to serve

Cut 8 squares of double-thickness foil. Peel and halve the bananas lengthwise, then place 2 halves on each foil square. Combine the butter, honey, brandy, and lemon juice in a pitcher and pour the mixture evenly over the bananas. Wrap securely and cook on the barbecue for 10–15 minutes. Unwrap the bananas, transfer to plates, and serve with almonds and cream.

8 servings

Caramelized Pineapple

1 large ripe pineapple, peeled and cut into ¾ inch thick slices

¾ cup molasses sugar

4 tablespoons white rum

chilled heavy cream, to serve

Lay the pineapple slices on a large plate. Combine the sugar and rum in a bowl, then brush the mixture on both sides of the pineapple. Cover and marinate for 30 minutes. Drain the pineapple slices, reserving the marinade, and place in a hinged basket. Grill, basting frequently with the marinade, for 5 minutes on each side. Serve with cream.

6–8 servings

Flambéed Pineapple

1 ripe pineapple, peeled

¼ cup/½ stick butter

⅓ cup molasses sugar

4 tablespoons dark rum

½ cup pecan nuts, roasted and coarsely chopped

Cut 4 squares of double-thickness foil. Cut the pineapple into 8 slices and stamp out the cores with a cookie cutter. Place 2 pineapple slices on each foil square. Melt the butter in a small pan, stir in the sugar, and heat until the sugar has dissolved. Divide the mixture among the pineapple slices, then wrap securely. Cook on the barbecue for 10–15 minutes. Open the packets carefully, spoon 1 tablespoon of rum into each, and ignite. Sprinkle with the pecans and serve.

4 servings

Barbados Baked Pineapple

1 large ripe pineapple, peeled and cut into ¾ inch thick slices

6–8 tablespoons brown sugar

½ teaspoon ground ginger

6–8 tablespoons shredded fresh coconut

6–8 strawberries, to decorate

Cut 6–8 squares of double-thickness foil, depending on how many slices of pineapple there are. Place a slice on each square. Evenly sprinkle with the sugar, ginger, and coconut. Wrap securely and cook on the barbecue for 10–15 minutes. Unwrap and decorate with a strawberry to serve.

6–8 servings

Baked Blueberry Packets with Almond Cream

6 cups ground almonds

4 cups mascarpone cheese

3 egg yolks

generous ½ cup superfine sugar

½ cup heavy cream

2 tablespoons Amaretto liqueur

6 cups blueberries

6 tablespoons vanilla sugar

6 tablespoons crème de cassis

Line a 7 inch strainer with a piece of cheesecloth large enough to overhang the edge by 4 inches and set it over a bowl. Beat the almonds with the mascarpone in another bowl. Beat the egg yolks with the sugar in a third bowl, until they are pale and fluffy. Fold the egg yolk mixture into the mascarpone mixture. Whip the cream in a bowl until it forms soft peaks, then fold into the mascarpone mixture with the Amaretto. Turn the mixture into the lined strainer, fold the overhanging cheesecloth over the top, cover with a small plate, and set a weight on top. Place in the refrigerator for 6–8 hours or overnight to drain. When you are ready to cook, cut 6 squares of double-thickness foil and divide the blueberries among them. Turn up the edges of the foil squares. Evenly sprinkle the blueberries with the vanilla sugar and crème de cassis. Bring up the sides of the foil and crimp the edges to seal. Cook on the barbecue for 8–10 minutes. Unmold the almond cream onto a large plate. Serve the blueberries with portions of the cream.

6 servings

Golden Fruit Slices

1 pound sliced fruit, such as apricots, plums, and peaches

2 tablespoons/¼ stick butter

2 tablespoons orange juice

2 tablespoons orange liqueur

2 tablespoons raw sugar

ice cream, to serve

Cut a large square of double-thickness foil and place all the fruit on it. Dot with butter, spoon over the orange juice and liqueur, and sprinkle with sugar. Wrap the fruit securely in the foil and cook on the barbecue for 5–10 minutes. Unwrap the fruit, tip the contents of the packet, including the cooking juices, into a bowl, and serve with ice cream.

4 servings

Fruit Kabobs with Honey-lemon Sauce

selection of peach slices, apricot halves, apple wedges, peeled banana chunks, pineapple chunks, seedless grapes, strawberries, and pitted dates

2 tablespoons lemon juice, plus extra for brushing

6 tablespoons honey

Cut the pieces of fruit to about the same size. If using apple chunks or banana slices, brush them with lemon juice to prevent discoloration. Thread the fruit onto 6 skewers. Heat the lemon juice and honey in a pan and brush the mixture over the fruit. Grill, turning occasionally, for about 5 minutes. Serve the fruit with the remaining sauce spooned over it.

6 servings

Maraschino and Mallow Kabobs with Dark Chocolate Sauce

12 pink marshmallows

12 white marshmallows

6 cocktail cherries

¼ cup/½ stick butter

¼ cup unsweetened cocoa powder

3 tablespoons light corn syrup

Thread the marshmallows and cherries alternately onto 4 skewers. Combine the butter, cocoa powder, and syrup in a pan and heat gently, stirring until smooth. Transfer the pan to the side of the barbecue to keep warm. Hold the kabobs, 2 at a time, just above the barbecue grid, for 1–2 minutes, until the marshmallows turn golden. Do not let them touch the grid. Serve with the chocolate sauce.

4 servings

Fruit Kabobs with Coconut Cream

3 tablespoons dry unsweetened shredded coconut

4 tablespoons boiling water

⅔ cup heavy cream, whipped

2/3 cup orange juice

1/2 cup lemon juice

scant 1/3 cup superfine sugar

1 pear, cut into 8 sections and cored

2 small firm bananas, peeled and each cut into 4 chunks

2 slices fresh or canned pineapple, cut into chunks

8 seedless grapes

4 small pieces of preserved ginger

2 tablespoons honey, melted

raw sugar, for sprinkling

2 tablespoons sliced almonds

Combine the coconut and boiling water in a bowl and let stand for 30 minutes. Strain into another bowl, pressing down on the contents of the strainer to extract as much liquid as possible. Discard the contents of the strainer and whisk the coconut milk into the cream. Combine the orange juice, lemon juice, and superfine sugar in a large bowl, add the pear, bananas, pineapple, grapes, and ginger, and stir well. Drain the fruits thoroughly and thread onto 4 skewers. Place the skewers on the barbecue grid, brush with melted honey and raw sugar, and grill for about 3–4 minutes, until lightly golden. Serve with the coconut cream.

4 servings

Sticky Rice and Ginger Cooked in Banana Leaves

1 cup short grain pudding rice

2 1/2 cups coconut milk

3 tablespoons superfine sugar

2 pieces of preserved ginger, finely chopped

banana leaves (optional)

Rinse the rice in several changes of water until the water runs clear. Drain well and place in a pan. Pour in the coconut milk and bring to a boil, then lower the heat, cover, and simmer gently, stirring occasionally, for 15–20 minutes. Transfer the rice to a bowl, stir in the sugar and ginger, cover, and cool slightly. Soften the banana leaves, if using, in boiling water, then drain, and cut into 8 strips, 3 inches wide. Use 2 crossed strips for each packet. Alternatively, cut 4 squares of double-thickness foil. Divide the rice mixture between the wrappings and then form into packets. Tie the banana leaves with soaked string, or crimp the foil to seal the packets. Cook on the barbecue for 4–5 minutes on each side.

4 servings

chapter 10

Drinks

Fruit Punch

¼ cup sugar

⅔ cup water

⅔ cup orange juice

⅔ cup pineapple juice

1¼ cups cold weak tea

fruit slices, such as orange, lemon, and pineapple

crushed ice

⅔ cup ginger ale

mint sprigs, to decorate

Put the sugar in a small pan and pour in the water. Heat gently until the sugar has dissolved. Remove from the heat and cool. Combine the cooled sugar syrup, orange juice, pineapple juice, and tea in a pitcher and chill for at least 2 hours. Add the fruit slices and crushed ice. Pour the punch in 4 tall glasses, top off with ginger ale, and decorate with mint.

4 servings

Summer Citrus Cocktail

2½ cups orange juice

2½ cups grapefruit juice

2½ cups ginger ale

2 tablespoons lemon juice

crushed ice

1 small orange, sliced

1 lemon, sliced

cocktail cherries

mint sprigs

Combine the orange juice, grapefruit juice, ginger ale, and lemon juice in a large pitcher. Add plenty of crushed ice and stir in the orange and lemon slices, cocktail cherries, and mint.

6 servings

Golden Fruit Punch

15 ice cubes

1¼ cups white grape juice

1½ cups apple juice

2½ cups pineapple juice

2 cups ginger ale

1 small pineapple, peeled and finely chopped

4 borage sprigs

Put the ice cubes into a large pitcher or punch bowl. Add all the remaining ingredients, stir well, and serve immediately.

6–8 servings

Fresh Lemonade

½ cup sugar

1¼ cups water

8 tablespoons lemon juice

ice cubes

club soda

4 mint sprigs and 4 lemon slices, to decorate

Place the sugar and water in a small pan and stir over low heat until the sugar has dissolved. Remove from the heat and cool. Put 1 tablespoon of the cooled sugar syrup in the base of each of 4 tall glasses. Stir 2 tablespoons of the lemon juice into each glass and add ice cubes. Fill the glasses with club soda and decorate with mint and lemon slices.

4 servings

Black Currant Fizz

3½ cups black currants

6 tablespoons superfine sugar

6 tablespoons lemon juice

5 cups sparkling lemonade, chilled

Place the black currants in a heavy pan, add the sugar, and cook over low heat, stirring occasionally, for 20 minutes. Strain the black currants into a bowl, pressing down gently to extract all the juice. Discard the contents of the strainer. Add the lemon juice and half the lemonade, whisking well together. Pour the mixture into a large pitcher and chill for 30 minutes. Whisk in the remaining lemonade and chill until required.

6–8 servings

Bloody Mary

1½ cups vodka

⅔ cup very dry sherry

scant ½ cup lemon juice

4 cups tomato juice

1 tablespoon Worcestershire sauce

1 teaspoon Tabasco sauce

½ teaspoon celery salt

ice cubes

salt and pepper

8 celery stalks, to decorate

Combine the vodka, sherry, lemon juice, and tomato juice in a pitcher and season with salt and pepper. Put the Worcestershire sauce, Tabasco, and celery salt in a screw-top jar, close the lid, and shake vigorously. To serve, half fill each glass with ice cubes, then pour in the vodka and juice mixture. Let guests help themselves to the spicy flavoring. Place a celery stalk in each glass for stirring.

8 servings

Champagne Strawberry Cocktail

¾ cup Fraise de Bois or other strawberry liqueur

1 bottle Champagne, chilled

strawberries, to serve

Pour the liqueur into a pitcher, then add the Champagne, stirring constantly but gently. Place a strawberry in the base of each glass and pour in the cocktail. Serve immediately.

6–8 servings

Sangria

1¼ cups red wine

2 tablespoons brandy

4 tablespoons orange juice, strained

1¼ cups lemonade

½ orange, thinly sliced

½ lemon, thinly sliced

1 apple, cored and thinly sliced

ice cubes

Pour the wine, brandy, orange juice, and lemonade into a pitcher and stir well. Chill for at least 2 hours. Stir in the fruit and ice cubes before serving.

4 servings

White Wine Punch

large block of ice or ice cubes

1 bottle medium-dry white wine, chilled

5 tablespoons brandy, chilled

5 tablespoons Cointreau or other orange liqueur, chilled

2 tablespoons lime juice

1¾ cups club soda, chilled

⅔ cup raspberries

1 peach, peeled, halved, pitted, and thinly sliced

8–10 lemon balm leaves, to decorate

Place the ice in the base of a large pitcher or punch bowl. Pour in the wine, brandy, and liqueur and whisk well. Add the lime juice and club soda, stirring constantly. Float the fruit on top, decorate with the lemon balm leaves, and serve.

6 servings

White Wine Sparkle

1 bottle dry white wine

1¼ cups lime cordial

4 tablespoons white rum

½ cup dry vermouth

8 ounce can crushed pineapple

1 lime, sliced

1 lemon, sliced

2 inch piece of cucumber, peeled and thinly sliced

6 cups sparkling lemonade

ice cubes

Combine all the ingredients, except the lemonade and ice cubes, in a punch bowl and chill until required. Add the lemonade and ice cubes and stir well.

12 servings

Citrus Ponets

15 ice cubes

6¼ cups white Rhine wine

⅔ cup vodka

2/3 cup club soda

juice of 6 oranges

juice of 2 large grapefruit

juice of 1 lemon

1 small pineapple, peeled and finely chopped

1/2 cup cocktail cherries

Place the ice cubes in a large punch bowl. Add all the remaining ingredients and stir well. Serve immediately.

6–8 servings

Red Wine Cup

large block of ice or ice cubes

1 bottle red wine, chilled

scant 1 cup Framboise liqueur, chilled

5 cups sparkling mineral water, chilled

1 small cucumber, very thinly sliced

6 borage sprigs with flowers, leaves coarsely chopped (optional)

Put the ice in the base of a large pitcher or punch bowl. Pour in the wine and liqueur and stir well. Add the mineral water, stirring constantly. Add the cucumber, borage leaves, and flowers, if using, stir once more, then serve.

6–8 servings

Chilled Claret Cup

crushed ice

1 bottle young claret or other dry red wine, chilled

½ bottle port, chilled

⅔ cup brandy, chilled

5 tablespoons orange juice

3 tablespoons lemon juice

½ cup confectioner's sugar

2 oranges, thinly sliced

1 lemon, thinly sliced

1½ cups club soda

6 mint sprigs, to decorate

Fill a large pitcher with crushed ice, then pour in the wine, port, and brandy, and stir. Whisk the orange juice, lemon juice, and sugar in a small bowl until the sugar has dissolved, then add the mixture to the jug. Add the orange and lemon slices and pour in the club soda, stirring constantly. Float mint sprigs on top to decorate and serve immediately.

10 servings

Brandied Coffee Cream

5 eggs

½ cup sugar

3 tablespoons brandy

1¼ cups milk

1¼ cups light cream

2½ cups strong black coffee

3 tablespoons heavy cream, stiffly whipped

2 tablespoons grated semisweet or milk chocolate

Whisk the eggs with the sugar until thoroughly combined. Combine the brandy, milk, light cream, and coffee in a pan and heat gently until hot but not boiling. Remove the pan from the heat and gradually whisk in the egg mixture. Pour the mixture into 8 heatproof glasses, top each with a little whipped cream and grated chocolate, and serve immediately.

8 servings

Mulled Wine

6¼ cups dry red wine

1 tablespoon finely grated orange zest

1 tablespoon finely grated lemon zest

1 cup sugar

½ teaspoon ground cloves

½ teaspoon grated nutmeg

1¼ cups brandy

Put the wine, orange and lemon zest, sugar, cloves, and nutmeg in a stainless steel pan and bring to a boil, stirring constantly. Remove from the heat and pour the mixture into a punch bowl. Warm the brandy in a small pan over low heat until hot but not boiling. Remove the pan from the heat and pour the brandy into the punch bowl. Ignite the punch, if you like, and serve when the flames have died down.

8 servings

Mulled Punch

9 cups hard cider

2 oranges, each stuck with 6 cloves

1 teaspoon ground cinnamon

2 apples, cored and sliced

4 tablespoons sugar

4 tablespoons brandy

Pour the hard cider into a large pan, bring to a boil, then simmer for 5 minutes. Add the oranges, cinnamon, apples, and sugar, bring back to a boil, stirring constantly, then add the brandy. Remove the oranges with a slotted spoon and discard the cloves. Thinly slice the oranges and return to the pan. Serve immediately.

12–15 servings

D

E

F

G

H

I

J

K

L

M

O

P

Q

R

S

T

V

W

Y

Z